How They
Were Taught

To My Wife

How They Were Taught

An Anthology of Contemporary Accounts of
Learning and Teaching in England
1800–1950

COMPILED BY

P. H. J. H. GOSDEN

BASIL BLACKWELL
OXFORD

First published 1969

Printed in Great Britain by
William Clowes and Sons Ltd, London and Beccles
and bound by
the Kemp Hall Bindery, Oxford

Contents

List of Plates

Acknowledgements

The compiler and the publisher wish to thank the following for permission to reproduce copyright material, full details of which are given elsewhere:

Allen & Unwin Ltd for an extract from *The Life of Frances Power Cobbe as Told by Herself*

Associated Book Publishers Ltd and Mr R. J. White for extracts from *Cambridge Life*; Associated Book Publishers Ltd and Mr Dacre Balsdon for an extract from *Oxford Life*

Basing School Managers and Mrs B. Beddington for an extract from *Basing Church of England School, 1866–1966*

The Bodley Head for extracts from *Memories of Sixty Years at Eton, Cambridge and Elsewhere* by Oscar Browning

Cambridge University Press and Miss M. K. Ashby for an extract from *Joseph Ashby of Tysoe, 1859–1919*

Chatto & Windus Ltd and Mr W. B. Gallie for an extract from *A New University: A. D. Lindsay and the Keele Experiment*

The Epworth Press for an extract from *The Story of Westminster College, 1851–1951* by Dr F. C. Pritchard

The Headmaster of Holy Trinity School, Ripon, for extracts from the school's log book

The Headmaster of Northam Junior School, Southampton, for extracts from the school's log book

The Controller of Her Majesty's Stationery Office for extracts from the *Report on the Differentiation of the Curriculum for Boys and Girls* and from *The New Secondary Education*

Mr C. P. Hill and the Governors of Bristol Grammar School for an extract from *The History of Bristol Grammar School*

Herbert Jenkins Ltd and Mr A. S. Neill for extracts from *That Dreadful School*

Miss A. Lawrence and the Governors of St Hild's College, Durham, for an extract from *St Hild's College, 1858–1958*

Macmillan & Co. Ltd for extracts from *The Life of Joseph Chamberlain*, vol. IV, by Julian Amery; *The Ancient Ways—Winchester Fifty Years Ago* by W. Tuckwell

Manchester University Press for an extract from *Portrait of a University, 1851–1951* by Mr H. B. Charlton

Oxford University Press for an extract from *Edwardian England, 1901–14*, edited by S. Nowell-Smith

Shrewsbury School Development Campaign and Mr W. F. Ewbank for an extract from *Salopian Diaries*

Times Newspapers Limited for articles entitled 'Reception Area Schooling' and 'Lancashire Children in Wales' which appeared in *The Times* on 18th September, 1939

Twentieth Century Magazine Ltd for extracts from an article entitled 'Leeds, 1929–34' by Rayner Heppenstall

West Riding County Council Education Committee for extracts from school log books in their possession

Mr H. M. Wilson, literary executor to the late J. H. Badley, for extracts from *An Educational Experiment at Bedales School* and for the extract from the *Report on Bedales School* by Alfred Hughes

Radio Times Hulton Picture Library for the photograph used in Plate 32

We have tried to trace owners of all copyright material, but in certain cases it has proved impossible to trace the probable owners of the copyright. In the event of this book reaching them we should be glad if they would let us know of any omissions so that we may make proper acknowledgement in future editions.

Introduction

The extracts which appear in this book are intended to illustrate
a few of the lines of development in the whole field of learning
and teaching during the last century and a half. It would be
quite impossible in a short collection of this nature to treat fully
all the significant developments and it has seemed better to
illustrate fairly adequately what appears to have been important
rather than to cover more ground sketchily. Consequently a
limited number of themes have been chosen, and within each
section the extracts concentrate on the main topics rather than
giving brief, fleeting glimpses of everything.

Since learning and teaching form an important part of the
life of the community, this book serves to illustrate an aspect of
our social history. It does not attempt to replace narrative
histories of education but rather to be complementary to them
by giving the reader the opportunity to view some of the
educational processes since 1800 through the eyes of contemporaries.

1 The Elementary Schools before State Aid

For the first part of the nineteenth century the educational needs of the children of the masses received increasing attention from the more influential sections of society, even though the state itself took no part in this. The lack of finance and the large numbers in need of some tuition led to the best known and possibly most ingenious system for educating large numbers of children, the monitorial system, propounded in rivalry by Lancaster and Bell.

The Monitorial School

Joseph Lancaster developed his system at a school he opened in the Borough Road, London, where by 1804 he had about 500 pupils. He was the only teacher and he organised his school through a large number of monitors chosen from among the pupils. Lancaster believed that he had found a way of overcoming successfully the twin problems of large numbers and expense. He was a Nonconformist as were his main supporters; the apparent success of his techniques encouraged similar developments among supporters of the established Church whose expert and publicist in this field was the Reverend Andrew Bell. Bell had experimented while in Madras, but he really developed an approach similar to that of Lancaster after his return to this country.

The importance of the rivalry between the two men and between their claims to priority as inventors lies mainly in that it marks the inauguration of the struggle between the National Society for Promoting the Education of the Poor in the Principles of the Established Church and the British and Foreign Schools Society, supported largely by Nonconformists. This struggle between Church and Dissent was to dominate Elementary education throughout the nineteenth century. Moreover the foundation and growth of these societies at this time had the effect of spreading schools organised on monitorial principles throughout the country so that they became the general pattern and persisted. The tradition of cheapness and mechanical methods of teaching formed an unfortunate legacy which the system bequeathed to the elementary school.

1. The principle of the Monitorial Method

SOURCE: Andrew Bell, *The Madras School or Elements of Tuition*, 1808.

This system rests on the simple principle of tuition by the scholars themselves. It is its distinguishing characteristic that the school, how numerous soever, is taught solely by the pupils of the institution under a single master, who, if able and diligent, could, without difficulty, conduct ten contiguous schools, each consisting of a thousand scholars.

2. A Description of the Monitorial School at Enmore

SOURCE: John Poole, *The Village School Improved*, 1813.

A. General Arrangements

The school consisting this day, twenty-third of March, 1812, of seventy children, of both sexes, is divided into eight classes; which are distinguished numerically, reckoning from the lowest upwards.

Each class is under the direction and tuition of its teacher. The teachers and their classes are under the inspection and superintendence of the monitor.

The schoolmistress watches and presides over the whole.

The school room is 27 feet long, and 16 feet wide. Parallel with its shorter sides are placed single moveable desks and forms; the ends of which are about $1\frac{1}{2}$ foot from the wall on one side of the room: on the other side there is a space, the whole length of the room, and about $4\frac{1}{2}$ feet in breadth, which is used for the common passage of the school, and for the classes to assemble in, to say their lessons. The desks being single, all the children sit facing one way; those in the eighth, or highest class, with their backs nearly close to the wall. At the other end of the room, in front of the first or lowest class, there is a space, 16 feet, the breadth of the room, by 7 feet, the distance of the first desk from the wall, where the classes also assemble, as in the space before mentioned, to say their lessons to their teachers. In these two spaces four classes, or one half of the whole school, can assemble, at the same time, with tolerable convenience. . . .

In front of each desk there is left room sufficient for a person to pass.

It is desirable that each class should have its separate desk:

but it frequently happens that the class is too large to admit of this; in which case the children at the bottom of the class are turned over to the desk next below their own. . . .

The children assemble at nine in the morning; go to dinner at one, during the summer; assemble again at two, and leave school at five: but in the winter, they dine at a quarter before one; assemble again at a quarter before two; and leave school earlier or later according to the length of the days; as some of the children live at the distance of three miles from the school.

Every alternate Saturday is a whole holiday: and a week's vacation is given at each of the three greater festivals.

The plan of instruction is carried on almost entirely through the agency of the scholars themselves; the school being divided, as was before stated, into eight classes; each under the tuition of a teacher. The teachers are supplied by the seventh and eighth classes. Most of the children in the seventh class, and all, except the head child, in the eighth class, take their turns for an hour at a time, as teachers to the other classes: and at the expiration of the hour, the children who have been acting as teachers are called back to their classes; and a new set is appointed. This change of teachers is under the direction of the head child of the school; who is the permanent teacher of the eighth class.

The monitor is selected from among the best and steadiest children of the eighth class; and is relieved at the same time, and by the same directions as the teachers. His usual station is at the inner extremity of the first or front desk; where either seated in the desk or standing on the form, and thus facing the classes, he has opportunity of observing accurately both their conduct, and that of their teachers. If a child offends in any way, the monitor instantly cautions him aloud; and if the offence is repeated, he is again cautioned, and his name is set down, with a mark opposite to it, on the monitor's slate: and for every new offence committed, the caution is repeated, and an additional mark set down. Before the school separates, the monitor's slate is examined by the schoolmistress; and if more than three or four marks appear opposite to any child's name, confinement, or some other punishment, is inflicted.

B. Learning the Alphabet

The children of the first class, having to learn the alphabet, are seated at their desk, which is nearly horizontal, and contains a sort of shallow trough (formed by thin slips of wood nailed to the top of the desk), covered with dry sand. Before each child or pair of children, is placed a pasteboard or card, containing, in large character, the printed letter which the children are learning, and which, to ensure their attention to its form, and to impress it on their minds, they are directed by their teacher to imitate with their forefingers in the sand. When each child has thus filled the space allotted to him, he names the letters which he has made, and counts their number to the teacher forwards and backwards, as he moves on in the front of the desk. This being done, the sand is immediately smoothed, the lines drawn, and the spaces marked out, by the teacher; and the class proceeds as before.

The capitals are taught in the following order; I, H, T, L, E, F, A, V, W, M, N, Z, K, Y, X, O, U, C, G, J, D, P, B, R, Q, S.

The small letters, according to the order of the alphabet.

During this practice in the sand, the children of the first class are called out by the teacher, three times at least, in the course of every hour, to some convenient part of the room, where a big pasteboard card of the whole alphabet is hung against the wall; and standing before it, in a semi-circle, are required, each in his turn, to name the letter to which the teacher points, or to find out the letter which the teacher names. For this latter purpose, the child is allowed to go close to the card. Should any mistake be made by a child, the one next below him is applied to; and so on, to the bottom, and if necessary through the whole, of the class; and the child by whom the mistake is rectified takes place of all those who have failed. The teacher himself in no case corrects an error, until the whole class has been applied to.

These regulations, with respect to correcting mistakes, taking places, &c. are strictly observed through all the classes.

By the strict and continued attention, both to the forms, and the names of the letters, which the exercises before mentioned require and ensure in the children, the knowledge of the alphabet is soon obtained: and when this is ascertained, by the school-mistress herself, to be the case, they are promoted to the second class.

C. Words of Command to be used in the school

BY MONITOR — General.

~~TEACHERS,~~ GIVE OUT COPIES: The teacher of each class receives copper plate copies from the schoolmistress or head child, and places one before every child in his class.

~~TEACHERS,~~ COLLECT COPIES: Each teacher collects his copies, and returns them to the schoolmistress or head child.

TEACHERS, BEGIN DICTATING: The teachers of the classes which write from dictation take their seats, and begin dictating their lesson, spelling, or mis-spelt words.

BY ~~TEACHERS~~ *Monitors*

CLASS, SHEW SLATES: the children of the class instantly raise their slates on the desk, with the written side outwards, and inclined a little to the end of the desk where the ~~teacher~~ gave the command.

CLASS, CLEAN SLATES: They rub out the inspected words with their spunges.

CLASS, TO LESSON; or OUT OF SCHOOL; or TO CHURCH: or TO CATECHISM; or TO CIPHERING: The children rise from their form, and, turning a little towards the end of the desk where the teacher stands, wait for the next command.

OUT: They step nimbly over the form, and stand behind it, keeping their eyes on their ~~teacher~~. The boys place their hands behind them; the girls hold theirs before them.

GO: They walk away rapidly, but quietly, under the conduct of their ~~teacher~~.

CLASS, TO YOUR PLACES, GO: They return in the same orderly manner to the space behind their form.

IN: They step over the form, and resume their seat.

3. Emulation and Rewards

SOURCE: Joseph Lancaster, *Improvements in Education*, 1806.

In spelling by writing on the slate, the performances of the scholars are inspected, sometimes by the monitor of their class, often by an inspecting monitor, and occasionally by the master.

Printing in the sand is inspected in the same manner as in the new method of teaching arithmetic. Every boy is placed next to one who can do as well or better than himself: his business is to excel him, in which case, he takes precedence of him. In reading, every reading division have the numbers, 1, 2, 3, &c. to 12, suspended from their buttons. If the boy who wears number 12, excels the boy who wears number 11, he takes his place and number; in exchange for which the other goes down to the place and number 12. Thus, the boy who is number 12, at the beginning of the lesson, may be number 1, at the conclusion of it, and vice versa. The boy who has number 1, has also a single leather ticket, lettered variously, as, 'Merit',—'Merit in Reading',—'Merit in Spelling',—'Merit in Writing', &c. This badge of honour he also forfeits, if he loses his place by suffering another to excel him. He also has a picture pasted on paste-board, and suspended on his breast; this he forfeits to any boy who can excel him. Whoever is in the first place at the conclusion of the lesson, delivers the ticket and picture to a monitor appointed for that purpose. The honour of wearing the ticket and number, as marks of precedency, is all the reward attached to them; but the picture which has been worn entitles the bearer to receive another picture in exchange for it, which becomes his own. This prize is much valued by the minor boys, and regarded by them all. Pictures can be made a fund of entertainment and instruction, combined with infinite variety. When a boy has a waggon, a whip-top, or a ball, one thing of the kind satisfies him, till it is worn out; but he may have a continual variety of pictures, and receive fresh instruction as well as pleasure from every additional prize. . . .

4. The Productivity of the System

SOURCE: Andrew Bell, *The Madras School or Elements of Tuition*, 1808.

In a word, the advantages of this system, in its political, moral, and religious tendency; in its economy of labour, time, expense, and punishment; in the facilities and satisfaction which it affords to the master and the scholar; can only be ascertained by trial and experience, and can scarcely be comprehended or credited by those, who have not witnessed its powers and marvellous effects.

Like the steam engine, or spinning machinery, it diminishes labour and multiplies work, but in a degree which does not admit of the same limits, and scarcely of the same calculations as they do. For, unlike the mechanical powers, this intellectual and moral engine, the more work it has to perform, the greater is the facility and expedition with which it is performed, and the greater is the degree of perfection to which it is carried.

5. The Weaknesses

Experience of the system led to disappointment as the drawbacks of monitorial schools became increasingly apparent. Their main weakness sprang from the limitations inherent in relying on child monitors or 'teachers'.

> SOURCE: Report of the Committee of Council on Education for 1845, vol. I, pp. 163–4. F. C. Cook, H.M.I., Report on Schools in the Eastern District.

We cannot reflect upon the age or acquirements of monitors without being struck with the absurdity of expecting any good results from the use of such materials. Taking the average age of monitors, they may be described as boys about $11\frac{1}{2}$ years old, reading with ease, but not much intelligence; writing from dictation, so as to give the sense of a passage, but without any regard to punctuation, or any practical knowledge of grammar; with more or less facility in working the ordinary rules of arithmetic to proportion or practice, but with little or no insight into its principles. The knowledge of geography, history, or general information, which the more intelligent of these youths may possess, is not called for in their employment as teachers of the lower classes; and it is hardly needful here to reiterate the severe but just observations which all writers upon our National Schools have made upon the tone and character of the religious instruction under monitors. It is equally prejudicial to the children, who are taught to confound the holiest things with the least important, and to themselves, since they are thus acquiring or confirming habits either of apathy or irreverence in dealing with those subjects which pertain to man's salvation.

We may surely, at present be permitted to assume, without further discussion, that the insufficient supply of qualified teachers, the small proportion which the numbers now employed

bear to the aggregate number of children under instruction, and the incompetency of the monitors to whom they are of
necessity compelled to intrust a considerable share of the teaching, are defects which ought no longer to be permitted to exist.

6. Dame or Common Schools

Although the national religious bodies established many schools on
monitorial lines, a considerable proportion of the children of the
labouring classes who attended any sort of day school were to be
found in dame schools or common schools. These were institutions
operated by untrained and sometimes unlettered individuals as a
means of getting for themselves a scanty living. In the 1830s, of
123,000 children attending elementary schools in Manchester,
Salford, Bury, Liverpool and Birmingham, some 50,000 were pupils
at dame or common schools. Conditions in these schools in the first
part of the nineteenth century are shown in this Report which was
based on reports made by local statistical societies.

> SOURCE: Report of the Committee of Council on Education, 1840,
> pp. 161–3. Baptist W. Noel, Report on the state of Elementary
> Education in Birmingham, Manchester, Liverpool and other
> towns in Lancashire.

The common schools, which are attended by children between
the ages of 5 and 14, are represented in the reports to be very
little superior to the dame schools with respect to instruction;
and, with respect to ventilation, often worse. The Birmingham
Report thus speaks of those which are in that town: 'Ventilation
is very little attended to in these schools, and, in some, cleanliness is equally neglected. There is generally a much greater
number of children crowded together than in dame-schools,
and the effluvia, arising from the mass of the scholars mingled
with the close air exhausted of its oxygen, and unfit for the purpose of comfortable or healthy respiration, under any long continuance in the school intolerable to a person unaccustomed to
it. The systems of instruction adopted are of the most imperfect
kind; the general principle of by far the largest number is that of
requiring the child to commit to memory a certain quantity of
matter, without any attempt being made to reach the understanding. . . . In only 29 out of the whole 177 schools of this
class, do the teachers profess to interrogate the children on what
they read and learn; . . . 8 out of the 29 who do interrogate their
children, admit that it is only done occasionally, when time and

opportunity permit. As in the dame-schools, corporal punishments form almost the whole of the moral training of these establishments.'

The Manchester schools are described thus: 'In the great majority of these schools there seems to be a complete want of order and system. The confusion arising from this defect, added to the low qualifications of the master, the number of scholars under the superintendence of one teacher, the irregularity of attendance, the great deficiency of books and the injudicious plan of instruction, or rather the want of any plan, render them nearly inefficient for any purpose of real instruction.' According to the reports, the schools of the same class in Liverpool, Salford, and Bury, are very similar to those of Birmingham and Manchester.

From the answers uniformly made to my inquiries on this subject among persons acquainted with the poor, I judge that the great majority, both of dame and common schools, in the Lancashire towns, answer to these descriptions; and the very few which my time enabled me to visit did not contradict that conclusion. In one of these dame schools I found 31 children, from 2 to 7 years of age. The room was a cellar, about 10 feet square and about 7 feet high. The only window was less than 18 inches square, and was not made to open. Although it was a warm day, towards the close of August, there was a fire burning; and the door, through which alone any air could be admitted, was shut. Of course, therefore, the room was close and hot; but there was no remedy. The damp, subterraneous walls required, as the old woman assured us, a fire throughout the year. If she opened the door the children would rush out to light and liberty, while the cold blast rushing in would torment her aged bones with rheumatism. Still further to restrain their vagrant propensities, and to save them from the danger of tumbling into the fire, she had crammed the children as closely as possible into a dark corner at the foot of her bed. Here they sat in the pestiferous obscurity, totally destitute of books, and without light enough to enable them to read, had books been placed in their hands. Six children, indeed, out of the 30, had brought some twopenny books, but these also, having been made to circulate through 60 little hands, were now so well soiled and tattered as to be rather the memorials of past achievements than the means of leading the children to fresh exertion. The only remaining instruments of instruction possessed by the dame, who lamented her hard lot, to be obliged, at so advanced an age, to tenant a damp cellar, and to raise the means of paying her rent by such scholastic toils, were a glass-full of sugar plums near the tattered leaves on the table in the centre of the room, and a cane by its side. Every point in instruction being thus secured by the good old rule of mingling the useful with the sweet.

Not far from this infant asylum I entered a common school. It was a room on the ground floor, up a dark, narrow, entry, and about 12 feet square. Here 43 boys and girls were assembled, of all ages, from 5 to 14. Patches of paper were pasted over the broken panes of the one small window, before which also sat the master, intercepting the few rays of light which would other-wise have crept into the gloom. Although it was in August the window was closed, and a fire added to the animal heat, which radiated from every part of the crowded chamber. In front of the fire, and as near to it as a joint on the spit, a row of children sat with their faces towards the master and their backs to the furnace. By this living screen the master, though still perspiring copiously, was somewhat sheltered from the intolerable heat. As another measure of relief, amidst the oppression of the steam-ing atmosphere, he had also laid aside his coat. In this undress he was the better able to wield the three canes, two of which, like the weapons of an old soldier, hung conspicuously on the wall, while the third was on the table ready for service. When questioned as to the necessity of this triple instrumentality, he assured us that the children were 'abrupt and rash in their tempers', that he generally reasoned with them respecting their indiscretion, but that when civility failed he had recourse to a little severity.

There was no classification of the children; and the few books in the school were such as some of the parents chose to send. Under such circumstances the poor man had an arduous task to accomplish; and, not knowing what situations might not be in our gift, he informed us that he would gladly avail himself of any opportunity of quitting an employment to which extrava-gance alone had caused him to descend.

2 Elementary Schools in the First Period of State Aid and Inspection, to 1862

1. Instructions for the Inspectors of Schools, 1840

In 1833 the first grants were made from public funds to aid elementary education. These grants amounted to no more than subscriptions to aid the National Society and the British and Foreign Schools Society with the cost of erecting school buildings. During the following thirty years the total amount of financial aid grew steadily and the types of grant multiplied in number. In order to ensure that value was obtained for public expenditure, the first of H. M. Inspectors were appointed in 1840. Dr Kay-Shuttleworth, Secretary to the Committee of Council on Education, directed the Inspectors to assist school managers and teachers and to encourage the development of the school as a community.

SOURCE: Report of the Committee of Council on Education for 1839–40, pp. 19 and 25, Minute of 4th January, 1840.

. . . the duties of Inspectors of Schools may be divided into three distinct branches.

1st. Those duties relate, in the first place, to inquiry in neighbourhoods from whence applications have been made for aid to erect new schools, in order to enable the Committee of Council to determine the propriety of granting funds in aid of the expenses proposed to be incurred, or to the examination of certain special cases in which claims of peculiar urgency are advanced for temporary aid in the support and improvement of existing schools.

2dly. To the inspection of the several schools aided by public grants issued under the authority of the Committee, and an examination of the method and matter of instruction, and the character of the discipline established in them, so as to enable the Inspector to report thereon to this Committee, for the information of both Houses of Parliament. . . .

The degree of attention paid to the moral training of the children, and the means which are adopted for this purpose, deserve the especial attention of the Inspector; he will particularly note to what extent the industrial instruction of females is carried; whether the master has any opportunity of becoming a companion to the children in their hours of relaxation; and whether he is in the habit of communicating with their parents, and procuring assistance from them in the regulation of the habits and formation of the characters of their children; the average attendance at the school, the number on the books, and the number of holidays in each week and year deserve to be noted.

2. The Training of Pauper Children in Workhouse Schools

The lack of facilities and the need for some sort of training were both more obvious in the case of pauper children than in the case of children who were not the object of that form of public care implied in workhouse residence. Under the reformed Poor Law, some sort of educational provision was extended to the majority of pauper children long before the same could be said to be available to the majority of children in this country. Early attempts to organise schools for pauper children ran into the difficulty of finding an adequate supply of suitable teachers and it was Kay-Shuttleworth's experience of this problem when with the Poor Law Board that led him to give urgent attention to providing training facilities when he became Secretary to the Committee of Council.

SOURCE: Report from the Poor Law Commissioners on the Training of Pauper Children, 1841, Appendix IX, pp. 391–3. Report by Edward Senior Esq., Assistant Poor Law Commissioner.

GENTLEMEN, *Grantham, 16th March, 1840*

In compliance with your instructions, dated 3rd February, 1840, in which I am directed to report on the state of the workhouse schools in my district, I desire to state,—

1st. That under the previous poor law the children in the workhouses were neither taught nor trained; they were usually placed under the care of an elder pauper, frequently himself unable to read or write, who was directed to look after them, and whose duties consisted in preventing the children from committing acts of mischief. So soon as the children reached the proper age, they were bound out as apprentices—always *out* of their own parishes—with a considerable premium, and thus the main object of the parochial authorities was obtained, the getting rid of the burthen.

More rarely the system of compulsory apprenticeship was adopted, and the different ratepayers were compelled, in turn, to take the pauper children, or to pay a fine; the latter alternative was generally preferred, until the collective amount of the fines tempted some needy tradesman to take them off the parish. The children had no motives to qualify themselves for service, which they disliked; the parochial authorities no interest in making them good members of society, the apprenticeship premium being the cure for all difficulties.

The children mixed with the adult, and too generally profligate, inmates; the boys naturally preferred the more exciting conversation of the poacher or the smuggler, and the girls that of the abandoned females. No attention was paid to the religious education of the children. . . .

With all the defects of the present system of education, it is unquestionably a great improvement on the previous management.

A schoolmaster or schoolmistress, or both these officers, have been appointed in almost every Union in the district under my care, and the children are to a great extent separated from the adults.

The children of both sexes are taught to read and write, and a knowledge of arithmetic is imparted to them.

The boys are employed in cultivating the workhouse grounds, and the girls are brought up to household employments.

The system of instruction adopted is usually that of the National School Society.

The Bible is in almost all the schools the only class-book, and the schools are deficient in the necessary elementary works on education, and corporal punishments are still in use; no system of rewards has hitherto been found practicable. . . .

The schoolmasters and schoolmistresses in the Union houses are usually very incompetent, and are frequently persons who have been unsuccessful in some other calling, and who have not been educated or brought up with the view of their becoming instructors.

Respectable candidates will not submit to the restraint of the workhouse, joined to the circumstance of their being under the control and authority of the master of the workhouse, and the fact of their being compelled either to take their meals alone, or to share them with the inferior officers.

Separate apartments for these officers are usually, but not always, provided for them.

The average salary in my district for a schoolmaster, where there is no schoolmistress, appears to be £18.

For a schoolmistress, where there is no schoolmaster, £16.

Average aggregate salary when both are employed, £47.

Average sum paid to instructors in the thirty-one Unions, £36.

During the last year I visited Scotland, with the view of making myself acquainted with the several methods of instruction made use of there, and endeavoured to obtain candidates for the office of workhouse schoolmaster; the terms, however, they required were so high, and the preliminary stipulation of being placed on a par with, and dining with, the masters of the workhouses, have hitherto prevented my obtaining any candidates from that country.

Not unfrequently the struggle between these officers leads to a collision; and during the last six months I have been engaged in assisting the guardians in inquiring into recriminatory charges which have been brought by these officers in two Unions, Spalding and Holbeach, which led in the former instance to the resignation of both officers, and in the latter will yet, I fear, interfere with the discipline of the establishment.

Under these circumstances I have no hope of being able to effect a further improvement on the present system, unless power be given to the Commissioners to unite Unions for the education and management of the children belonging to them, with a joint Board of Management, elected by the several Unions. I feel persuaded that such a system would not only be followed by an improvement in the education of the children, but would also effect a considerable pecuniary saving in the establishment charges from the diminution in the number of schoolmasters and schoolmistresses.

I have the honour to be,

Gentlemen,

Your obedient servant,

EDWARD SENIOR,

Assistant-Commissioner.

3. The Lack of Teachers and the Poverty of Schools, 1845

The increase in the number of schools which was encouraged by government building grants made more acute the problems of finding enough adequately trained teachers and of the poverty of schools. The new grants introduced in 1846 were designed to meet these needs.

SOURCE: Report of the Committee of Council on Education for 1845, Vol. 1, pp. 258–61. Report by the Rev. Henry Moseley, F.R.S., H.M.I. on Elementary Schools of the Midland District.

The systems of Bell and Lancaster were introduced at a period when public opinion on the subject of education was not so far advanced as it is now, and when public aid was not, to the same extent, contributed for its support. If to the other difficulties opposed at that time to the introduction of popular education, the expense of maintaining it had been superadded, the spirit of antagonism then abroad would probably have been successful. It was, therefore, hoped to make it self-supporting; and although this expectation has been but in very few cases realised, yet the method of Dr Bell (the monitorial system) has been found by experience to be pre-eminently a cheap method of instruction; and could no other reason be alleged, this is sufficient to account for its adoption by those eminent persons, who then so perseveringly and so successfully laboured in its cause; and for the hold which it has so long had upon the education of the country. It is a reason which now, however, that a due value is set upon popular instruction, has lost much of its authority.

I believe that the opinion which I have expressed here is held substantially by the great body of the friends of education, and that the public mind, so far as it is interested in this matter at all, is fully ripe for a change.

To the state of educational progress, indicated by this fact, the action of the Committee of Council on the public opinion of the country, during the last few years, has greatly contributed; and it is for this reason that a grave responsibility seems to me to rest upon it as to the system by which that now about to fall into disuse is to be replaced.

To take away from the master his monitors, and expect him to teach, unaided, the crowd of ignorant children intrusted to his charge, would be to assign him a hopeless task. It would be to disorganise his school.

It is for these reasons that, in another part of this Report, I have brought the subject of organisation specially under your notice.

It is sufficient for me here to state, that all plans for that object involve an increased expenditure in the maintenance of schools, by the introduction of a greater number of adult teachers into the business of elementary instruction, and the employment of a class of paid pupil-teachers, supposed to be preparing for the office of master.

Every such plan supplies, moreover, new and higher functions of the master than have hitherto been assigned to him. These will, in few instances, be efficiently discharged, unless he have received some previous instruction in a training college of a professional character; and they suppose considerable enterprise and energy of character and a high standard of general attainment. Masters of this class cannot be procured, or at least kept, on the stipends which have been found sufficient to retain the services of the master of an ordinary monitorial school, so that, not only in respect to the number of adult teachers, but in respect to the stipend of each, does this change involve, in every school, an increased expenditure.

I believe that the additional funds necessary to this purpose cannot be raised by local contributions, unless that stimulus be superadded which Government aid can alone supply. . . .

The deplorable state of poverty [of the schools] operates to their prejudice in various ways. In the first place, it has led to the introduction, and perpetuates the employment, of a class of schoolmasters who are wholly unequal to the duties intrusted to them. Schoolbuildings are now erected by the aid of your Lordships grants and those of the National Society, with comparatively little difficulty. The embarrassments of the clergyman begin when the schoolroom is completed. Finding himself completely unable to guarantee the salary required by a master instructed in one of the training colleges, he is obliged to accept the services offered to him, perhaps by some person upon the spot, whose chief recommendation next to the indispensable one of a high personal character, may be his disqualification for any other pursuit in life. Under the auspices of such a teacher, the school drags on a spiritless, if not a lifeless, existence, . . . an obstacle to the cause it is established to promote rather than a means to its advancement.

The poverty of schools is, in the second place, to be seen in the inadequate supply of school books . . . I know of nothing which would more advance the cause of education than to render easy the purchase of books.

Another evil, resulting from the difficulty in maintaining schools is, that the clergy are deterred by this difficulty from undertaking the responsibility of establishing them.

And last and chiefly, it is the poverty of the schools, by which the monitorial system—of the inefficiency of which this Report and that of every other Inspector supplies your Lordships with the evidence—is perpetuated in them.

With a view to the remedy of these evils, I beg respectfully to submit, that the principle upon which the public funds are made to contribute towards the erection of *school buildings* is applicable to the *maintenance* of the schools and that it would be found in practice to be equally free from objection. The great danger to be guarded against in respect to all such aid is, lest it should dry up those sources of private benevolence, which, however inadequate, are in their amount considerable, and which are not only of importance in diminishing the public expenditure required for this object, but as the exponents of local sympathies, and the means of calling forth local co-operation. By the particular expedient adopted in respect of grants in aid of the building fund, the amount of local contributions to that fund has, however, been largely *increased*. And there can be no question, that the sum raised locally every year for the *maintenance* of schools, would, in like manner, be greatly augmented in amount, if government aid were, by the same judicious expedient, offered to meet it.

Among the many advantages which would result from such a measure, it is not the least, that by the facilities which it offers for the *support* of schools, when established, it would lead to the establishment of many new ones.

I know of no other measure, which, in its practical operation, would more entirely meet the views and wishes of the promoters of schools, or contribute more directly to the progress of elementary education, than one for contributing to the support of apprentices or pupil-teachers. It is a recommendation of this measure, that it will provide for the more liberal maintenance and support of the training colleges, and to the supply of a continual succession of candidates qualified for admission to them.

4. The Use of Corporal Punishment

The controversy over the value of corporal punishment in schools is of long standing; this extract contains some interesting evidence from schools of their practices in the 1840s.

SOURCE: Report of the Committee of Council on Education for 1845, Vol 2, pp. 164–6. Report by the Rev. F. Watkins, H.M.I.

... It has long been a question whether such punishment be necessary; very different opinions are held on the subject;
'Adhuc sub judice lis est'

Now the answers made by 163 places are these: That in 145 of them it is made use of. That in 18 it is dispensed with. Of the 18 places in which there is no corporal punishment—

      6 are schools of girls only,
      2 are schools of girls and infants,
      2 are schools of infants only,
      5 are schools of boys and girls mixed,
      1 is a school for boys only,
      2 are schools for boys, girls and infants separate.
      —
     18.   Of these only three are large schools.

In the six girls' schools the discipline is admirable; in four of them the children's progress in their studies is highly satisfactory.

The same may be said of one of the infants' schools, the other has been lately re-opened, and cannot be judged fairly in these respects.

The two schools of girls and infants are equally pleasing in these points.

Of the remaining eight schools, one is excellent in all respects, two are tolerable, the five others are wretched in discipline and very deficient in progress. ...

I now turn to the other side of the question and take the 27 places ... where corporal punishment is used most frequently, and, as far as I can judge, the most severely. What is the result?

At 20 of them are schools which are notoriously lacking in

discipline, some of the worst, if not the very worst, in the Northern district.

Of these, 15 are in an equally wretched state, as to moral tone and intellectual progress.

At the other seven places, the schools of three are in a satisfactory state in all respects, and may be called good.

The remaining four are only tolerable, with a discipline of fear rather than of love; where the children are not making great progress in their studies, but are not remarkably backward in them.

I subjoin a list of these 27 schools, with the answer made to the question about corporal punishment in the master's own words. I should say that the instruments of punishment are the cane, stick, ferule or ruler, strap or taw (i.e. strap with three, five or seven tails), and birch rod.

1. 'Strap very often'—a tolerable school, rather deficient in discipline.
2. 'Cane very frequently'—a bad school in almost all points.
3. 'Cane every day'—a good school on the whole.
4. 'Cane very frequent'—a very bad, undisciplined, and ignorant school.
5. 'Cane daily'—a poor school without any character.
6. 'Cane every day'—a restless set of boys and girls mixed.
7. 'Cane very frequently'—a very ignorant school of gaping, heavy children.
8. 'Little stick once or twice per day'—a few grossly ignorant and inattentive children.
9. 'Cane freely'—the worst school (I think) in moral tone and discipline in the whole district.
10. 'Cane and strap frequently'—a fair village school, but the children are inattentive and nervous.

Such are briefly the characteristics of the schools in which there is the greatest amount of corporal punishment: Do they seem to commend it to our judgement?

The offences for which it is inflicted are many and various; they are chiefly these, as returned by the teachers of the schools: 'Talking or laughing in school'; 'gross inattention or disobedience'; 'coming late frequently'; 'playing truant'; 'telling lies'; 'bad language'. In comparatively few cases 'stealing';

3

'robbing orchards'; 'trespassing on neighbours' property'; 'being mischievous in the streets', &c.

There are, I think, very few of these offences which would not be much diminished by an increase of the number and improvement in the character of teachers, by inclosed playgrounds, and by cheerful companionship of the teachers with the children during their times of relaxation. In girls' schools, it is now the general opinion, that corporal punishment is not only unnecessary, but actually mischievous. In the best of those which are under my inspection, such as that at Clifton (York), Mrs Burdon's Castle Eden, Beverley, St Mary's (Sheffield), Richmond, Northallerton, Alston, Stalybridge, Manchester (St Anne's), Seaton Carew &c, it is, I believe, a thing unknown, or almost unpractised. A mistress who cannot rule her school without a rod may well doubt whether she is fitted for that particular situation.

In boys' schools it is doubtless more difficult to dispense with it. There are natures amongst the wretched, uncultivated, and almost brute-like occupants of some of our boys' schools to which this 'last appeal of force' seems the only one to which they will attend; but it is plainly the duty of a master to attempt to win them by all other means; and it is plain, that the *charm* of the rod loses its power in proportion to the frequency of its use. I have seen schools in which the master never lays the cane down, but walks about with it, as his sceptre, bestowing a smart tap with it here and a sharp cut with it there, as may seem to him most needful. Such schools are almost always of an inferior description. The boys are cowed by the master's eye and the master's hand; but when he is absent for a moment, or his back turned, it is easy to see how little education is progressing there.

5. The Good Waitress, 1849

Nineteenth century class books were rich in moral and practical advice expressed both in prose and verse.

SOURCE: *Lessons on Industrial Education for the Use of Female Schools, by A Lady*, 1849.

> The servant who at table waits,
> Should have a ready eye;
> For 'tis not all, to hand the plates,
> And silently stand by.

The table neatly to set out,
As it before was planned;
To move with noiseless step about,
To serve with gentle hand.

To cast a look from side to side,
And read in every face
If any want is unsupplied,
Or unfill'd any space.

To have whatever's call'd for near;
To speak no useless word;
To hear, yet never seem to hear,
What passes at the board;

These, of a clever parlour maid,
The special duties are;
And she who hopes to be well-paid,
Must make them all her care.

6. The General Condition of Elementary Schools about 1850

These descriptions of conditions in schools indicate some of the difficulties confronting schools at this time and serve to emphasise the need for better teachers.

SOURCE: Report of the Committee of Council on Education for 1850–51, Appendix C, pp. 421–3, Report by the Rev. M. Mitchell, H.M.I., on schools in the Eastern Counties.

B . . .

A very painful visit, I hardly know how to satisfy both my own conscience and the managers. The apparatus, books and slates are all of the worst description, and very defective in both schools.

The discipline in the boys' schools is most imperfect. The master has not the least idea of system, and the most confused idea of school-keeping. He is entirely untrained, and needs at least six months to qualify him to communicate knowledge. He has, however, a third class first division certificate. I don't know what to do about it. He seems a good sort of man, but in no respect a schoolmaster, and I feel really annoyed both at declining to authorise his augmentation, and at permitting it.

The girls' school is much better. But I wonder at the managers being satisfied with the apparatus and books. They must be taught that if the Committee of Council aids schools, it is only on the conditions being fulfilled. I cannot express how annoyed I have felt at the imperfections of these schools,—each with certificated teachers and two pupil teachers, and they are the worst in the neighbourhood. I think they must be dealt with severely.

It is sought to obtain for these schools of 140 mere infants,

	£	s	d
For the master's certificate	18	0	0
Two pupil teachers	20	0	0
Teaching ditto	9	0	0
Mistress's certificate	11	0	0
Two pupil teachers	22	10	0
Teaching ditto	9	0	0
Total	89	10	0

Neither the school nor the place warrants such an expenditure of public money.

C ...

This ought to be a better school than it is from the attention paid to it. The tone of the scholars is good. The children are very fond of it, but the master says that he cannot get on with his own system, and that the clergyman does too much &c. I think the school would be even better under an inferior master, and the present man would do better in a school less under the immediate teaching of the clergyman. They sing very nicely, but there is too little life or spirit among the children, who were, however, terribly afraid of the Inspector, which shows imperfect training, for if a school is so conducted that the scholars cannot, through nervousness, put out their forces when required, the system must be deficient. The pains and attention of the clergyman cannot be too highly commended, and the tone of the children is excellent, as regards a submissive discipline, but I doubt whether such training is equal to the task of making them able to stem the rude roughness of ordinary life, or really to fit them to contend with and overcome the actual trials of their necessary existence. Nervous sensibility appears to me the last thing to be encouraged in a hardy labourer. A manly spirit of proper independence is the real tone to excite. On a recent inspection of this school, I am happy to state that everything is very much improved, and that sickly sort of sensibility is now entirely removed.

D . . .

Nothing can be more miserable than these schools. The master and mistress, Man and wife, are totally incompetent. The children are shamefully ignorant and the supply of books and apparatus is lamentably defective. No school at all would be better. Only two of the boys could work any sums. Nine of the others attempted addition, but failed entirely. Their scripture knowledge is equally defective.

A good mistress might be secured for the salary of the present very inefficient people, being £40.

Norfolk.—It is evident, from this week's work, that this part of Norfolk is in a most lamentable state of un-education, arising from defect of funds, consequent bad teachers, and deficiency of books and maps, &c., which the teachers would not, however, know how to use, even if they had them. . . .

O . . .

A small village school of humble character. The acquirements of the mistress are insufficient to take pupil-teachers. In 14 lines she made 7 false spellings.

P . . .

At the examination, the mistress, highly recommended by the clergyman of —— has made a most disgraceful failure in her paper-work. In 23 lines of writing she made 17 false spellings. The salary which is paid, £20, cannot secure a competent person.

Q . . .

There are many women equal to the conducting of a small school fairly, who are totally inadequate to train pupil-teachers or stipendiary monitors.

R . . .

A very wretched school under a youth who was dismissed from
St Mark's College after a year's residence, because the surgeon
refused him his certificate. His training has not profited him at
all. The instruction is very meagre. The school is totally un-
provided with books or apparatus, and the fittings are very indifferent. A part of the ceiling has given way. £20 towards the
support comes from the clergyman.

S . . .

Examined the pupil-teachers. The master's papers are not equal
to a good pupil-teacher's of the second year. I observe few pupil-
teachers can answer the questions in mechanics or mensuration,
but the geography is much improved. These pupil-teachers have
only had half a year, instead of the whole, and their papers are
imperfect.

T . . .

The master, an old sea-captain, is not the man to impart a good
moral tone; and he not having been trained, and having taken
to the profession late in life, is unequal to the management of so
large a number of children.

7. The Half-Time System in Bradford and Rochdale, 1861

Under the Factory Acts children between the ages of 8 and 13
employed in factories—mainly in textile mills in these two towns—
were required to attend school on a part-time basis. This description
by J. S. Winder, an Assistant Commissioner, gives some idea of the
educational worth of the arrangement. Half-time education was not
completely abolished until after the First World War.

> SOURCE: Report of the Royal Commission on Popular Education
> (Newcastle Commission), 1861. Reports from Assistant Com-
> missioners, pp. 228, 231.

The mode in which the half-time system is carried out is almost
universally as follows: Every child between the ages of 8 and 13,
working in a factory, spends half the day, from 6 a.m. to 12
noon, or from 1 p.m. to 6 p.m. in the mill. During the other half,
i.e. from 1.30 p.m. to 4.30 p.m. or from 9 a.m. to 12 noon it is in

school. Periodically, in some cases monthly, in others weekly, the morning and afternoon batches of children in each mill change turns, so as to effect an equitable division of school time and work. On Friday the schoolmaster makes up for every mill, from which short-timers are sent to him, a record of the attendance or absence of each child for every day of the past week; without this certificate of previous school attendance, it is illegal to continue to employ a child. If absence has extended to the whole week, the child cannot be employed at all; if it has been but partial, for one or two days, it is the practice to compel the offender to make up for the lost school time by an additional attendance of an equal, or, as the rule is in some factories a double time, by way of compensation. Schools, being open only five days in the week, a short-timer is in school something less on average than 15 hours a week, from which must be deducted for each day not less than half an hour for prayers, an interval of recreation and various interruptions. The time, therefore, during which a short-timer is under effective instruction is very short indeed; short as it is, however, in the case of girls, a large portion is abstracted for teaching sewing. Mixed schools devote usually about an hour and a half, girls' schools about an hour and three quarters, to this purpose daily; and, as in a majority of cases, by a stupid arrangement, the needlework lesson is given only in the afternoon, a mill girl may, during her afternoon turn, lasting a week or a month, as the case may be, have not more than an hour a day for intellectual instruction. Indeed, in not a few private, and some public schools, needlework takes up the whole afternoon, and the girls may be left for a whole month without even having a reading lesson. . . .

It seems to me that in many public schools in which the two kinds of scholars are mixed, the interests of the half-timers are made to bend too much to those of the day scholars. The time-table is often so arranged that there is no equitable division of lessons between morning and afternoon, and in consequence a half-timer may go on a whole week or a month with little or no instruction in writing or some other important subject. Needlework is certainly a difficulty even under the best arrangements, but in very few half-time schools is any attempt made to intersperse it amongst the other instruction in a rational way. A few teachers divide it fairly between morning and afternoon, but much more frequently it is assigned exclusively to one portion of the day, so that the half-time girls during one half of their time have no sewing at all, during the other half, hardly anything else. The half-timers are, it is easy to see, very frequently looked on as a nuisance. Generally speaking, they spring from a lower grade of society than the day scholars,—have somewhat ruder manners and give more trouble, without being more profitable, than half their number of full-time children. Some of the schools in receipt of government aid, as the Bradford Borough West British schools and the Rochdale Wesleyan school refuse to take them at all.

The private factory schools in the Rochdale district are on the whole very unsatisfactory. I did not find a really good one, though two or three were fairly efficient. At least five which I visited, two close to the town and the rest in outlying districts, are schools only in name, and a complete fraud upon the Factory Acts. In two, taught in cottage rooms by old incapacitated weavers, hardly any of the children learnt writing, and none could do more in the way of reading than scramble through an easy verse in the New Testament. Yet one of these schools provided education for 50 and the other for 18 part-time children. In another I found not less than 60 girls, chiefly short-timers, crowded into a frightfully hot room so tightly that it was almost impossible for them to move, with desk room for about 10, and apparently hardly any instruction given except a little reading and sewing. Schools like these answer the purpose for which they were established, of giving formal certificates of school attendance,—and so long as they have the support of the neighbouring mill owners they may set at nought the competition of better schools and the remonstrances of parents whose children they sacrifice. The Factory Inspectors may undoubtedly refuse to accept the certificates of a very inefficient school,—but the standard of competency which they feel themselves authorised to exact is very low, and their authority in this matter to be very sparingly exercised.

8. An Elementary School for Children of Skilled Artisans

Some schools charged rather more weekly pence than was usual and drew their pupils from among the children of skilled workmen and small tradespeople; their programmes of instruction tended to be fairly ambitious. Many of these schools were attached to the non-conformist British and Foreign Schools Society.

SOURCE: *Some Habits and Customs of the Working Classes by A Journeyman Engineer*, 1867, pp. 14–20.

Take the case of a well-to-do mechanic's son. Having been taught to read in a woman's school, or in a national infant school, he is at seven or eight years of age removed probably to one of those schools known as British schools; in which the general body of pupils pay from fourpence to sixpence a week each, and an 'upper class' a shilling a week each in consideration of learning 'extras'. On the day on which he is to enter his new school, the hope of the Joneses, attired in the cloth suit which up to the previous day has done duty as his 'Sunday clothes', and with hands and face as clean as water and soap can make them, and hair carefully oiled and brushed, is taken to the school by his mother, it being necessary that one of his parents should have an interview with the master. On coming into the master's presence, Mrs J. makes her best curtsey, and explains that she wishes her boy to be enrolled as a pupil in that school; whereupon the schoolmaster having taken a look at Master Jones, and blandly asked him whether he is a good boy, proceeds to take down his name and age and the address of his parents. He next asks whether he has been to school before, and if so, where; and then tests his power by putting him to read a few sentences aloud; after which he assigns him a class. The boy being thus disposed of, the master addresses himself to the mother, telling her in the first place that they are very strict as to the personal cleanliness and regular attendance of their pupils, and she having expressed her approval in these matters, he goes on to inform her that 'our course' consists of reading, writing, arithmetic, grammar, geography, including the use of the globes, the Scriptures, astronomy, composition, history, elocution, singing, and elementary science; in addition to which, French, Latin, and geometry are taught in the upper class, for admission into which however, Master Jones will not be qualified for some time to come. Mrs Jones listens to the recital of this numerous and high-sounding list of studies respectfully but appalled—wondering why the master should enter into all these details with her; but she is speedily enlightened upon this point by his going on to say that they find some of the books, but that her son will also require a number of books which they do *not* find, but with which he will be happy to supply her at the same price as the booksellers. Mrs J. of course takes and pays for the books, which are duly handed over to her son, who may then be considered fairly established in his new school. And now let us look at the plan of education followed in the school. The hours of attendance are from nine in the morning till four in the afternoon, with an hour and a half for dinner, and half an hour—a quarter of an hour morning and afternoon—for play; besides which each pupil has 'night lessons', the preparation of which will take from one to two hours, according to the length of the lessons and powers of memory of the learner. The pupils are divided into from seven to ten classes, irrespective of the upper class; and taking it that our illustrative school has ten classes, we will suppose that our new pupil is placed in the fifth. This class will be 'taken' by pupils from the first class, or the younger pupil-teachers, boys destined for the teaching profession, but who as yet are mere schoolboys, whose inaccessibility to the corrupting influence of marbles cannot be relied upon, and many of whom, it is well known in schoolboy circles, are given to secretly eating the toffee that has been taken from pupils who have been detected devoting greater attention to it than their lessons; and who openly make favourites of some pupils, and take 'picks' at others. One of these boys will in the morning 'take' the night lessons and sums, this operation consisting in examining the sums, and seeing that a certain percentage of them have the right answers, and listening to the repetition of the lessons, passing those who are tolerably perfect in them, and making those who are very imperfect or totally ignorant 'stand on the line', in order that the master may deal with them. After the taking of the night lessons, come (say) the scripture lesson, which consists in the reading—each boy in the class taking a verse in his turn—of one or more chapters in the Bible, and the asking of a number of questions by the teacher to test the *memory* of the boys concerning what they have been reading. When this has been gone through, it will be time to go into the playground. On assembling in school again, the whole of the pupils are formed into one large class for a singing lesson, at the end of which they break up into their ordinary classes for their writing lessons, which last till dinner time.

After dinner, the time up to the hour for going into the play-ground will be occupied by grammar and geography lessons, which in the fifth class will be taught, the former by the pupil repeating in a monotonous sing-song tone after the teacher, 'There are nine parts of speech—article, noun, adjective, pro-noun,' &c.; and the latter by their repeating in the same tone and manner, that the Earth is divided into two hemispheres and four continents; that an island is a piece of land entirely sur-rounded by water, and a peninsula a piece of land almost surrounded by water. On returning from the playground, the remainder of the afternoon will be taken up by the reading lessons, consisting, in the fifth class, of 'moral lessons in words of two syllables', and the setting of the night lessons, which last will, in the case of our young friend, be confined at this time to the working of half-a-dozen sums, and the learning by heart of a table of weights and measures, and a column of 'spellings'. But even with this limitation in the matter of night lessons, Master Jones's scholastic task will be a tolerably heavy one for an eight-year-old boy, fond of play, and having to go to bed at eight o'clock in the evening. This, however, is only the beginning of his educational sorrows. We will suppose that he is a moderately good and intelligent boy, that he does not get 'put on the line' with unusual frequency, that he never gets sent home for having dirty shoes or face, that he does not occasionally spend his school wages, play truant for a week, and bring a forged note of excuse for his absence; that when he gets a caning he grins, or howls, and bears it, and does not go home crying, and bring his mother with him on the following morning to indignantly state in the face of the assembled pupils, 'which her boy is as good a boy as ever breathed, and she ain't a-going to have him beat black and blue to please any nasty puppy of a teacher;'—we will suppose all this, and that he gradually rises from class to class, and takes prizes at the half-yearly examinations, until, at twelve years of age, he reaches the first class, and the full force of the cramming system is brought to bear upon his devoted head. His night sums will now be in the higher rules of arith-metic, which he finds exceedingly difficult, from his having been forced through the earlier rules without being taught the principles of their application; and the lessons will embrace half a dozen different subjects besides. These and his day lessons tax his powers of memory to an unnatural extent, while leaving his other faculties dormant. But still the system enables him to shine at the heavily crammed and oft-rehearsed half-yearly examinations, to take the prizes at them, and to cover himself and his master with glory in the presence of the parents of the pupils and others who attend such examinations. Having so distinguished himself, it is considered advisable by his proud and gratified parents either to remove him to a 'finishing school' (generally a 'genteel academy' at from one to two guineas per quarter), or place him in the upper class of the school he is already attending; the latter plan being the most usually adopted. In consequence of this proceeding, lessons in mathematics and a couple of languages are added to the boy's already cruel mode of educational misery. He will now have little or no time for play; his memory will be strained to a stupefying degree; he will begin to sincerely hate school and all pertaining thereto, and urge his parents to send him to work; and when he is sent to work his sense of relief at being freed from the thraldom of lessons will give an additional zest to the general feeling of joy and importance which all boys feel on first going to work.

Nor is it at all surprising that such a system as I have attempted briefly to describe should produce a hatred rather than a desire for education in the minds of those who suffer under it. In the first place it attempts too much. A moment's consideration must make it evident that boys of from twelve to fourteen years of age and only ordinary strength of mind, cannot simultaneously study ten or twelve subjects—several of which really are, and all of which as they are taught to them appear to be, wholly distinct—with any reasonable probability of attaining a useful proficiency in them all; while the distraction of mind consequent upon this multiplicity of studies makes it very improbable that they will learn any of them well. The mode of teaching practised under this system, and indeed necessitated in order to secure its *apparent* success, is also utterly objectionable. Its chief aim is to produce prize pupils and organize showy public examinations, rather than to lay the foundations of a good education. By this mode only the barest and driest outlines of each subject are taught: no attempt is made to interest the pupil in his studies by teaching him the broad principles or general applications of the various branches of knowledge which those studies embrace, or to amalgamate or generalize such of the studies as admit of it. Under this system of teaching, proficiency is sought to be attained by cramming the pupils to bursting-point with definitions, dates, and figures, all of which, though of the utmost importance as parts of the subjects to which they pertain, and essential to the thorough understanding of them, are wholly uninteresting and practically useless to students having no further knowledge of those subjects. Let any person look, for instance, at the class-books from which history and geography—the two most interesting branches of an ordinary English education—are taught in those schools more particularly devoted to the education of the children of working-men, and they will find that the best of them are little better than chronological tables recording the dates of the births and deaths of sovereigns, and the names and dates of famous battles and sieges, and catalogues of the principal countries, rivers, and mountains of the earth. These books are a good illustration of the striving-to-do-too-much feature which disfigures the system to which they belong, for they profess to give a *detailed* history, or geographical description of the world, in a small volume of about a hundred and twenty pages. That a knowledge of the physical sciences and the ancient and modern languages is a highly desirable thing there can be no doubt, but the circumstances of working men do not admit of their boys being taught these branches of education, and the attempt to teach them during the last year or so at school is a mere waste of time. The smattering he gets (and that is the utmost he can hope to gain) is not sufficient to induce him to continue the study after he has left school, and the smattering itself is speedily forgotten.

Speaking from experience, I have no hesitation in saying that the children of the working-classes must under the most favourable circumstances leave school at fourteen years of age, and many of them much earlier; it is a mistake to attempt to extend their school studies beyond the plain foundations of reading, writing, and arithmetic. But these, and more especially the first of them, might be taught in so comprehensive a manner as to embrace a useful general knowledge of a variety of subjects. Working men cannot be made *scholars*, but by reading they may gain knowledge, and to create and to direct a taste for reading should be the chief aim of their education. Under a system having this object in view, the education of the working-classes would be continued after they left school; for literature of all kinds is so abundant and easy of access that no youth or man who has a taste for reading experiences much difficulty in gratifying it.

3 Elementary Schools in the Era of Payment by Results and the School Boards, 1862-1902

The rapid increase in the cost of grants for education during the middle years of the nineteenth century led to the setting up of the Newcastle Commission to inquire into the 'State of Popular Education in England'. The Commission reported in 1861 and found, among other things, a need for a greater concentration on teaching the elementary skills of reading, writing and arithmetic and a simplification of the grant system.

1. The Revised Code, 1862

Robert Lowe, Vice-President of the Committee of Council on Education, was determined to meet the situation described by the Newcastle Commission with a remedy which was largely of his own devising, by applying the principle of payment by results to government grants. The multiplicity of grants which had grown up were to be replaced by a single grant based partly on the attendance of scholars and partly on the results of annual examinations in reading, writing and arithmetic. In spite of a storm of opposition, the Revised Code came into force in 1862 and continued, with various modifications, until nearly the end of the century.

> SOURCE: Report of the Committee of Council on Education for 1862, pp. XXI–XXIII. Revised Code of Minutes and Regulations of the Committee of the Privy Council on Education, 1862. Chapter II, Grants to Maintain Schools, Part I, Section I.

39. Schools which do not meet more than once daily cannot receive grants.

40. The managers of schools may claim at the end of each year, defined by Article 17:
- (a) The sum of 4s per scholar according to the average number in attendance throughout the year at the *morning and afternoon* meetings of their school. . . .
- (b) For every scholar who has attended more than 200 morning or afternoon meetings of their school:
  - (1) If more than six years of age 8s, subject to examination.

(2) If under six years of age 6s. 6d., subject to a report by the inspector that such children are instructed suitably to their age, and in a manner not to interfere with the instruction of the older children.

44. Every scholar attending more than 200 times in the morning or afternoon, for whom 8s. is claimed, forfeits 2s. 8d. for failure to satisfy the inspector in reading, 2s. 8d. in writing, and 2s. 8d. in arithmetic.

46. Every scholar for whom the grants dependent upon examination are claimed must be examined according to one of the following standards, and must not be presented for examination a second time according to the same or a lower standard.

48.

	Standard I	Standard II	Standard III
Reading	Narrative in monosyllables.	One of the narratives next in order after monosyllables in an elementary reading book used in the school.	A short paragraph from an elementary reading book used in the school.
Writing	Form on blackboard or slate, from dictation, letters, capital and small, manuscript.	Copy in manuscript character a line of print.	A sentence from the same paragraph, slowly read once, and then dictated in single words.
Arithmetic	Form on blackboard or slate, from dictation figures up to 20;	A sum in simple addition or subtraction, and the multiplication table.	A sum in any simple rule as far as short division (inclusive).

48.—*cont.*

	Standard I	Standard II	Standard III
Arithmetic *cont.*	add and subtract figures up to 10, orally from examples on blackboard.		

	Standard IV	Standard V	Standard VI
Reading	A short paragraph from a more advanced reading book used in the school.	A few lines of poetry from a reading book used in the first class of the school.	A short ordinary paragraph in a newspaper, or other modern narrative.
Writing	A sentence slowly dictated once by a few words at a time, from the same book, but not from the paragraph read.	A sentence slowly dictated once, by a few words at a time, from a reading book used in the first class of the school.	Another short ordinary paragraph in a newspaper, or other modern narrative, slowly dictated once by a few words at a time.
Arithmetic	A sum in compound rules (money).	A sum in compound rules (common weights and measures).	A sum in practice or bills of parcels.

49. The grant may either be withheld altogether or reduced for causes arising out of the state of the school.

4

2. Matthew Arnold on Payment by Results, 1869

The Reports written by H.M.I.s in the years following 1862 indicate that they were as divided as educational opinion generally on the value of the new system. One who was a consistent opponent was Matthew Arnold.

SOURCE: Report of the Committee of Council on Education, 1869–70, pp. 290–3. General Report for the Year 1869, by Matthew Arnold, H.M.I.

During the School year more than 25,000 children passed under my inspection; of these, about 13,000 were presented for examination grants.

The total rate of failure which in 1866–7 was 13 per cent., rose in 1867–8 to 14·56 per cent., but declined in 1868–9 to 11·3 per cent. Of last year's failures 20 per cent. were in arithmetic, 7·7 per cent. in writing, and 6 per cent. in reading.

This gradation not ill represents the degrees of difficulty in teaching by rote the three matters of arithmetic, writing and reading. I have repeatedly said that it seems to me the great fault of the Revised Code, and of the famous plan of *payment by results*, that it fosters teaching by rote; I am of that opinion still. I think the great task for friends of education is, not to praise *payment by results*, which is just the sort of notion to catch of itself popular favour, but to devise remedies for the evils which are found to follow the applications of this popular notion. The school examinations in view of *payment by results* are, as I have said, a game of mechanical contrivance in which the teachers will and must more and more learn how to beat us. It is found possible, by ingenious preparation, to get children through the Revised Code examination in reading, writing, and ciphering, without their really knowing how to read, write, and cipher.

To take the commonest instance: a book is selected at the beginning of the year for the children of a certain standard; all the year the children read this book over and over again, and no other. When the Inspector comes they are presented to read in this book; they can read their sentence or two fluently enough, but they cannot read any other book fluently. Yet the letter of the law is satisfied, and the more we undertake to lay down to the very letter the requirements which shall be satisfied in order to earn grants, the more do managers and teachers conceive themselves to have the right to hold us to this letter. Suppose the inspector were to produce another book out of his pocket, and to refuse grants for all the children who could not read fluently from it. The managers and teacher would appeal to the Code, which says that the scholar shall be required to read 'a paragraph from a reading book used in the school,' and would the Department sustain an Inspector in enforcing such an additional test as that which has been mentioned?

The circle of the children's reading has thus been narrowed and impoverished all the year for the sake of a *result* at the end of it, and the *result* is an illusion.

The reading test affords the greatest facilities for baffling those who imposed it, and therefore in reading we find fewest failures, but the writing test is managed almost as easily. Let us take the middle of a school, generally the weakest part, and the part which requires most careful teaching—the scholars in the third standard. There are books of the third standard which, what with verse, pages of words for spelling, exercises for dictation, and sums, contain for the prose reading lesson less than fifty pages of good sized print. The writing test for scholars of the third standard is to write from dictation a sentence from that same lesson of their reading book in which they have just previously been set to read. Verse is not commonly used for the reading of the third standard; an examiner would hardly choose to set the very dictation exercises given in the lesson book; there remain the fifty prose pages which the scholar has been reading and re-reading all the year. His eye and memory have become familiar with them; he has just refreshed his acquaintance with one of them by reading it; from this page he is now set to write a sentence slowly dictated to him by a few words at a time. Can it be said that because a child can spell this sentence tolerably and thus produce the required result, he may therefore be set down as able to write easy sentences from dictation? and must we not own that this *result* also is in great measure an illusion? We see accordingly, that though the rate of failure in writing does exceed that in reading, yet it exceeds it very slightly, and both are quite inconsiderable.

In arithmetic, the rate of failure is much more considerable. To teach children to bring right two sums out of three without really knowing arithmetic seems hard. Yet even here, what can be done to effect this (and it is not so very little) is done, and our examination in view of *payment by results* cannot but encourage its being done. The object being to ensure that on a given day a child shall be able to turn out, worked right, two out of three sums of a certain sort, he is taught the mechanical rule by which sums of this sort are worked, and sedulously practised all the year round in working them; arithmetical principles he is not taught, or introduced into the science of arithmetic. The rate of failure in this branch also will thus, in all probability, be gradually reduced, but, meanwhile, the most notable result attained will be that which has been happily described by my colleague, Mr Alderson, when he says: 'Unless a vigorous effort is made to infuse more intelligence into its teaching, *Government arithmetic* will soon be known as a modification of the science peculiar to inspected schools, and remarkable chiefly for its meagreness and sterility.' . . .

The Minute of February 20th, 1867, was meant to correct that impoverishment of the instruction, which was due to the mechanical routine brought in by the Revised Code examination.

But it proceeds just in the same course as that examination proceeds. It attempts to lay down, to the very letter, the requirements which shall be satisfied in order to earn grants. The teacher, in consequence, is led to think, not about teaching his subject, but about managing to hit these requirements. He limits his subject as much as he can, and within these limits tries to cram his pupils with details enough to enable him to say, when they produce them, that they have fulfilled the Departmental requirements, and fairly earned their grant. The ridiculous results obtained by teaching geography, for instance, under these conditions, may be imagined. A child who has never heard of Paris or Edinburgh, will tell you the measurements of England in length and breadth, and square mileages, till his tongue is tired. I have known a class, presented in English history, to take the period from Caesar's landing to the Norman Conquest, and to be acquainted in much detail with the Roman invasion of Anglesey; but Carnarvon, on the coast opposite Anglesey, being mentioned, they neither knew what Prince of Wales was born there, nor to whom the title Prince of Wales belonged. Another class took the period from Caesar's landing to the reign of Egbert, and knew the history of this period, or what passes for its history, minutely, but only one of them had heard of the Battle of Waterloo. It is true, for this sort of unsound performance Inspectors pluck candidates for the supplementary grants much more freely than they pluck candidates for the main grants. But this is only because these supplementary grants are so insignificant that managers and teacher care comparatively little whether they are obtained or not, and meanwhile, the object of the Department, to counteract the narrow, unintelligent mode of instruction encouraged by the Revised Code, is not attained.

3. How to Conduct the Annual Examination, 1871

These rather detailed instructions to inspectors were issued at a time when the number of children in schools and the number of inspectors required to examine them were both increasing rapidly. The need for uniformity of practice among inspectors arose from the necessity of attempting to ensure that all schools were treated equally fairly.

SOURCE: Education Department, Administrative Instructions, 1877, p. 7.

Circular No. 18

8 May 1871

SIR,

Many of Her Majesty's Inspectors will long ago have considered and come to their own conclusions on the chief points of detail, connected with the examination of children under the standards; but the following practical hints, which past experience has suggested, may be useful, at a time when so large an addition is being made to the staff of officers employed in inspecting schools.

STANDARD I.—Using the book in which the class has been taught to read, each child may be tried in *two* or *more* places in the book. This has been done rapidly in some cases thus: all the children in the standard are formed into a line according to their places in the schedule, and not having anything in their hands but their slates, on which they have done their sums and transcription, they pass the Inspector one by one; as each comes up he hands his slate to the Inspector, who gives him the book open, and points where he is to read; while listening to the reading, the arithmetic and writing can be marked on the schedule; the Inspector turns rapidly over a few pages of the book and the child reads again; he then gives back the book, takes his slate, and goes to his place, while the next child comes up, gives his slate, and is dealt with in the same manner.

The writing, which in this standard will generally be on slates, should be chiefly judged as *handwriting*, and the handwriting and correctness of transcription and dictation should jointly determine *a pass*. They ought in this stage *both* to be satisfactory in order to pass.

It is best to dictate the sums; if the children are too close to-together for satisfactory examination two sets of sums should be given alternately, so that each child's neighbour may have sums different from those which he has himself. When cards are used this trouble is avoided, but numbers printed in words, and not in figures, are likely to puzzle the younger children in this standard, and looking over the sums is more tedious. The results of two sums in addition and two sums in subtraction may be easily carried in the memory, and no more are wanted for the dictation of a double set.

No mechanical devices, however, will stop dishonest practices on the day of examination, in a school which has not been carefully and honestly taught throughout the year. An Inspector will be justified in recommending a reduction of the grant to a school in which the children are found to have copied from each other.

4. A Pupil's View of School in the 1860s

This account of his schooling in the 1860s was told to his daughter by Joseph Ashby. Its interest lies largely in that it gives a consumer's view of what a village school offered in the early days of payment by results.

SOURCE: M. K. Ashby; *Joseph Ashby of Tysoe, 1859–1919*, Cambridge University Press, 1961, pp. 16–21.

All this time, indeed since his fifth birthday, Joseph had been a schoolboy attending 'the new school', which he was to leave in the springtime before he attained eleven years. I do not remember his telling any tales of school until the time when the old schoolmaster left after forty years of his office. Turning out the cupboards Mr Dodge gave my father two old reading books, the very texts he had read in Standards I and II. As he handled them the doors of this old cupboard of memories swung slowly open, and urged by his children's questions he took out a good deal.

He even remembered something of the infant class. The children sat together, taught by a boy monitor, Charlie Reason, at the 'bottom end' of the girls' wing, near the girl's door, a great draughty door of the same size and shape as the south door of the church. The chief business of the infants was to learn to chant the alphabet and the numbers to one hundred. In the next class they chanted tables and recited the even numbers and the odd. When the children were unbearably fidgety ('fidget' was the word spoken most often by the teachers), Charlie would tell them to sit up straight; when he could hear a pin drop they should say their rhyme again. He would drop a pin and pretend he heard, through the hubbub of six classes, and then the children would chant all together Charlie's own poem, waving their hands to mark the rhythm,

Infants never must be lazy
On to work and up-si-daisy.

There was another recitation Joseph recalled:

O-n, On; b-o-n, bon; c-o-n, con,
L-o-n, lon; d-o-n, don; London.

But then the new schoolmaster came and the children said:

Ride a cock-horse to Banbury Cross

instead of 'Up-si-daisy'. And as Banbury was not far away that seemed somehow important and natural.

Right up the school, through all the six standards (there was a special class of a few boys and one or two girls above this) you did almost nothing except reading, writing and arithmetic. What a noise there used to be! Several children would be reading aloud, teachers scolding, infants reciting, all waxing louder and louder until the master rang the bell on his desk and the noise slid down to lower note and less volume.

Reading was worst; sums you did at least write on your slate, whereas you might wait the whole half-hour of a reading lesson while boys and girls who could not read struck at every word. If you took your finger from the word that was being read you were punished by staying in when others went home. A specially hard time was the two 'sewing afternoons'. While the girls were collected together for sewing, the boys merely did more sums or an extra dictation, just the sort of thing they had been doing all morning. As they craned their necks to see what sort of garments, what colours, were coming out of the vicarage basket of mending, they were unusually tiresome to the poor pupil-teacher, losing their places over and over again, or misspelling words they knew perfectly well—forgetting everything. He rapped with a stick; he shouted; he called out, 'Jack, Tom, stay in half an hour!'—a rather effective threat. To remain in school was the thing above all others the children did not want to do. But the most extraordinary thing about sewing afternoons was the quiet that fell on half the school. The girls and their teachers seemed to be talking almost as if they were at home or in a shop, and that made a strangeness in the school atmosphere where contrariwise, the unnatural was customary. The new master, Mr Dodge, had not made so very much difference, though he was college-trained and eager to work. After all, there were a couple of hundred children and he was busy teaching the top class.

Two inspectors came once a year and carried out a dramatic examination. The schoolmaster came into school in his best suit; all the pupils and teachers would be listening till at ten o'clock a dog-cart would be heard on the road even though it was eighty yards away. In would come two gentlemen with a deportment of high authority, with rich voices. Each would sit at a desk and children would be called in turn to one or other. The master hovered round, calling children out as they were needed. The children could see him start with vexation as a good pupil stuck at a word in the reading-book he had been using all the year, or sat motionless with his sum in front of him. The master's anxiety was deep, for his earnings depended on the children's work. One year the atmosphere of anxiety so affected the lower standards that, one after another as they were brought to the Inspector, the boys howled and the girls whimpered. It took hours to get through them. But the older children looked beyond the examination; the moment the Inspectors had finished the school would be closed. Well, not quite at that moment; time would be taken to open a hamper of great, golden rare fruit, of which each child would presently have a specimen cupped in his own two hands—oranges! A traditional kindness this, paid for by 'the Marquis'.

'Was there no interest in school?' we asked our father. Sometimes there was. Mr Dodge, the master, might come and take your class for a few minutes, and he was never as dull as the pupil-teachers. He might give you a real sum about some boy's father's garden; it was known that if he gave a dictation he would alter the book's familiar paragraph to catch you out; and he would come out and play, on rare occasions, at rounders, and couldn't he run!—a tough little man, always. There were 'object' lessons now and then—without any objects but with white chalk drawings on the blackboard—an oil-lamp, or a vulture, or a diamond might be the subject. Once there was a lesson on a strange animal called a quad-ru-ped—cloven-footed, a chewer of the cud; her house was called a byre (but in Tysoe it was not); her skin was made into shoes and from her udder came milk. It burst upon Joseph that this was one of the creatures he would milk after school, part of Henry Beasley's herd. He would milk three or four cows, and Robert Philpott, stronger and quicker in the hand, would milk the other six, though in school the latter was a famous dunce, always in trouble.

How dull school was! My father summed up. And yet, no, not *dull*. One didn't learn much but the place was full of feeling. It was so easy to get a beating for one thing. Some boys couldn't get through a day without 'holding out their hands' or a week without a real thrashing. While a thrashing proceeded the school simmered. Would a boy cry? Was the master hitting harder than usual? It might be oneself soon. Life was uncivilised in school, and yet there was plenty of conscience. For example the master never caned a girl, no matter how maddening she might be. There was the emphasis on duty. Whatever people didn't know about the children's health or how to teach them, they knew the children's duty. What a tremendous standard was set them! They ought to be silent, they ought to march in and out in orderly fashion, they ought to attend—above all to attend—to whatever the master or the Vicar or the pupil-teachers or even the monitors might put before them or upon them. The very height of the standard impressed the children.

They felt it sincerely prescribed by the master (they were not so sure of the others) and that there were sins, such as untruth, that really hurt him. Standards could be very inconsistent: for example, children dared not come late to school, but they absented themselves altogether for every sort of reason. Girls could be kept at home on the weekly washing day; boys would go to every flower show, every meet of the hunt within seven miles. When the cowslips bloomed both boys and girls would be taken out by their mothers to pick the flowers for wine and for a cowslip pudding. Some families stayed away, too, on all the old traditional festivals—St Valentine's Day, Plough Monday, and on the Club Days or patronal celebrations of villages round about.

School was so unreal. That explained the truancy and the caning and much else, and yet there were only one or two families whose children did not go at all, twenty years before compulsion came. All the parents wanted their children to learn to read, and the National School had put out of business all the dame and gaffer schools, and had absorbed the old Feoffees' School.

Though reality only trickled into school, fate would come crashing. Whenever there was an epidemic some child would die—sometimes more than one, and, on one occasion, several—and the master would be stricken and even the pupil-teachers 'upset'.

Enough about the school! One was always glad to get out of it, my father said. But that was a complex, vexing business, getting out. All the children in a class came out together—or rather in order—to a series of commands. One! and you stood in your desk. Two! and you put your left leg over the seat. Three! and the right joined it. Four! you faced the lane between the classes. Five! you marched in the spot. Six! you stepped forward and the pupil-teacher chanted, 'left, right, left, right, left, right'.

5. The Education of Pauper Children, 1873

In his Report for 1873, E. Carlton Tufnell, included a number of letters from persons who had passed through workhouse schools as children and had later made good. In introducing this particular letter he wrote 'it must not be considered in any way exceptional'.

The writer and his sister had lived in Woolwich with their mother after being deserted by their father; on the death of their mother, they went to live with their widowed grandmother who could not afford to keep them.

SOURCE: Local Government Board, Report on the Metropolitan District for the year 1873 by E. Carlton Tufnell.

My uncle James came back, but vowed he would not do anything for us unless grandmother would take us to the Union. She would not, and at last James left us altogether. I often saw him in the street, but did not dare speak to him: he was very cruel indeed. He afterwards opened a shop near the hill and sold fish. I must not forget to mention that once or twice a week we got a good dinner from a soup kitchen which was opened. My sister about this time was always ill. At last I remember we went before a lot of gentlemen (the Board of Guardians) and they asked me several questions. Where that occurred I do not remember, but I do remember shortly after being put into an omnibus with my sister, and leaving my grandmother crying and clinging to my uncle on Market Hill. We were put down at a Union workhouse on the west side of London. I was then nearly eight years old.

I must say that my grandmother took a great deal of trouble to get myself and sister thoroughly clean before we went to the Union. My uncle James also bought us some new clothes, and I remember looking at my little sister with some feelings of pride to see her dressed so neat and clean. We were put down from the bus opposite the gate, and the conductor took us in. We were shown into the female receiving ward, and after waiting some time had dinner. It was on a Saturday, and we had pudding for dinner; we neither of us could eat it all, and for some time after admission I could seldom eat all the meal served out; in fact, I had not been used to regular meals, but got a little when I could. Hence I was often very hungry indeed between meals, but could not eat all when it came.

After dinner an old woman came and took all my clothes off, and then showed me into a bathroom, telling me to get in and not be afraid. I should think I was not afraid, indeed; I had been too much used to water. I was in the bath in a moment with a jump, but the next moment my screams and yells could be heard far and wide. The fact was that the water was hot; to me it appeared scalding hot. Mr Willis, the master, came, and several more, but could not get me in again. They lifted me, smacked me, coaxed, and at last used sheer force. I was never so afraid in all my life; I thought they were going to kill me. Never before had I had such a thing as a hot bath, and never shall I forget it. They thought I was afraid of the water; it was not the water but the heat. I must not forget to mention that a string of not very refined language was largely mixed with my screams. I was a marked boy from that time.

When at last I got dressed in the uniform, Mr Willis himself marched me off to the school, and, with a full and facetious account of my bath, left me in the custody of Mr Darley, the schoolmaster. It was Saturday afternoon, and the boys were 'kept in' for previous bad behaviour. They were all standing stock still round the school, and as quiet as could be. I looked at them and wondered at seeing so many and so still. Mr D. asked me my name, I wouldn't answer. He asked me two or three times, but no answer. At last he got me off the stool at the desk, and took hold of my shoulder, and said, 'What is your name'. I was out of his reach in a moment, and shouted out as loud as I could, 'Find out, carrots'. He had red hair. There was a titter all round the school, and one of the monitors caught me by the collar, and got a punch in the head for his pains, which did not seem to hurt him in the least. He was a big boy and had me up to the desk in no time. Mr D. opened the desk and brought out a cane, and told me to look at it. I looked at the cane, but paid far more attention to the monitor who had hold of me. Mr D. again wanted my name, and I wanted the monitor to leave go of his hold and then I would tell. The monitor was ordered to leave go, and I sulked out in answer to the repeated query, 'Billy'. At last he got my name, and to his credit he never touched me then to hurt me. It turned out that I was the smallest boy in the school, and had to stand at the end, as we were all in our sizes. I remember marching down the long passage into the dining hall to tea, and wondered whatever had become of my sister. When we got into the dining hall, the thought struck me I might possibly see her: but no. I found out after that she was on the infants list, and they did not attend the hall. All this time I had been very sulky, and when at last I had my bed pointed out, and when Mr Waters, the shoemaker, had undressed me and put me into bed I felt so relieved. The boys soon began to make a noise in the bed-room, but not so myself. I remember putting my head right under the bedclothes and having such a quiet cry. Night after night I did the same, and used to long for the night to come so that I might cry without being noticed. The next day, Sunday, we went to church—the dining hall. Everything seemed very strange indeed. I had never before heard prayers of any kind, and of course did not understand them. I had often heard songs sung in a public house, and wondered to hear everyone singing here. It did seem strange altogether.

I remember also when we came out of church the monitor came and pulled me out in front for having been fast asleep in church. Several others were 'stood out' as well as myself. I had also been talking, and that, coupled with what I had done the day before, I suppose it was, determined Mr Waters, the shoemaker, to punish me. He had a small cane behind his back when he told me to put up my hand. I had not the least idea what he meant doing, and when he took my hand and himself put it out, I simply looked sullenly at my own outstretched hand. Presently, and without my being aware of it, down came the cane upon my outstretched palm. The pain to me was intense. I yelled and flew at him, and before he was aware, had given him one or two good kicks. He then belaboured me in pretty much the same style I had been used to, viz., all over, but not one touch seemed to hurt me so much as that stripe on the hand. After giving me a good caning, he wanted the other hand, but it was no use, he did not get it. It was sheer fright that made me obstinate.

After it was all over, and we had returned from dinner and got into the playground, I seemed to make friends with some of the boys, especially one big boy named Lloyd, who knew me before I went there. There were also several boys, I might say about half a dozen, who knew me before I went there. The boys were walking very orderly about the playground, but I longed to go to the little room in Woolwich again and see my grandmother. I fully made up my mind to tell her about the beating I had received. It might be about three o'clock when Mr Waters showed himself in the yard. I little dreamed that I was as much in his power as ever, for directly I saw him I flung a stone at him and ran away. He never moved and the stone never hit him, but I was wholly surprised to see three or four boys run after me, and in spite of my utmost efforts to release myself, I was brought face to face with Mr Waters. He caught hold of me, boxed my ears well, and took me into the schoolroom, and made me stand on a form all the afternoon. There I was in the schoolroom all alone, and did not dare get off the form. In very truth I began to see that there was no back door to get away, and that I must very much alter. As the pain wore off, I began thinking of home, to me a happy home, about all connected with it, and more than all, about my sister. How I did wonder what had become of her. All the time I kept on crying, till at last the door opened and a lady came in; it turned out to be Mrs Maurice, the schoolmistress. She began talking to me and I listened. She spoke kindly; I seemed to like her, and showed her my hand, where I had had the stripe. She gave me a deal of advice, and went and begged me off the form. She had prevailed upon me to stop sobbing, but no sooner had she gone than I was at it again. We had divine service again in the evening, and I got into trouble again for being asleep. This time I was let off, and so got quietly to bed, to again put my head right under the clothes and cry quietly, and wonder whatever had become of my sister. Thus my second night in the Union was like my first, in that I cried myself to sleep.

I believe I have a very good memory, and now that I attempt to write this out on paper, it seems as though it were only yesterday it all happened. The next day, Monday, opened my eyes very considerably. All passed off well until nine o'clock, when we went in school. I was put in the lowest class with the other little boys, but soon got tired of it. I longed to be about the streets again, and wondered when it would all come to an end. It seemed as though I must get into trouble, for that day I got a stripe on each hand from Mr Darley. This system of cutting the hand with a cane was certainly a new thing to me, and it seemed also to hurt me more than any other method of punishment could. I had never, before going to the Union, had a beating without seeing father or uncle, or some of them who were beating me very much out of temper; but here the operator, let him be who he would, and we were subject to three, the tailor, shoemaker, and schoolmaster, always took it so coolly. It made me most awfully afraid of them.

I may as well here make a short digression to show how the school was managed. The schoolmaster and pupil teacher, together with four monitors, who were dressed differently to the rest, had entire charge of us during school hours. Apart from school time we seldom saw the schoolmaster, except in the dining hall, but were under the control of either the tailor or shoemaker, or both, together with pupil teacher and monitors. The tailor and shoemaker had just the same power of caning as the schoolmaster. Between the three, there was a great deal of caning, and I shall have occasion to speak of it again presently.

I looked upon all three as brutes, and as far as the shoemaker is concerned I have not yet altered my opinion. He did really seem to me to love to flog the boys. I once saw a boy with the two sides of his face black and blue. He showed it to the master in the dining hall, and I believe Mr Waters, the shoemaker, got into trouble over that. I also saw him once in the shoemaker's shop offer a boy a penny to take four cuts on one hand without flinching. The boy put out his open hand on the cutting board and took the four cuts, but Mr Waters would not give him the penny. I could give other instances of this man's, what I call, cruelty, but am afraid of being tedious.

I have been thus far rather minute, because I think it is to get the first impression which school discipline has on the poor little street boy that you particularly want. To sum it up shortly, I must say that in my case it was *fear*. The utter impossibility of getting away, and the terrible certainty of the cane for misbehaviour, inspired me with terror. I had it more for bad language than for anything else. It was no use trying to love the masters, I dreaded them. I seldom joined the boys in play for a long time, and it was not long after that I was in the Union that I was put in the infirmary. I was taken ill, and I believe that it was brought on by fretting. My old home, humble, and indeed almost uninhabitable as it was, to me seemed the happiest place in the world. . . .

By-the-by, boys under twelve at this Union are, or were, under fed; four ounces of sop bread for breakfast, four ounces of bread and butter for supper, and dinner in proportion is not enough. I know it because I have gone through it.

6. History and Geography about 1870

Considerable emphasis was placed upon factual learning in such subjects as History and Geography. The catechism form was often employed by writers of textbooks, pupils being required to memorise answers.

> SOURCE: The Rev Dr Brewer, *My First Book of English History*, pp. 71–2 (undated, about 1870).

Who was Henry VIII?
Son of Henry VII.

What was his character?
As a young man, he was bluff, generous, right royal, and very handsome.

How was he when he grew older?
He was bloated, vain, cruel, and selfish.

What title did the Pope give him?
'Defender of the Faith'.

Why did he so call him?
Because Henry wrote a book to defend the Roman Catholic Religion.

Why did he afterwards quarrel with the Pope?
Because he wanted to put away his wife, and the Pope would not give him leave.

How did Henry resent this refusal?
He sided with the reformers, and said the Pope should never again have any power in England.

What was the result?
The reformed religion was adopted by the Crown.

What is the reformed religion called?
The Protestant religion.

How many wives did Henry VIII marry?
Six.

What became of them?
Two he put away, two he beheaded, one died, and one outlived him.

SOURCE: The Rev Dr Brewer, *My First Book of Geography*, pp. 21–3 (undated, about 1870).

The Counties of England

How are Great Britain and Ireland divided?
Into counties.

How many counties are there in each?
Fifty-two in England and Wales, thirty-three in Scotland, and thirty-two in Ireland.

How may the number of counties in England and Wales be remembered?
It is the same as the number of weeks in a year.

Who divided England into counties?
Alfred the Great.

For what purposes?
That persons might more easily refer to places, and that order might be more easily preserved.

How may the Counties of England be grouped?
Into northern, southern, and midland.

How many are grouped in the north?
Six.

Name the three to the east or right hand.
North-umber-land, Durham, and York.

Name the three to the west or left hand.
Cumberland, Westmore-land, and Lancashire.

How many of the English counties are grouped south of the Thames?
Ten.

Name those which face the English Channel.
Cornwall, Devon, Dorset, Hampshire, Sussex, and Kent.

Name the remaining four.
Somerset, Wiltshire, Berkshire, and Surrey.

How many form the eastern group.
Nine.

Name those that face the sea.
Lincoln, Norfolk, Suffolk and Essex.

Name the five inland counties of the eastern group.
Cambridge, Huntingdon, Bedford, Hertford, and Middlesex.

5

How may the remaining counties be grouped?
Into a centre triangle enclosed in a square.
What three counties form the centre triangle?
Stafford, Worcester, and Warwick.
What three counties form the north side of the square?
Cheshire, Derby, and Nottingham.
What three counties form the east side of the square?
Leicester, Rutland, and Northampton.
What three counties form the south side of the square?
Buckingham, Oxford, and Gloster.
What three counties form the west side of the square?
Monmouth, Hereford, and Shropshire.
What is worthy of notice in the position of these three counties?
They form (with Cheshire) the border of Wales.
What is the climate of England?
Moist, but healthy.
What is the character of the English people?
Brave, intelligent, and very persevering.
What is the size of England?
About 430 miles long and 320 broad.

A Method of Teaching History

SOURCE: *Metrical England*, a textbook in verse, by John Box
c. 1860.

Each line of *Metrical England* states one historical fact: the
metre of that line denotes the century in which the event
occurred (e.g. Iambic – thirteenth century: anapaest – fifteenth
century): and the initial letters of the first two words of the line,
by a special code, indicate the tens and units figures of the date.
The code is:

a – 1; b – 2; c – 3; d – 4; f – 5;
s – 6; v – 7; 1 – 8; n – 9; o – o.

Thus:

1066   Swiftly sweeping o'er the sea, the
        Norman brings his chivalry.

1170   Vile outrage stretched Becket in
        blood at the altar.

1215   All freemen joined the tyrant to
        defeat.

1314   A day of glory Scotland won at
        Bannockburn.

1415   Agincourt's famous fight is the pride
        of his reign.

1660   Sailed over the sea to the throne of
        Charles the Second.

1759   Feared naught brave Wolfe who fell in
        victory's hour.

7. The Arrangement of Schoolrooms

A usual feature of schools built in the mid-nineteenth century was the inclusion of a gallery or tiered arrangement for desks so that the teacher could see more easily the whole of the group he was demonstrating to or addressing. When Inspectors' districts were reorganised after the Education Act of 1870, Inspectors who had hitherto been confined to the schools of their own denomination found they were responsible for all schools in a district; some of them had not been accustomed to arrangements favoured by other denominations and commented unfavourably. The illfeeling this caused led the Education Department to issue this circular.

Source: Education Department, Administrative Instructions, 1877, p. 18.

Circular No 44

5 June 1872

Sir,

The attention of the Education Department has been drawn to reports of H.M. Inspectors, in which they recommend the removal of galleries from the principal rooms of schools visited by them for the first time, since the re-arrangment of their districts.

It appears that several of these schools have been erected with aid from the Parliamentary grant; that the gallery has been in constant use in them for many years, during which annual grants have been regularly paid; and that in some training systems great importance is attached to oral teaching, which is most conveniently given, when the numbers are large, on a gallery, grouping together as many children as possible. The scholars are more under the eye of the teacher, and this arrangement of them is evidently best suited for the conversational tone of an oral lesson.

In small schools the advantage is not so great, but even in them, for lessons of a general kind, to awaken attention, to secure simultaneous effort, to concentrate the teacher's influence, the gallery is useful.

On behalf of the gallery system much can be said, and in the hands of teachers trained to make the right use of it, it is a valuable element in the organisation of a school.

H.M. Inspectors, whose experience has been heretofore limited to one kind of school organisation, should endeavour to make themselves acquainted with the best methods which have been adopted in other schools, and when they can conveniently do so, they should visit those training schools where the traditions of what is familiarly known as the 'Stow system' are kept up.

An Inspector may reasonably object to the organisation of a public elementary school which seems to be selected because of its usefulness for non-scholastic purposes.

A schoolroom, where the convenience of the teaching is subordinate to the arrangements made for some non-educational parochial purpose, or where the arrangements seem primarily intended to promote some work other than primary instruction, should certainly be objected to; and the Inspector should everywhere insist with the managers on this essential condition under which a school is recognised as a public elementary school, viz., that instruction of children is the main purpose to which the buildings are put, and for which they are fitted up.

Having secured this, it would be unwise to recommend or insist upon one particular form of organisation exclusively. If satisfactory 'results' be obtained, no adverse criticism should be made on the method. If the Inspector is convinced that he can advise the managers how to improve their school, he should confer with them on the subject, but if the 'results' are good, he need not be urgent for changes in the fitting up, which would very probably be a hindrance in the case of a teacher trained under another system.

The introduction of extra subjects, and especially of science subjects, will require much oral teaching. By this means the general intelligence of children in our schools will be improved, and those teachers who have been accustomed to use the gallery frequently for collective lessons in reading, geography, history, explanations of arithmetical rules, mental arithmetic, singing and science subjects, should rather be encouraged to persevere than hindered by recommendations of changes in the fitting up of their schools.

I am, &c.

F. R. SANDFORD

To H.M. Inspectors of Schools.

8. Inspectors, Teachers and School Boards, 1884–8

One consequence of Payment by Results was that the Inspector's task seemed increasingly to be to catch the teacher out. At the same time managers and school boards were very anxious that their teachers should so impress the visiting Inspector as to earn the maximum grant. The following extracts indicate what could happen when these rather delicate relationships went wrong.

SOURCE: Log Book of Askern Board School, South Yorkshire.

1. Log Book entries, 1884.
   Visit 3rd October, 4.10. The children were dismissed before 4 o'clock. Time for dismissal is *4.10.*

   There is yet no partition wall to separate the two yards, and doors are still required for the offices—see last report.

E. H. Howard, Sub-Inspector.

An Explanatory Vindication
   The Master wishing to leave Askern by the 4.13 train (a very rare occurrence) had left the school when H.M. Inspector called. He wishes to say that (by his watch, set at noon to Askern Railway Time) *required* school work was carried on in strict accordance with Code and Time Table *till 4* o'clock. His having to travel as just stated, then necessitated a somewhat rapid dismissal. He regrets Mr Howard was *too late* to see the children and thus test the accuracy of the registers.

Oct 6th, 1884. J. Dodson.

2. Further entries, 1888.

Verbatim Copy of Summary of H.M. Inspector's Report on the School, Received 9th June, 1888.

'Increase of staff and diminution of scholars have not been attended by the improvement in attainments that might have been expected. The Infants receive justice and needlework shows improvement, but the general level of attainments in Elementary subjects (which alone are presented for examination) is not satisfactory. My Lords have again directed a deduction of one-tenth to be made from the grant for continued faults of instruction.'

June 19th. The Master trusts it will not be considered '*irregular*' in him here recording that since the recent Examination he has received several gratifying assurances from parents that though their children have failed to pass they are much pleased with their progress and the instruction imparted.

Oct 25th. The Master and Assistant Mistress received notice from the Board last Saturday (without any assigned reason) that their services would not be required after the 29th of January.

9. Misdemeanours

Great emphasis was placed on moral training in Victorian Schools and penalties for shortcomings were both drastic and immediate.

THE BOY WHO STOLE

SOURCE: Log Book of Holy Trinity National School, Ripon.

1882

Monday, December 18th. Found this afternoon that 1/6d had been stolen out of a cupboard sometime last week. Enquired from the children who had spent money. Communicated with the parents of the boy suspected.

Tuesday, December 19th. Found that money taken last week and 6d the week before had been stolen by one sixth standard boy. Sent for the Rev. J. H. Goodier who told me to dismiss the boy at once and write to ask the father to

meet us at the Vicarage in the evening. Found also that 3/-
had been stolen again last night after school hours.

Thursday.   The Rev. J. H. Goodier and Mrs Goodier visited
the school in the morning and the former dismissed the boy
from school who had stolen the money. Gave prizes to all
who had not been absent from school since midsummer.
Eight children were entitled to receive a prize. Gave a
reading book to each child who has not been absent from
school more than three times. Broke up for the Xmas
holidays.

    2 weeks.

1883

January 8th.   Reopened the school after the Xmas holidays.
Attendance not satisfactory. Sent after all absentees.
Several children absent on account of illness and many
others are not able to pay the school money. The boy who
owns to stealing 2/- out of the school has been told not to
come to the school again. The brother and sister have also
left the school.

AMY BALCHIN'S FLOUNCES AND ATTENDANCE

SOURCE: Minutes of the School Attendance Committee of the
Guildford Union, Surrey, 13th January, 1883.

A letter was read from the Rev'd Geo Chilton of Littledon
respecting the refusal of the managers of Wanborough School
to admit Amy Balchin on the score of finery of dress and Mr
Chilton attended and further explained the circumstances
relative thereto. And it was decided to issue a summons against
the parent of Amy Balchin and that a letter be sent to that effect
to Mr Chilton with an intimation that the School Attendance
Committee will expect him to appear in support of the
summons – of the reasonableness of the rule made by the
managers of the School and of the breach of such rule.

10th February, 1883.

The Clerk reported that on hearing of the summons against
the Parent of Amy Balchin the Chairman of the bench said
the rule as to neatness was a very proper one. The dress of the

child did not appear to be out of the way but it did not suit
the taste of the Managers. The bench would not inflict a fine
but Defendant must either take off the flounces or send the
child to another school.

10. Teachers' Salaries, 1887

In general the salaries paid by the large city school boards were
higher than those paid by voluntary school managers and the small
school boards. Even so, the salaries of head teachers were often related to the degree of success with which they ran their schools as
measured by earnings under the payment by results system—as in
this case at Bristol. Most of the assistant teachers would be paid as
'Ex-Pupil Teachers'.

> SOURCE: Second Report of the Royal Commission on the Element-
> ary Education Acts, 1887, Appendix C, p. 1025.

BRISTOL SCHOOLBOARD
SCHEME OF SALARIES
HEAD TEACHERS

Salaries of Head Teachers consist of (1) a payment on average
attendance during the school year; (2) the merit grant; (3) a
proportion of the school fees; (4) payment for instructing pupil
teachers; and (5) the grant for drawing.

Average Attendances	Boys	Girls	Infants
	£	£	£
100 or under	110	50	40
101–125	115	55	45
126–150	120	60	50
151–175	125	65	55
176–200	130	70	60
201–225	135	75	65
226 and over	140	80	70
Merit Grant	All	All	Half

One fourth of the fees paid by the parents or remitted by the
board will be paid to the teacher during the first four years of

the engagement; three-eighths during the second four; and one-half after eight years' service.

Fees to be reckoned at 2d per week whether collected or remitted.

For one pupil-teacher, £5; for two £9; for each additional pupil-teacher after the second, £3.

This payment will only be made in respect of pupil-teachers who pass a fair (or good) examination.

One half of the grant under Article 119 (Code 1884) will also be paid to the teacher.

The grant earned by passes in drawing [will also be paid].

NOTE.—The guaranteed salary is £120 for masters and £70 for mistresses; but when the managers are satisfied that the total salary will not be less than £150 and £90 respectively, the board will authorise monthly payments at the latter rates.

ASSISTANTS

Assistants will be paid in accordance with the following scale:

Year		1st	2nd	3rd	4th	5th
		£	£	£	£	£
Certificated and	Males	75	80	90	95	100
Trained	Females	55	60	70	—	—
Certificated but	Males	65	70	80	85	90
Untrained	Females	45	50	60	—	—
Ex-Pupil	Males	50	55	60	—	—
Teachers	Females	30	35	40	—	—

11. Religious Instruction in Bradford Board Schools

Religious instruction was given by most school boards and normally consisted of studying the Bible without any interpretation that could be said to be dogmatic. This satisfied most non-conformists but was manifestly unsatisfactory to Anglicans and Roman Catholics. Because of the controversial position of religion in the schools, detailed regulations and syllabuses were usually issued on the lines of these from Bradford. The pedagogic value of instruction on the lines set out in paragraphs 4 and 5 might, perhaps, be open to doubt.

SOURCE: Second Report of the Royal Commission on the Elementary Education Acts, 1887, Appendix C, pp. 1023–4.

Scheme of the Bradford School Board for Religious Observances
and Instruction.

1. The board attach very great importance to the religious instruction in their schools. Their intention is that it shall be carefully and regularly given, in order that the knowledge imparted
to the children about the facts and principles of Holy Scripture
may be comprehensive and thorough.

2. The order for opening the morning school must *invariably* be
a hymn, the Lord's Prayer, and Bible lesson; and for closing the
afternoon school, a hymn and the Lord's Prayer. These observances shall take place in the principal room, in the presence of
all the teachers and scholars, and shall be conducted only by the
head teacher, except as provided for by rule 4.

3. The course of scriptural instruction shall commence at the
beginning of the twelfth month of the school year and terminate
in the eleventh month of the following school year.

4. In schools with an average attendance exceeding 150, the
school management committee may, on application from the
head teacher, allow the assistant teachers to read *without comment* to *classes selected by the head teacher*, the portions of scripture
laid down in the scheme. The explanation on the passages read
to these classes must be afterwards given by the head teacher.

5. In upper departments it is recommended that the scholars
repeat the more important passages simultaneously after the
teacher. This will not only secure the attention of the children,
but will also familiarise them with Bible phraseology.

6. The subjects selected for infant's departments are those most
generally illustrated by pictures, and head teachers are advised
to use these in the daily Bible lessons.

7. Monday mornings shall be reserved for oral questions on the
work of the previous week and instruction in sacred geography.

8. In the explanations and instruction given the provisions of
the Elementary Education Act, in sections 7 and 14, shall be
strictly observed both in letter and spirit, and no attempt shall
be made to attach children to any particular denomination.
Head teachers shall give such information on geographical sub-

jects as will enable the children to understand the passages of scripture in which persons, places and events are mentioned, or in which allusions are made to the institutions or circumstances in the life of the Jews or other ancient peoples.

9. An examination of the junior teachers and scholars will, at the discretion of the school management committee, be held in the eleventh month of the school year, of which due notice will be given. Other examinations may be held, without notice, in any part of the school year, when a proportionate part of the year's work will be expected. These examinations are solely to test the knowledge acquired respecting the facts of the Bible and of scripture history.

10. The examinations will take place between 9 and 9.45 a.m.

11. During the religious observances and scriptural instruction no secular work of any kind shall be conducted, except as provided for by rule 12.

12. Any parent may object to his or her child being present during the time of religious teaching, or religious observance; and any children withdrawn from such teaching or observance shall receive instruction in secular subjects in a separate room by an assistant teacher.

Upper Departments
Old Testament
(Tuesday and Thursday)

When the examination takes place in a year with an *odd* number.

Gen. i. ii. iii. iv. 2–16, vi. viii. ix. 1–20, xi. 1–9, xiii. xiv. xxi. xxii. 1–19, xxiv. xxvii. xxxi. xxxii. xxxiii. xxxvii. xlii. xliii. xliv. xlvi. xlvii. xlviii. xlix. 1.

Exod. i. ii. iii. iv. v. vii. ix. x. xi. xii. xiii. xiv. xv. xvi. xvii. xviii. xix. xx.

When the examination takes place in a year with an *even* number.

Numb. xiii. 17–33, xiv. xxi. 4–9, xxii. xxiii. xxiv.
Deut. xxiv.
Josh. i. ii. iii. iv. v. xxiii. xxiv.

1 Saml. i. ii. iii. iv. xvii. xix. 1–13, xxiv. xxvi. xxxi.
1 Kings xvii. xviii. xix.
2 Kings i. ii. iv. v.
Psalms lxxviii. cv. cvi.
Daniel vi.
Jonah i. ii. iii. iv.

NEW TESTAMENT
(Wednesday and Friday)

When the examination takes place in a year with an *odd* number.

St. Luke's Gospel and Acts i. to xiii. inclusive.

When the examination takes place in a year with an *even* number.

St. Mark's Gospel and Acts xiv.–xxviii. inclusive.

In all years, St. Matthew v. vi. vii.

In half-time departments only half the above is required, but the second half must be taken before the first half is repeated.

INFANTS' DEPARTMENTS
OLD TESTAMENT
(Tuesday and Thursday)

The Creation– – – – – – –	Gen. i. ii.
Death of Abel – – – – –	Gen. iv. 2–15
The Flood and Noah's sacrifice	Gen. vi. vii. viii. ix. 1–20
Tower of Babel – – – – –	Gen. xi. 1–9
Offering of Isaac – – – – –	Gen. xxii. 1–19
Jacob's Dream – – –	Gen. xxvii. xxviii. 6–22
Joseph in the pit – – – – –	– Gen. xxxvii
Visit of Joseph's Brethren – – –	Gen. xlii. to xlv.
Birth of Moses – – – – – –	Exod. ii.
Passage of the Red Sea – – – –	Exod. xxiv. xv.
Manna – – – – – – –	Exod. xvi.
Giving of the Law – – – – –	Exod. xix. xx.
Brazen Serpent – – – – –	Numb. xxi. 4–9
Call of Samuel – – – – –	I Saml. i. to iii.
David and Goliath – – – –	I Saml. xvii.
Elijah – – – – –⎫	I. Kings xvii. xviii. xix.
Elisha mocked by the children ⎰	II. Kings i. ii.

Elisha and the Oil, &c. –   –   –   –   II. Kings iv.
Naaman   –   –   –   –   –   –   – II. Kings v
Daniel in the Lion's Den   –   –   –   Daniel vi.

NEW TESTAMENT
(Wednesday and Friday)

Birth of Christ   –   –   –   –   –   Matt. i. 48–25
                                          Luke i. 25–26
The Shepherds   –   –   –   –   –   Luke ii. 1–20
Wise Men and Flight into Egypt   –   –   Matt. ii. 1–23
Christ in the Temple at twelve years of age   Luke ii. 40–52
Preaching of John the Baptist –   –   –   ⎧ Matt. iii.
Baptism of Christ –   –   –   –   –   ⎨ Mark i. 1–13
                                      ⎩ Luke iii. 1–22
Cleansing of the Temple –   –   –   –   –   John ii.
Woman of Samaria   –   –   –   –   –   John iv.
Healing Sick of the Palsy   –   –   –   ⎧ Mark ii.
                                          ⎩ Luke v. 16–39
Widow's Son at Nain   –   –   –   –   –   Luke vii.
Calming of the Storm   –   –   –   –   Luke viii. 22–25
Feeding 5,000   –   –   –   –   –   ⎧ Mark vi. 30–44
                                       ⎩ John vi. 1–13
Christ walking on the Sea   –   –   –   Matt. xiv. 22–36
Healing the Man born Blind   –   –   –   –   John ix.
The Good Shepherd   –   –   –   –   John x. 1–18
Raising of Lazarus –   –   –   –   –   –   John xi.
The Good Samaritan   –   –   –   –   Luke x. 25–37
Prodigal Son –   –   –   –   –   –   Luke xv. 11–32
Pharisee and Publican   –   –   –   –   Luke xviii. 9–14
Christ blessing the Children   –   –   –   Mark x. 13–16
Entry into Jerusalem   –   –   –   –   Luke xix. 28–48
Widow's Mite   –   –   –   –   –   Mark xii. 41–44
Agony and Betrayal   –   –   –   –   Mat. xxvi. 36–56
Trial   –   –   –   –   –   ⎫
Crucifixion   –   –   –   –   ⎬
Burial –   –   –   –   –   ⎬ John xviii. 28–40, xix. xx.
Resurrection –   –   –   –   ⎬ Acts i. 9–11
Ascension   –   –   –   –   ⎭

12. Attendance

School boards were established in 1870 to provide school places where there was a deficiency, their work was essentially preliminary to the introduction of compulsory attendance a few years later. The problem of getting unwilling children, or the children of unwilling parents, to attend school was not solved by legal compulsion alone. Both the unsatisfactory attendance and some of the expedients used as incentives are illustrated in the school log books of the time. The unhelpful attitude of some magistrates is shown in the following extracts from the Minutes of the London School Board.

    (a) SOURCE: Log Book of Holy Trinity National School, Ripon.

1889

Friday, April 5th.   Examined the upper standards today and was much disappointed with the work. They passed only 70 per cent. The children are so very irregular in their attendance that it seems almost impossible for them to do their work well. Some weeks the attendance of the class does not reach 70 per cent. This week it is only 74 per cent.

1891

Friday, June 12th.   Examined standards I, IV, and III boys. There was a little improvement in both St I and St IV but the work of the boys in St III was very unsatisfactory, especially the dictation and spelling. The attendance has been better this week. There are two boys on the Register who have not been present since the present school year began. They are running about the streets and the School Attendance Committee seem to be unable to make them attend. Their names have been reported each month.

1894

Friday, 20th July.   The Rev. J. H. Goodier came to school this morning and gave prizes to those who had earned them for regular attendance, punctuality and good conduct.

Friday, 21st December.   Attendance very poor yesterday, only 102 present in the afternoon. This is owing to the Thursday before Christmas being a special market day.

    (b) SOURCE: Second Report of the Royal Commission on the Elementary Education Acts, 1887, Extracts from the Minutes of the London School Board.

On the 19th February, 1886, the mother of Charles Bull, 12, of 14, Springfield Street, Clerkenwell (a widow), was summoned at Clerkenwell Police Court, for the son's irregular attendance at school. At the hearing of the summons, the defendant stated that she required the boy at home whilst she was out obtaining the living. The magistrate (Mr Barstow) held that the services of the boy were necessary, and dismissed the summons. The defendant is a charwoman, earning about 12s a week, and there are two children in the family, the boy in question, who has passed Standard III, and a younger child. The family live in one room, and the visitor reports that the boy runs the streets all day.

On 8th December, 1886, at the Woolwich Police Court, Mr Shiel imposed a fine of 1d, to be recovered by distress warrant, or, in default, one day's imprisonment, under the following circumstances: Jeremiah Donegan, 6, Rush Grove, Woolwich, was summoned for the irregular attendance of his son William, $12\frac{1}{2}$, Standard I. Defendant stated that the boy was 13 last July. The visitor explained that the mother had told him the boy was born on 2nd January, 1874. Mr Shiel stated that the case had better be dropped, as there was quite enough to do to look after the younger boys.

On 8th December, 1886, Mr Biron, at the Thames Police Court, dismissed a summons against Edward Lecomber, fruiterer, of 44, Brick Lane, for employing his daughter, Maud, 13. Upon being asked on what grounds he dismissed the summons, Mr Biron said, 'I am not bound to give you my reason, but I dismiss it because the girl looks to me to be over the age'. The child failed in two subjects in the third standard, has not made five years' attendances, and has not been to school for over six months.

Woolwich Police Court, 22nd December, 1886. A man named Thomas Bird was summoned, but there was no appearance, and he was fined 2s 6d, or, in default, three days imprisonment, but in the decision no order was made. The superintendent then called the magistrate's attention to section 8 of the Summary Jurisdiction Act, and asked him, as he had made no express order otherwise, that he would direct the fee paid for the summons to be repaid to the board. Mr Shiel replied, that it was his invariable practice not to allow costs or fees to the Board and that he should always adopt this course. The fact was that he wanted the public to know what these prosecutions cost, to which he (the superintendent) replied that any ratepayer could have this information, as, under the Act of Parliament, all the Board's books were open for inspection at any reasonable time. He (the superintendent) further pointed out to Mr Shiel that he was really placing a penalty upon the School Board for carrying out the duties imposed upon it by Act of Parliament; and that it seemed the Board was placed upon a different level to any other informant. The magistrate replied that this was so, the Board *were* on a different level, and as to the question of losing their fees, he did not think there was much in that, as it was merely a question of account, and it did not matter if it came out of one pocket or the other. He (the superintendent) urged upon Mr Shiel that it really did matter, so far as the Board were concerned, and that he could be no party to any understanding. He felt bound to make a special application in each case, inasmuch as, according to his reading of the section, it was clearly contemplated that the court was to exercise a discretion in the matter. He could not see what discretion was used when the magistrate made it a rule to allow no costs in this or in future cases. The application was, however, refused, but he renewed it in every other case before the court, to which Mr Shiel simply replied 'No'. Adding that, he understands from Mr Gedge, that this would be an express order otherwise, and therefore the Board appears to have no remedy in the matter.

13. The Dangers of Mixed Schools, 1894

An increase in the number of mixed elementary schools as a consequence of financial difficulties and resulting closures led the Chief Inspector to discuss the question of mixed schools in his General Report for 1894.

> SOURCE: Report of the Committee of Council on Education for 1894–5, Appendix Part I, pp. 41–2. General Report for the Year 1894 by C. H. Parez, H. M. Chief Inspector.

... One kind of change in the constitution of schools—of questionable advantage has recently become somewhat frequent; I mean the merging of a boys' department and a girls'

PLATE 1

A Regency Governess.

PLATE 2

A COLON, marked thus :

The Colon consists of two dots, as you see ;
And remains within sight whilst you count one, two, three :
'Tis us'd when the sense is complete, tho' but part
Of the sentence you're reading, or learning by heart.
As " Gold is deceitful : it bribes to destroy."
" Young James is admired : he 's a very good boy."

A PERIOD OR FULL STOP, marked thus .

The full-fac'd gentleman here shown
To all my friends, no doubt is known :
In him the PERIOD we behold,
Who stands his ground while four are told :
And always ends a perfect sentence,
As " Crime is followed by repentance."

THE EXCLAMATION POINT, or Note of Admiration !

This Youth, so struck with admiration,
Is of a wondering generation,
With face so long, and thin and pale,
He cries, " Oh! what a wonderous tale !"
While you count four, he stops, and then,
Admiring! He goes on again.

A QUOTATION " "

Two commas standing on their heads,
Their orders are obeying :
Two others, risen from their beds,
Their best respects are paying :
These four are ushers of much use,
As they great authors introduce.

Part of a page from *Punctuation Personified, Or Pointing Made Easy: by Mr Stops*
—dated 1822.

PLATE 3

BINGLEY
Free Grammar
SCHOOL.

AS Misconceptions have prevailed respecting the Manner in which Education at the FREE GRAMMAR SCHOOL, in BINGLEY, is conducted, we, the undersigned, being a Majority of the Trustees of the School,

At a MEETING

HOLDEN THIS DAY FOR THE PURPOSE, DO ORDER, THAT

THE FOLLOWING RULES

BE PUBLISHED,

For the Information of those who may be entitled to send Children to the said School.

Joshua Crompton,	*C. F. Busfeild,*
William Busfeild,	*William Penny,*
Thomas Leach,	*William Twiss,*
Edward Ferrand,	*William Ellis.*
Walker Ferrand,	

1. No Boy shall be admitted to be taught as a Free Scholar in this School, upon what Pretext soever, unless he be able to read the Testament sufficiently well to be forthwith promoted to the Latin Accidence; this being the Practice of the Wakefield and Sedburgh Schools, to which the Charter refers.

2. The Hours of Attendance at School, shall be from *Seven* in the Morning to *Eight* before Breakfast; from *Nine* to *Twelve* before Dinner; and in the Afternoon from *half-past One* to *Four* in *Winter*, and *Five* in *Summer*.

3. The Duties of the School to begin, as usual, with Prayers.

4. The Church Catechism to be taught and explained to the Scholars, as has heretofore been done, three Times a Week, till they are perfect in it, and afterwards to be repeated by them *once* every Week.

5. Select Portions of the Holy Scriptures, and English Books of moral Instruction, to be read in Classes by the Scholars, at convenient Intervals between their Latin and Greek Lessons.

6. The Scholars to come to School neat and clean, with *Shoes* on their Feet.

7. No Boy to absent himself from School, unless a good and sufficient Reason be given by his Parent or Guardian, in Person or Writing, to the Master.

8. As it has always been the Usage of this School, for the Free Scholars to be classed and taught with the Boarders, according to their respective Progress in Classical Learning, the Trustees expect that the same Line of Conduct be pursued by the Master.

BINGLEY, November 3d, 1814.

NICHOLSON, PRINTER, BRADFORD

Rules for Bingley Free Grammar School, 1814.

PLATE 4

Harrow School Room *c* 1810, from a drawing by Pugin.

PLATE 5

Ladies' School, Milan Home,

WOODHOUSE LANE, LEEDS,

CONDUCTED BY

THE MISSES GILES,

AND VISITING MASTERS.

The Course of Instruction includes Reading, Writing, Arithmetic, English Literature, and Composition, Needlework, &c., &c., Accomplishments, French, German, Music, Singing, Painting, Drawing, Dancing, Calisthenics, Wax Flower Making, &c. Private lessons given in the Accomplishments.

The House is very large, pleasantly and healthily situated, one School-room being thirty feet long, and very lofty. Spacious dormitories and bath. The number of resident Pupils being limited, every comfort is afforded. The domestic arrangements are under the superintendence of Mrs. Giles, and are those of a private family.

Terms for Day and Resident Pupils on application.
A Class for Little Boys.

REFERENCES

KINDLY PERMITTED TO PARENTS OF PUPILS, MINISTERS
AND GENTLEMEN.

Advertisement for an Independent Girls School, 1873.

PLATE 6

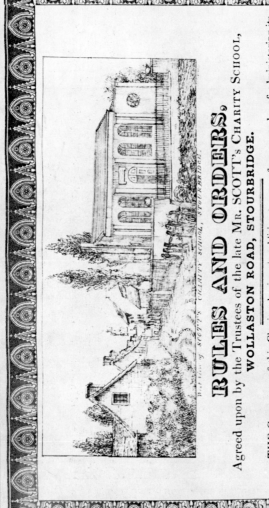

West View of SCOTT's CHARITY SCHOOL, STOURBRIDGE.

RULES AND ORDERS,

Agreed upon by the Trustees of the late Mr. SCOTT's CHARITY SCHOOL, WOLLASTON ROAD, STOURBRIDGE.

THE Governors of this Charity, having, in addition to some former modes of administering its funds, established a distinct branch, Midsummer, 1821; consisting of a Day School for sixty Boys, on the British System; unanimously resolved upon the following General Rules and Orders; and also adopted the Rules herein contained, for its daily regulation.

Regular attendance on Public Worship shall be required of the Scholars, under the superintendance of the Governors and Teachers; in addition to which, they are also required to meet at the Charity School on the Morning and Afternoon of the second Sunday in August; and likewise on the second Sundays in January, April, July, and October, at six o'clock in the evening; being the times appointed for quarterly meetings of parents, children, visitors, and others; when applications for admissions are received.

PLATE 7

Holidays are appointed from time to time, at the discretion of the Trustees; and occasional examinations of the Scholars take place, in the presence of the friends of the institution.

The Master is required to keep an accurate Register of Scholars, noting every circumstance worthy of observation, with a view to the formation of a full and permanent Record.

Monitors shall be selected from the Scholars in attendance, and instructed in such a manner as to qualify them to become useful assistants in conducting the business of the School.

As it is the intention of the Trustees to form this branch of the Charity as nearly as possible upon the model of the British Free School in Severn-street Birmingham; they have caused the following Rules of that Institution to be printed for their use.

RULES, to be observed by the Children of Scott's Charity.

1. To attend School constantly at Nine in the Morning and Two in the Afternoon.
2. To attend School with Hands and Face clean, Hair combed, and Shoes brushed.
3. On all occasions to speak the Truth.
4. To behave with particular and solemn reverent Quietness when reading the Holy Scriptures.
5. To behave with Solemnity in all Places of Public Worship.
6. To be obedient at Home to Parents and Friends.
7. To avoid all bad Company.
8. Never to use bad Words or ill Names.

9. To avoid all Quarrelling and Contention.
10. Never to mock lame or deformed Persons, and to be kind to all men.
11. To avoid Cruelty, and never teaze or in any way harm brute Creatures.
12. To be silent in School.
13. To enter and leave School orderly.
14. To obey the Rules and Orders of the School.

Whenever a Boy is about to leave School, it is expected that he will inform the Master.

Rules of a 19th century Charity School.

PLATE 8

The Dormitory, Westminster School, c 1820.

PLATE 9

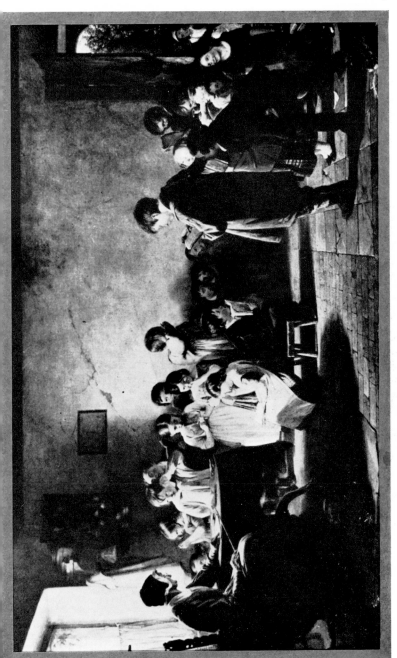

A Dame School *c* 1845, from a painting by T. Webster.

PLATE 10

Queen Elizabeth's Free Grammar School, Wakefield, 1854.

PLATE 11

Monitorial School in the East End of London, 1839.

PLATE 12

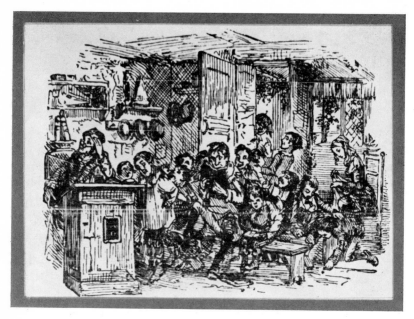

An English Village School in 1840.

Mickleham New National School, Surrey, 1840.

PLATE 13

ESTABLISHMENT FOR YOUNG LADIES,

MACKENZIE PLACE, BROOMHALL, SHEFFIELD.

MISS IRELAND

Respectfully announces to the Gentry of Sheffield and its vicinity, that she receives a limited number of Young Ladies, to Board and Educate. Her house, which is commodious, and has a garden attached, is delightfully situated in a healthy and highly respectable locality, a short distance from the town.

She is experienced in tuition, having been engaged in it during twelve years, in London and its suburbs : her time is entirely devoted to her Pupils, their studies and amusements being soley under her personal direction. Every attention is paid to their health, morals, and domestic comforts, which are superintended by her mother, MRS. IRELAND, who resides with her.

TERMS,

A liberal English Education, including Religious Instruction, Ancient and Modern History, Use of the Globes, Mapping, Writing, Arithmetic, French, Drawing, Dancing, and Plain and Fancy Needle-work.

	Guineas.			
Yearly Boarders	30	0	0	per annum.
Do. under twelve years of age	25	0	0	,,
Weekly Boarders	20	0	0	,,
Day Pupils	6	0	0	,,
Piano-Forte and singing, each	4	0	0	,,
Harp	8	0	0	,,
Italian	4	0	0	,,
Use of Piano	1	0	0	,,

References are kindly permitted to MRS. SHARPE, 57, Wentworth Terrace, Sheffield; W. B. ANDERSON, ESQ., Rectory Cottage, Shacklewell Lane, London, and 21, Billiter Street, London, &c.

Advertisement for a finishing school for young ladies.

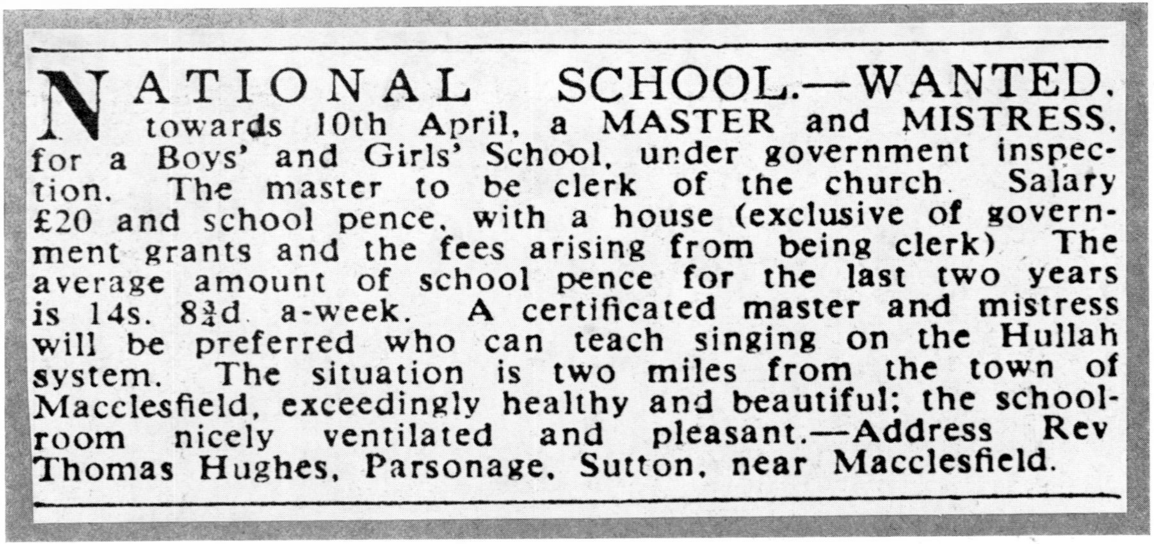

PLATE 14

NATIONAL SCHOOL.—WANTED.
towards 10th April, a MASTER and MISTRESS.
for a Boys' and Girls' School, under government inspection. The master to be clerk of the church. Salary
£20 and school pence, with a house (exclusive of government grants and the fees arising from being clerk) The
average amount of school pence for the last two years
is 14s. 8¾d. a-week. A certificated master and mistress
will be preferred who can teach singing on the Hullah
system. The situation is two miles from the town of
Macclesfield, exceedingly healthy and beautiful; the schoolroom nicely ventilated and pleasant.—Address Rev
Thomas Hughes, Parsonage, Sutton, near Macclesfield.

Advertisement for a schoolmaster for a National School in the 1860s. Church duties were often required as a condition of appointment.

PLATE *15*

Great Gaddesden School Board.

Hemel Hempsted,

June, 189 .

Sir,

I am requested by the School Board to inform you, that in case you should require any Boys for Hay-making during the present season—upon filling up and signing the Form enclosed herewith, and sending it to either of the Teachers of the Gaddesden Row Board School—the Great Gaddesden National School—or the Potten End School; leave will be given to such Boys as you may require, for a period of 4 weeks.

Your obedient Servant,

W. GROVER,

Clerk.

Copy of a circular sent annually by a school board to all farmers in the district.

THE THREE R's; OR BETTER LATE THAN NEVER

Chairman of the Board—'Well my little people, we have been gravely and earnestly considering whether you may learn to read. I am happy to tell you that, subject to a variety of restrictions, certain clauses, and the consent of your vestries—YOU MAY!' (*Punch, 1870*).

department into one for boys and girls mixed. In some cases the change has been made voluntarily by managers from motives of economy, in other cases it has been found to be the only way out of the difficulties involved in the endeavour to bring unwieldy premises into conformity with the wholesome requirements which have recently been insisted upon, and to be practically unavoidable. From one cause or another it seems probable that similar conversions may become not infrequent. Opinions differ upon the question whether congregation of boys and girls is advisable in our schools. Whether the presence of the female element exercises a benign and softening influence upon the harsher sex without itself receiving injury, or on the other hand the rough, or worse than rough, manners of the boys are sure in the long run to predominate; this will be determined to a great extent by different persons in accordance with their own idiosyncrasies. Experience exists indeed, deductions from which, it might have been supposed, could be ascertained; but as the results are not always palpable, and as the experiments are tried under varying circumstances, some doubt must always remain, and answers which are given must be affected to some extent by prejudice. The matter, however, is one of some importance, and one on which, especially as the mixed system is likely to be on the increase, all who are interested in the moral welfare of our children should keep a watchful eye. In America, it may be remembered that Bishop Fraser reported that public opinion, though not unanimous, was on the whole favourable to mingling boys and girls in the primary schools. In New York the general system seemed to be to have a mixed primary school with separate departments for older boys and girls either in the same building, or, which is thought preferable, in different localities. Yet even the principal of one of the most esteemed high schools near Boston considered after 16 years' experience that the mingling was distinctly advantageous, and that in consequence of it the children seemed to meet more on the footing of brothers and sisters. The genius of American institutions may, however, demand greater freedom, and withal ensure greater safety than our more primitive social habits can tolerate or guarantee. Most of our own country schools after all, and a fair proportion of our town schools are of the mixed kind, and, though managers and persons who have to come into daily

7

contact with the children and watch them as they grow up into manhood and womanhood may be best able to give an opinion of the actual results of the mixed and separate systems, and to say whether or not companionship of boys and girls in school is a healthy prelude, under favourable circumstances of course, in respect of discipline and control, to the social relations of adult life, still the Inspector is able to form a pretty good idea of the tone that prevails in a school, and can judge pretty well whether the mutual regard is a little too free, or is characterised by something of shyness and constraint. It is a good sign among us, even if it would not be thought so across the water, when, upon a class of lads and lasses being called up together for a common oral examination, a sort of atomic repulsion appears to exist between the two portions of the class, so that a considerable amount of elbow room is left where the two approach each other. On the part both of boys and girls there is a sort of natural timidity and bashfulness which keeps them apart. This is a healthy sign. On the other hand the want of retiringness in school does not speak hopefully for the nature of the relation that must exist outside. The influence within the school walls brought to bear day by day, and having the sanction of authority, cannot fail to produce an impress for good or for evil on the life outside. Whether the children meet together in school or go into separate buildings, scope remains on the way to and fro for misconduct and rough manners. From time to time in the log-books occurrences of this kind and complaints made by children are noted, and reprimand or punishment is mentioned as being meted out according to the circumstances of the case. This is of course as it should be, and may happen in the best of schools, though less likely to occur where it is known that severe notice will be taken. But where discipline is lax, where, even without flagrant disorder, whispering and talking are allowed, where movements in changing lessons are not carried out in an orderly way, and the system of lessons is not such that each child knows always what he has to do and is kept fully employed, where the influence of the master's eye is not felt, irregular habits and practices soon creep in and, under cover of these, it is impossible to say how much of evil may not be allowed to shelter. The responsibilities of managers are no doubt serious, but, especially in mixed schools, it is of immense importance that they should be careful to have disciplinarians at the head, and to keep this consideration in view when a new master is being appointed.

14. Some Incidents from School Life

There are certain incidents in the life of a school which do not form part of the planned existence of the institution but which, nevertheless, are essentially the product of bringing people together as members of a community. The flavour of some of these incidents in the later nineteenth century may be savoured best from entries in school log books. It would probably be wrong to print accounts of some of the typical episodes without eliminating such references as would make the characters identifiable; accordingly the following extracts—which have a humorous as well as a serious aspect—are reproduced after the removal of evidence which would permit identification. They are all from the log books of schools in Yorkshire, mostly in the West Riding.

A. A HEADSHIP FORCEFUL AND BRIEF

1873

July 7th.   I commenced my school duties here this day.

July 11th.   The order of the school is, at present, very far from being satisfactory. The children take little notice of commands, it is not intentional disobedience but indifference. Want of respect for their masters and those who teach them seems to be the course. I hope in time to gain both their respect and good feelings and thus to gain obedience.

July 18th.   Have had a hard, tough, week's work. The ignorance as well as the state of discipline is very discouraging, and a hard year's work is before me. On testing the whole school on Friday only three boys in the I and II Standards could work a simple addition sum correctly, and in the three upper Standards, III, IV and V, *not one* scholar could work a sum in addition of money consisting of eight lines in the space of half-an-hour. Plenty of work before me . . . Have commenced this week with drilling, the best aid to discipline.

July 25th.   Honoured with a visit from H.M. Inspector Barring-
ton Ward Esquire who gave me wholesome hints and advice. Highly recommended drilling as an aid to obtaining
discipline in the school. His kind and valuable suggestions
shall be faithfully observed and acted upon.

Wednesday and Thursday testing Standards III, IV and
V in Arithmetic, commencing with I Standard cards. I
find *no one* can even put the sums down, they are utterly at a
loss to know how to set about them, that is of the III
Standard scholars, and only one of the IV and V Standards
could set about them without having the measure of the
wording of the sums, in simple subtraction, explained to
them. The boys come very late to school, and some of the
latecomers have to leave early to take dinner to the Works
for their fathers; these sort of scholars are a great drawback
to the progress of the school.

November 7th.   John Henry—very stubborn and disobedient.
I spent 1½ hours over him in teaching him the word
'Expectant'. I cut it up into syllables, gave him the words
Collect, Connect, Suspect, Expect; told him numerous
times and at the end of two hours he persisted in calling the
word 'exp*lain*ant'. I punished him smartly after asking the
scholars present if they thought he did it purposely or not;
and they all said he did so—that he used to do such tricks
in the former Master's time.

Tuesday afternoon (Nov. 11th).   Rang the School Bell at 1½—
waited until 2 o'clock, no scholars came: have all gone to
the Statute Hirings 'to see'.

1874

January 9th.   A very poor beginning for the New Year, only
45 at school opening after the Xmas holidays. Fewer girls
than ever. A general desire exists for sending boys to the
Grammar School, and girls to Miss Pickergill owing to the
uncertainty of the Master's remaining. 'They no sooner
get settled than they are shifted'—so say the parents.

January 15.   The Vicar having threatened to take £10 off my
salary if my wife failed on Monday last to resume the sewing [lessons]: also to report me to the Committee of
Council: from whom, I believe, I should receive some con-

sideration under the circumstances which has been refused
by the Vicar.

January 16th.   The logbook of the school has been shown to
me today by the Vicar. The entries made by the Master on
15th January and 9th January are not suitable, and notice
will be taken by the Education Department if any similar
remarks are again inserted. The logbook is simply intended
as a record of school events, and it cannot be made the
vehicle for personal attack upon the Managers.

M. J. BARRINGTON-WARD

H.M. Inspector.

January 26th.   I will not again make any entries in the Log
Book but what have to do with the progress of the school:
the treatment of the Master by his Vicar however, *does very
materially* affect the progress of the school.

February 19th.   School only small—lessons well done. The
majority in each Standard are well prepared for the Government Inspection, and are very well up in their work.

February 20th.   Have this day finished work in [this school].
The New Master will commence his duties on Monday the
23rd inst.

February 23rd.   Find the children very unruly and also very
backward. No homework appears to have been done for
many months.

Arithmetic is moderately fair.

Reading very poor throughout the school.

Writing has been utterly neglected, and the extra subjects never touched.

B. DIFFICULTIES WITH THE NEW HEATING

1881

October 11th.   The Rev. G. O. B— visited the school on
Monday. On the same day Mr. T— and a gentleman came
to find the cause of the stove smoking. They sent Mr. G—
to alter it. It has smoked very much since the alteration, so
I have not had a fire today (Friday).

October 18th. On Monday Mr. T— came to see about the stove smoking, and on Wednesday I had a mason in school all day who tried to alter it. It was rather better on Thursday but today (Friday) it is as bad as ever. The three Misses B— visited the school today and I told them about the stove, and in the afternoon a clergyman who is assisting the vicar visited the school.

October 25th. On Wednesday morning a man came and examined the stove.

November 1st. The Rev. J— visited the school on Monday afternoon. The two Messrs Ledgard on Wednesday morning and again in the afternoon. Rev. J—, Dr. B— and a Mason were in school on Wednesday afternoon from 2.30 to 3.30 examining the stove. On the same day we received the new harmonium. There has not been any fire in the school this week because they now go out as soon as they are lit.

November 5th. Today being 5th November the children were given a half holiday to go to the fire. Mr. T— visited school and lit the fire, but it smoked so much that he put it out immediately. A man also came and painted the boys' gate.

November 15th. Rev. J— visited the school on Monday morning, Tuesday morning, Wednesday morning, and on Thursday morning and afternoon Mr. T— came with him. The smoke has been very bad this week, some larger pipes were laid in the floor to try and prevent it, but it has not succeeded. Some workmen came this afternoon (Friday) in order to raise the pipes, and I allowed the children to go home at once.

November 19th. On Thursday afternoon two joiners came to school and laid a plank in the floor in place of the iron grates, and took out the pipes which are not needed now as the stove pipe has been made to ascend and not descend. The school has been very warm and comfortable, and quite free from smoke ever since.

1882

April 24th. There has been no fire in school today, as the fire has begun to smoke again.

C. A LOCAL POLITICIAN

1885

November. On Tuesday morning a large number of boys
attending this school marched through the Boys' Porch into
the playground singing a Political Song from handbills
supplied to them by Mr. George 'Smith', one of the
Members of the Board.

The handbills on one side had 'Why I am a Liberal'
signed Geo. 'Smith', and on the other the political song
'Brighter Days in Store'.

Before the work of the school could proceed I had to request their being put away and to prevent contention, etc.,
I also requested the removal of bits of yellow and blue
ribbons. At the same time I forbade the wearing of them
in the school and playground. In the afternoon I had to
repeat my request, many wearing bits of yellow ribbon
which had been given them at Mr. 'Smith's' office during
the dinner-time—several only gave a dogged obedience,
Abraham Carter being the principal.

On Thursday morning Abraham Carter came to school
wearing a yellow tie and a piece of yellow ribbon attached
to his jacket. On his disobedience in not removing the
ribbon when requested I gave him a smack on his cheek
with my open hand. He then left the room hurriedly
muttering threats whom he'd tell.

At the close of morning lessons the boy Carter and Mr.
'Smith's' office boy were in the street in front of the school
and were quickly joined by a number of the bigger boys on
their leaving it.

The boy Carter met Mr. 'Smith' on his return from Hull
and evidently a large number of children knew he was
going to do so, because at the time of opening school in the
afternoon they disregarded both the school bell and my
whistle and waited in the street until Mr. 'Smith' led the
way with Carter.

On Mr. 'Smith's' entrance to the school room at the
head of a most disorderly crowd of boys he demanded the
log book in a loud, dictatorial manner before all the school.
Under the circumstances I refused to give it to him but

said he would be able to see it at the Board Meeting next Tuesday night (December 1st, 1885).

Mr. 'Smith' then assaulted me in the presence of the children and teachers—called me a lunatic—said I was not fit to be in school—that I was a big coward—dared me to thrash Carter now and he'd thrash me—struck at my face with his yellow handkerchief and called me a Tory scamp— Addressing Carter he said his father would be quite right to summons me. Told the children they could wear either yellow or blue in the school and playgrounds.

He also told the children and teachers as I would not give him the log book they were to go home as there would be no school that afternoon.

A large proportion of the children took him at his word, ran out of school shouting and consequently it was impossible to hold school.

The Registers were not marked. Immediately after the above scene Dr. Arbuckle visited and I reported the above proceedings to him.

The school had holiday on Friday, the room being used as a Polling Station for the Election of a Member of Parliament.

D. MORE TROUBLE WITH A FIRE

1895

January 30th.   A thick snow on Monday morning which has prevented many children from coming the distance. Today is extremely cold and both fires have smoked and have had to have one door open all day.

February 6th.   We have had to have one door open on account of the smoke ever since last Wednesday. The schoolroom is very cold and draughty at all times, but a door open and smoke makes it very disagreeable, and really not fit for the children to be in. Proper lessons cannot be done as we have to crowd round the fire. The Vicar and another member of the Board came to look at the stove today but nothing has been done to make it any better.

February 8th.   The large room is really not fit for the children to be in at all so we are all doing the best we can in the classroom.

February 11th. The weather is still fearfully cold. The stove has been mended so we are able to have the door shut. Still the schoolroom is very cold and neither teachers nor children can work.

February 22nd. Considering the severity of the weather the children have really attended well but the rooms have really not been sufficiently warm. We have done our best but have been obliged to let the children play and drill very often to help them keep at all warm.

E. THE MADNESS OF MAUD E—

1900. Maud E— had another outbreak of madness this a.m. and persisted in singing loud snatches of comic songs interspersed with wild patter. Without violence she could not be induced to leave her classroom until 10.45 when she sang 'God Save the Queen', bade the children 'good morning' and after intoning a solemn 'amen' left the school.

4 Secondary Schools before 1902

Secondary education in the nineteenth century presented a very varied picture. It included the movement of the public and endowed grammar schools from their unreformed condition to a considerable state of efficiency—spurred on in their endeavours by government commissions, the efflorescence of private secondary schools and the establishment of secondary schools by elected public bodies for the first time.

1. Life at Winchester in the early Nineteenth Century

SOURCE: W. Tuckwell, *The Ancient Ways—Winchester Fifty Years Ago*, Macmillan, 1893.

'I became virtually a scholar of Winchester at three days old. My Father, playing whist in New College common room, was congratulated on the birth of his son! Yes! said he jestingly, "and how pleasant if one of you some ten or twelve years hence were to nominate him on the foundation at Winchester". A Mr. Gifford who was present took him at his word, the promise was kept in mind and carried out and in July 1842 I went down with my father as a candidate or "Candlestick" to the Winchester election. The railroad was not opened to Oxford; we drove on a three-horse coach to Steventon, a small station on the Great Western; by rail to Reading, thence in another coach to Basingstoke, and so again by rail to Winchester. We travelled second class; the carriage had neither cushions nor glass windows; and the third class carriages were open to the sky like coal trucks. . . .

'The court was filled with "Candlesticks" and their "Paters"; for though the election was a farce, and the six or seven scholarships were known to be bespoken, men brought their sons on the chance of unexpected vacancies, or to awake interest in their behalf for following years. . . . the "Candlesticks" were ushered into the election chamber; where sat in awful state the two wardens, of New College and Winchester, the sub-warden

Heathcote, the two posers, Ogle and Stephens, arrayed the one in a velvet-sleeved proctor's gown, the other in a silk law gown, and Dr. Moberley. I had prepared with great care 100 lines of Virgil, but had not construed three before the examiner said, "That will do; can you sing?" I stared and answered, "Yes". "Say", he continued, "All people that on earth do dwell"! I recited the line. "Thank you, you may sit down". My examination was over, and I was elected. By the founder's statutes the scholars were to be practised in singing, that they might take part in the chapel services. No doubt at some time in the history of elections their vocal attainments had been tested by a verse of the Old Hundredth. The practice had been discontinued, but the form remained, quite in harmony with the unreality of the whole proceeding.

A day in the life of a Junior

'The seventy college boys slept in seven chambers, situated on the ground floor and opening into the court; dedicated not only to sleep, but to eating, drinking, study from six p.m. till six a.m. Ten boys more or less lived in each; owning a bedstead with a coarse brown quilt, to which clean sheets, or "clean straw", as with delightful historic suggestiveness it was called, were vouchsafed only in the beginning and middle of the half-year; a cupboard or "toys" and a chest or in some chambers a set of drawers for clothes. The chamber was warmed by wooden faggots four or five feet long, supported on iron dogs in a vast open fireplace, four faggots being the nightly allowance in wintertime. Round the "post" which supported the roof ran a set of bookshelves, containing the chamber library. The inmates were two, possibly three, prefects; the special fag or "valet" of each; certain boys who were neither fags nor prefects; and the "junior in chambers" who was the common drudge. When the chambers were settled for the half-year I found myself "junior in fourth". Let me describe a day of my life in that capacity. It is half-past five in the morning, and the junior is haply dreaming of home, when a harsh voice calls through the keyhole of the locked door, "First peal in the Fourth, Mr. Tuckwell, first peal". Mr. Tuckwell, an urchin of twelve years old, starts up, throws on hastily a pair of braces or some such light attire, unlocks the door, and admits "Rat Williams", a little old man shouldering a hamper, who with his colleague "Martin" bears away the dirty boots. Remitting ablutions as irrelevant, Mr. Tuckwell lights a fire, "sweeps up", fills the basin, calls the boys,—a process requiring nice discrimination, since imperfectly roused sleepers take vengeance on the omission to awake them, and those who are too rudely disturbed respond with a missile or a blow. . . .

'Breakfast was at half-past eight in hall and here the junior had a two-fold function to discharge: he was "breakfast-fag" to some prefect, for whom probably butter was to be washed, and pork chops or sausages to be fried, and he was "junior at end"; slave, that is, to a group of eight or ten boys, whose table or "end" was to be served. These offices performed, he might forage for his own trencher, roll, pat of butter, at the three butteries or "hatches", known as Purver's, Dear's, Colson's. Fierce was the struggle at their breast-high doors, at the bread hatch especially where Dear, the old Artopta, was waggish, garrulous, and slow. Once in this contest a boy, whom we looked upon as "cracked", and who died shortly afterwards, drew his knife across my finger, nearly severing the joint and leaving a scar for life.

'The tea was obtained in mugs from La Croise's table. It was wet, and it was hot, and that was all; and one drank warily after the first few sips, to avoid disturbing the bank of sand with which the "bargy" or brown sugar, selling in those days for sixpence a pound, had been adulterated by the thrifty confectioner. Knives were scarce articles; a junior mostly went without, digging into the butter with a sharp edge of crust, and eating it in fragmentary lumps alternate with the bread. Physiologically, I suppose, it made no difference; but the system lacked repose.

'From half-past nine to twelve was Middle School, a comparatively peaceful time. "Twelve to one" was sacred to games. The fags "watched out" at cricket in summer, 'kicked in" at football in winter: it is hard to say which ordeal was the more hateful. To a little boy a cricket-ball swiftly bowled or "swiped" was as terrible as a cannon ball. The first time a "pila icto bacillo", as old Christopher Johnson calls it, came my way, I deftly let it pass and ran after it; I can hear today the strident, high-pitched voice of V. C. Smith, the Captain of the Eleven, whose bat had propelled it, "Fetch up that ball and then come here". I stood before him, a big strong boy of nineteen or twenty; for being "Founder's Kin" he remained at school after the usual age of superannuation. "Why did you shirk that ball?"—and as he spoke he gave me a "clout" or box on the ear which knocked me down and left the glands swollen and painful for days. I have seen "middle stump" laid heavily on the loins of a little boy for the same offence. Per contra a fag who made a catch was released for the rest of the hour. The result was that with whatever detriment to fingers, skin, chest, or face, we somehow stopped the balls. . . . "Kicking in" was not less irksome; football was played between two rows of low posts threaded with ropes, and lined on the outside with juniors, whose business was to kick in, prevent the ball, that is, from rolling out of bounds. In its abrupt and rapid turns this was difficult for the fags stood five or six yards apart, liable to the summary vengeance of a player who had the ball before him and found himself defrauded of his kick. But I think the bitter and persistent cold was worse than the casual pommelling. We were not allowed to wear our gowns, but stood in jacketless sleeved cloth waistcoat which was the college uniform, shivering in a December day, looking anxiously to the cathedral clock face visible from one or two points through the plane trees of the "Meads" or playground. On Fridays, when there was a chapel service from eleven to twelve, the word used to be passed round amongst the fags in all seriousness, with some recollection perhaps of the Tishbite on Mount Carmel, to "pray for rain". The abandonment of "kicking-in", and the substitution of high canvas walls to the football course, was another of the good deeds with which later on I shall decorate the memory of Charles Wordsworth.

'From one to a quarter past was given to preparation for dinner; the seniors washed and dressed in a lavatory scripturally designated "Moab"; the fags kept out of the way both of the seniors and of cold water. At 1.15 we went up in hall. Six days of the week the dinner was mutton: two Southdown sheep were brought into the kitchen daily; the saddles, legs, shoulders, supplied the higher tables; the juniors had "the racks". I have never been able to determine the anatomy of these helpings or "dispers" as they were called: they consisted of a long bone with a small piece of meat attached, through which the spit had passed, leaving a large green scar. We had a quarter of a pound of bread, potatoes in a pewter dish or "gorner", beer brought up from the cellar in mighty leathern "black jacks", and served in pewter "forums". At the end of the hall was an iron-bound "tub" or cask. Into it the uneaten food was thrown pell-mell to be divided amongst the poor who thronged the court after we had left the hall. Let us hope they consumed the racks: we found them altogether inedible.

'Afternoon school lasted from two till six; in the vast school-room, lighted at that time only by candles in sconces; the boys sitting at their "scobs" or movable desks, while commoners were accommodated also at friendly scobs, or sat at two long "commoner tables". Against the walls were the "Tabula Legum", or rules of the school, and the curious "Out disce" tablet, offering a threefold alternative of study, with a mitre as its reward; timely withdrawal to wield the lawyer's pen or soldier's sword; the "sors tertia" of the rods, which stood throughout school time in a compartment of the Headmaster's seat, and were used when school ended. Order was preserved by two prefects, the "Ostarius" or doorkeeper, and the "Bible-Clerk", exempted from lessons for police work, and armed each with his ground ash. At six o'clock we rose and stood in ranks, while the prefect of school read a form of thanks for the "religion and good learning" which, by the bounty of our Founder, we had imbibed throughout the day; and the junior relapsed once more from the student into the bondslave. . . .

'In 1847 I was made "Prefect of Hall", captain that is and commandant of the whole school both college and commoners. It was said by them of old time that there were three absolute rulers in the world; the Great Mogul, the captain of a man of war, and the prefect of hall at Winchester. Even in my time his power for good or evil was incalculable, sustained by centuries of precedent, and by the whole force of magisterial authority. Once only a boy, too big for me to coerce physically, rebelled against my power. I referred the matter to Moberly, the boy being a commoner and under his jurisdiction: he was flogged and vanished from the school. I met him afterwards at Oxford, and he bore no malice. . . .

'In 1848 I won the Queen's Silver Medal for Oratory and Gold Medal for English Composition. I proudly preserve them both, and I have also the victorious essay. Its subject, "The

Moral Effects of the Love of Praise", is still pencilled in my school Horace as I took it down from Moberly's lips; it reads to me as a very fair performance. When the Electors came down in July, I received them as the head of the school with the "Ad Portas" a Latin oration at the College gates. . . . The severe ordeal of the election followed; I have the roll of elected scholars in the old Warden's handwriting with my name at the head,— for which, according to custom, I gave a guinea to his butler who brought it to me. So I left Winchester for New College; and nothing was left of me except my name on a marble tablet above the prefect of halls' bed in sixth chamber.'

2. A Defence of Unreformed Eton

The Royal Commission on the Public Schools began its inquiries in 1860 and reported in 1864. Eton received detailed attention and the Commissioners' attitude was critical of the school's curriculum and general arrangements. Some of the values of education offered by the school in 1860 are set out here by Oscar Browning.

SOURCE: *Memories of Sixty Years at Eton, Cambridge and Elsewhere,* pp. 62–70.

I have said in a previous chapter that, after having marked out for myself a course of life inconsistent with my being a school-master, I accepted first a mastership at the Liverpool Institute, where I remained a fortnight, and then a mastership at Eton, where I remained fifteen years. There was a great contrast between the two places, not altogether to the advantage of Eton. At Liverpool I found small classes, enthusiastic and devoted students, close friendship among the staff, careful supervision by the Head Master, Dr. Howson. The short time that I spent there is even now vivid to me. Anything that I did for the boys received its full acknowledgment, and I well remember that when my form was offered a holiday during my second week, they asked that it might be deferred till after my departure, because they did not wish to lose any of my teaching. At Eton, where I went to take the place of the Rev. W. B. Marriott, who had been master in College when I was a boy, and was now incapacitated by illness, everything was in confusion. The divisions were far too large, there was no organization, and no control. The Head Master set an excellent example of industry and conscientiousness, but each tutor was suffered to go his own way, and would probably have resented interference.

I found myself at the age of three-and-twenty, after a fortnight's experience of teaching, standing in the place of a parent to forty pupils, some of them only a few years younger than myself, and set in charge of a division of eighty boys, many of them very unruly. Perhaps I should have been less incompetent to deal with these duties if I had felt myself more incompetent. But my assurance was complete; I was convinced, not only that I could meet these obligations, but that I could meet them better than they had ever been met before. My division work was certainly, for the time, a failure, but I succeeded with my pupils, and I believe that I have now no firmer friend than the first boy who had the courage to entrust himself to my incompetent hands, Charles Edward Buckland.

The condition of Eton in 1860 is well known to the world at large, certainly to all those who are interested in the history of English education. It was the year in which the Royal Commission on Public Schools, which reported in 1864, began its investigations. The state of Eton at that time, as represented in the cold, unsympathetic language of a Commission Report, was entirely indefensible. The education was purely classical, little mathematics were taught and no science. Modern languages did not form a part of the regular curriculum, and boys who had learnt them at home with their sisters soon forgot what they had thus acquired. The Prince Consort's Prizes, for the encouragement of these studies, were generally won by boys of fifteen who had been instructed by the family governess. Harry Tarver, the French master, when asked to describe the position which he held in the school answered in the immortal phrase: 'I suppose that I am an "objet de luxe".' The divisions were unwieldy; there was no proper system of promotion. The condition of the College foundation was worse than that of the school. The Provost was generally an ex-Head Master, apt to interfere dangerously with the work of his successor, the fellowships were usually given to masters after twenty years' service, unless they had made themselves obnoxious by too much zeal. Their principal duty was to attend the Chapel services, and to preach to the boys, whose nature they had lost the power of understanding. Their sermons were atrociously bad. I remember a few choice phrases: 'What do you do when you receive anonymous letters? Of course you don't read them; of course you throw them into the fire.' 'You would have smiled, my young friends, at the maps which we used to do in those days.' 'What did they do in the French Revolution? They fell down and worshipped the Goddess of Reason.' A little idolatry in that direction would not, in my opinion, have been altogether inopportune. Occasionally the Head Master preached, and to him the boys lent a willing ear. Hawtrey's addresses on the Catechism, delivered as Head Master, printed, but never published, attained a very high level of literary excellence. Thus Eton, when placed on the rack by a Royal Commission, had nothing to say for herself; there was no need to turn the windlass. She confessed everything, and was found in everything wanting. But really this was a great mistake. Eton in those days was a very fine educational institution; but she was out of touch with the age; her most ardent supporters did not understand her, and did not know how to defend her. When I now read over the evidence given before the Royal Commission, I am forced to the conclusion that the Public School education of that time aimed at a much higher level, and secured a far greater success than that of the present day. After fifty years, Public School Reform has resulted not in improvement but in failure. . . .

Eton education, in the year 1860, in its most favourable aspects, was one of the best educations that has ever existed, although it had grown up by accident, and its full excellence was not understood or appreciated by those who had to work it. For this reason, when it was attacked, it was protected by a clumsy and inadequate defence. It was of course entirely classical, resting on the foundation of the Greek and Latin languages. But education must rest upon some basis, some study must be made principal and other subordinate, and a classical foundation is as good as any other and better than most, so long as it remains in harmony with the spirit of the age. An Eton boy's education was given to him by two sets of teachers in two different places, by the division master in school, and by the tutor in his pupil-room; one the law, the other the equity of instruction. The school work, as it was called, was absolutely rigid, confined to certain Latin and Greek books read again and

8

again, until they were learnt by heart. This rigid system continued up to the Head Master's division, where it became less
formal and more personal, the Head Master having no pupils of
his own, and exercising, if he was a man of power, a real influence on those immediately under his control. Side by side
with this school teaching was the work of the tutor, a thing
difficult to explain to, or to be understood by, any one who has
not personally experienced it. Every boy going to Eton was
committed to a tutor, to be placed either to reside in his house
or to be under his care while he resided at a dame's house. The
tutor was in the place of a parent, and did more for his charge
than many parents do or can do. He had complete control of the
boy, body, mind, and spirit, for six years. His duty was to know
him thoroughly, to understand his character, the quality of his
disposition, and how he might be trained and moulded to the
greatest advantage.

The first duty of a tutor would be to supervise the school work
of his pupil, to see that he knew the lessons which he had to
prepare for the division master, and to correct his Greek and
Latin exercises, prose and verse. But besides this he supplied the
deficiencies of the regular curriculum. Twice a week his pupils
came to him for what was called 'private business', the reading
of Greek and Latin authors, apart from the ordinary course.
This work took many forms. One term I read out in English to
my upper pupils the twenty-four books of Homer's Iliad, the
boys following in the Greek text. We got through a whole book
in a two hours' sitting, but I must admit that book Epsilon was
a hard struggle. The whole of the Sunday teaching was in the
tutor's hands. At Eton there was no school on Sunday, and the
deficiency was supplied by the tutor. Three or four sets of
'private business' held on that day were a heavy burden, indeed
Sunday was to us the hardest day in the week. The Sunday
teaching was of very various descriptions. I read with my upper
pupils, at different times, Ewald's History of Israel, St. Paul's
Epistles in Lightfoot's edition, Scrivener's Textual Criticism of
the New Testament, and Dante's Divina Commedia in the
original Italian. I have also known Eton tutors instruct their
pupils in French, German, Italian, History and Literature, and
provide courses of scientific lectures for them out of their own
pockets. Tutors, whether clerical or lay, prepared their pupils

for confirmation, and I always regarded this as a most valuable privilege.

Besides the teaching of the division master and the tutor, there were a number of extra masters in different subjects, whom the boys could attend. All these were under the direction of the tutor, who gave tickets to his pupils to go out of the house after 'lock-up', signed by himself and the teacher whom they attended. A good tutor rarely punished his pupils, but no boy could be punished without his tutor knowing of it, technically, indeed, not without his permission. There was very constant and intimate communication among the masters about the boys with whom they came into contact, and much time, indeed too much time, was spent in these conversations. Before each lesson, the masters assembled in the Head Master's Chambers and exchanged information and ideas. Theoretically, they should have met together a quarter of an hour before the school lesson, and have gone into school punctually, but in practice the time thus spent was taken out of the lesson, and it was a curious sight to see every day a long string of black-gowned masters walking slowly into school a quarter of an hour late, the boys waiting for them in the court outside. The conversation of the masters with each other was almost exclusively about their pupils, and I often thought that, if the boys gossiped about the masters as much as the masters gossiped about the boys, there must be a superfluity of scandal in the school. These frequent meetings undoubtedly served to bring the masters together, and to encourage friendship and camaraderie between them, a great contrast to the isolation of the University Don. The tutors were in the closest communication with the parents of their pupils, and visits were constantly paid to the pupils' homes in the holidays. I was glad to take advantage of this opportunity to know the family surroundings of my pupils, as I felt that it made me understand them better. Also, tutors frequently took their pupils with them as companions in foreign travel. The wealthy Etonian parent did not object to pay for the improvement or amusement of his son in this way; but the University Don who takes an undergraduate abroad has generally to pay his companion's expenses as well as his own, as the undergraduate, whether wealthy or not, has an allowance, which he does not care to exceed.

From what I have said it will be seen that Eton possessed two elements, which are essential parts of a good education, the firm and uniform course of the school curriculum, determining the character of the training and the place of the learner in the school, and the work of the tutor's pupil-room, subtle and adaptable, fitted for every kind of mind and capacity. It must not be supposed that the system was always accompanied by a performance equal to its highest level or promise; it required good men to execute it. There were some lazy tutors, and some incompetent division masters, but I maintain that, properly carried out, under favourable conditions, the old Eton education has never been surpassed. Some further remarks should be made about it. It exacted great devotion and untiring labour from those who carried it out. There was a very high tone amongst the Eton tutors of my time; no one thought of his leisure or his comfort. So long as anything could be done for the advantage of their pupils, they were always ready to do it. My own work generally lasted from six in the morning to half-past ten at night, and the only exercise I could reckon upon was three hours of dull walking in two days. In the summer half there was more leisure, and a happy combination of Saints' Days might give one a day's hunting in the winter. Again, much was left to the boy himself. It is obvious that the narrow classical school curriculum could not give a liberal education by itself. Its very limitations forced those who received it to enlarge it by their own efforts, and there was, consequently, a great deal of private reading, not only in Classics, but in every branch of literature. In the present day the prevailing feeling, both at school and University, is that nothing can be known which is not consciously taught; in the times of which I write a boy was trained to believe that if he wished to acquire knowledge he must gain it by his own exertion. The skill of the tutor was shown, not by superimposing new knowledge, but in the maieutic art, the art of the midwife as Plato calls it, of bringing to birth knowledge already generated in the mind of the pupil, and yearning to be born. Also, the characteristic note of the education which had given so many statesmen to England had not ceased to sound. The tradition of interest in public affairs, of care for the reputation and honour of the country had not died out. Classical studies did much to foster these feelings. The merit of Latin prose literature, as exhibited in Caesar, Cicero, Livy, and Tacitus, is that it teaches the intrinsic importance of human affairs, and inculcates dignity of character and conduct. To men who have the chance of a public career, open to so many Etonians, this is a priceless benefit, and the fact that India has for so many years been governed by Etonians, and that Etonians hold so many important positions in the State, apart from the advantages given to them by their birth, is due, I believe, largely to the Classical education which they received, an education which it is quite impossible that mathematics or science should supply.

3. An Endowed Grammar School in the 1860s

The Schools Inquiry Commission, whose Report was issued in 1868, did much to help the process of bringing the ancient endowed grammar schools into line with contemporary conditions, but in some cases the trustees of the schools had shown themselves aware of the need for change for many years. This was the situation at Leeds Grammar School where Lord Eldon's famous judgement had prevented much modification of the curriculum until the trustees obtained a special Act of Parliament in 1847. J. G. Fitch wrote the section of the Report from which this extract is taken in his capacity as Assistant Commissioner to the Schools Inquiry Commission.

SOURCE: Report of the Schools Inquiry Commission, Vol. IX, 1868, pp. 167–71.

LEEDS GRAMMAR SCHOOL
Mr. J. G. Fitch's Report

This rich and important school has long enjoyed a high reputation. Its foundation dates from 1552, but it has received considerable augmentations of income from time to time, and its present gross revenue from endowment is £2,454. In Carlisle's 'Endowed Schools' a long description is given of the amounts and terms of the several bequests, and it is stated that at the time of publication (1818) there were 70 boys in the school. There were then two departments, of which the one was preparatory to the other, sending up its pupils to the upper school as soon as they were perfect in the rudiments of Greek. The Charity Commission in 1826 reported that there were then 100 scholars receiving higher instruction; and the list of persons educated at the school includes the names of a judge, a bishop, and several eminent scholars and heads of colleges.

The famous decision of Lord Eldon, so often cited as a precedent, determining the legal definition of a 'grammar school,' was given in the suit, Attorney-General v. Whiteley, in 1806, after an application from certain inhabitants of Leeds to the Court of Chancery, to permit the appropriation of part of the funds of this charity to the payment of masters for French and German, and other subjects likely to be useful to the inhabitants of a commercial town. The report of the Master in Chancery had stated that in his opinion there 'was nothing in the original institution and endowment of the charity which necessarily excluded the teaching of any useful kind of learning; that it would be beneficial to the inhabitants to employ part of the funds towards teaching things useful in trade and commerce, and that he therefore approved of adding to the establishment three additional masters, one to teach German, one for French, and the third for algebra and mathematics.' The Lord Chancellor declined to sanction this arrangement, and sent back the Master's report for revision, after enunciating the following memorable judgment:

'Taking upon me now to correct the omission of this decree, and to declare what this foundation is, I am of opinion, upon the evidence now before me, that the Free School in Leeds is a free grammar school for teaching grammatically the learned languages, according to Dr. Johnson's definition; upon circumstances without variation in fact since the year 1553, to which I cling as better interpreters of the real nature of the charity than any criticism I can form, or constructing upon the instruments; for, with the exception of the highway, the original founder proposed to the inhabitants the benefit of this donation by his will for a free school, and to this time every charity given by these instruments has been by inquisition and decrees upon them applied in fact for the benefit of the Free School in Leeds, in which nothing has been taught but the learned languages; and under such facts the result of the evidence is, that the Free School in Leeds is a free grammar school for teaching grammatically the learned languages. The reason of my opinion is, that I do not apprehend it is competent to this court, as long as it can find any means of applying the charitable fund to the charity as created by the founder, upon any general notion that any other application would be more beneficial to the inhabitants of the place, to change the nature of the charity. A case may arise in which the will cannot be obeyed, but then the fund will not go to the heir; upon the principle that an application is to be made as near as may be, growing out of another principle, that you are to apply it to the object intended if you can. It must therefore appear by the Master's report that the court must despair of attaining that object, or the court cannot enter into the question, in what other way the fund is to be applied:

'Declare, that the charity intended to be established by the first donation mentioned in the master's report is the sustentation and maintenance of a free grammar school for the teaching the learned languages; that the Free School in Leeds is a free grammar school for the teaching grammatically the learned languages; and that it appears to the court that the free teaching thereof is the charity intended to be established by the several donations mentioned in the report, so far as the same relate to the school. With that declaration let the Master review his report as to any plan they may think proper to lay before him, and it will be open to him to consider what is proper and necessary, not for the benefit of the inhabitants of Leeds, but for the benefit of the charity, declared to be such upon this record.'

The effect of this decision was to postpone for several years any enlargement of the curriculum of the school; and it was not until the year 1847 that the trustees were enabled by a special Act of Parliament to fulfil the wishes of the inhabitants in this respect. The scheme of the Court of Chancery which now governs the school came into force in 1855, and the new schoolhouse and residences were erected as recently as 1859. As there has been a change in the head mastership since that date, it is probable that all particulars respecting the condition of the school in 1865 represent very inadequately the true importance of the institution and the services which it is destined to render to the higher education of the north of England.

The new premises are on Woodhouse Moor, the healthiest site in Leeds, and have been erected on an unusually grand and costly scale. The school rooms are capable of accommodating at least 300 pupils; there are an excellent residence for the headmaster, with rooms adequate for the reception of boarders; nine acres of playground; and a school chapel. No statelier or more commodious school buildings are to be seen in the county. The staff of teachers has been constituted on an equally liberal scale. Besides the head and second masters, there are three assistants, who are graduates, and special teachers for physical science, for modern languages, for writing, and for drawing. There is also a special master in charge of the modern department.

The scheme provides for the annual examination of the upper forms of the school by examiners from the universities. At the time of my visit this examination was being conducted with great care and minuteness by Mr. Hansel, of Magdalen College, Oxford. The report of that gentleman addressed to the trustees is as follows:

'The head form have been examined by me in the following subjects and books:

'Divinity.—Questions were given in the history of the Old and New Testaments; these have been satisfactorily answered by nearly all in the form.

'A paper was also set in the Greek text of St. Matthew's Gospel and the Epistle to the Hebrews; the average of marks gained by the form generally was higher in this than in the former paper.

'In classics the books brought up for examination were, in Greek, two orations of Demosthenes, two books of Homer's Odyssey, and the Trachiniae of Sophocles; in Latin, two books of the histories of Tacitus, five books of Virgil's Æneid, and the Satires of Juvenal. With regard to these books, I notice with pleasure that the high standard of accurate and at the same time spirited translation which impressed me so much last year has been fully maintained this year. I would wish to name especially the renderings from Demosthenes and Tacitus, the latter a book which presents peculiar difficulties to an English translator. The higher number of marks has been reached in the translations from the Latin, some of the pupils having obtained full marks, others nearly full marks, but the translations from the Greek are quite satisfactory. The paper of critical questions has been creditably answered. Each pupil was examined separately both in Greek and Latin viva voce, in parsing as well as in construing.

'I am glad to notice a very decided improvement this year both in the Greek and Latin prose; the verse compositions are also much better than they were, and I see no reason to doubt that in no very long time the same high standard may be reached in composition which has been already attained in translation.

'In mathematics the three highest forms have been examined, according to the extent of their reading, in Euclid, algebra, trigonometry, and conic sections, geometrical and analytical. In each subject problems have been given to test how far the pupils could apply their book-work. I have no doubt at all about the soundness and efficiency of the instruction given in this department; both matter and form are good, and the solution of independent problems shows that the principles have been mastered. I am glad to observe that conic sections have been mastered geometrically.

'For the exhibition a distinct examination has been held in divinity, classics, and mathematics, the relative value of each subject having been settled by a previously arranged proportion. The questions in divinity were set by myself; those in the other two subjects were taken almost entirely from papers recently given in college scholarships at the University.

'Taking the whole examination from first to last, and comparing the result with that of last year, I feel myself justified in coming to the conclusion that no ground has been lost, that some very important ground has been gained, and that a full amount of solid work has been done in the course of the year.'

At the time of my visit the school contained upwards of 200 boys, of whom 50 were in the lower or commercial department. Throughout all the classes the boys were working with steadfastness and method, and I was particularly impressed by the frankness and manliness of tone which pervaded the school. Much of this is evidently attributable to the personal influence of the head master, who takes an active share in revising and directing the work of the lower forms, as well as in the teaching of his own special department. Some of the tests which he was applying to the mathematical work were exceedingly skilful and expeditious, and the entire organization struck me as being more compact than that of many great schools in which the number of masters causes each class to be practically severed from the rest.

The scheme of instruction provides that French shall be taught in all but the lowest form: and 22 of the boys are learning German. In the upper forms, boys are allowed to substitute certain branches of science for Greek; 36 are studying chemistry, and nearly an equal number are receiving systematic instruction in other branches of physical science. There is an excellent laboratory and ample apparatus and other provision for the teaching of these subjects. Drawing is a part of the regular routine of the school, and an unusual proportion of the boys pay the extra fee for instruction in it. They are taught under the direction of a master connected with the Leeds School of Art, and I have seen in no other grammar school so much interest evinced in drawing. I learn that the school has secured a good number of prizes from the Department of Science and Art.

These arrangements appear to have been most judiciously devised to meet the objections so commonly urged against an exclusively classical education for the upper classes of a commercial town. In practice, however, all the best teaching power of the school is concentrated upon the teaching of Latin and Greek, and all the traditions and feelings of the school are naturally in favour of the supremacy of those studies. There is less demand on the part of the boys and their parents than was anticipated for instruction in chemical and other science; and on the whole the experience of the new scheme, so far as it has worked hitherto, seems to prove that in a rich commercial community like Leeds there is great readiness to appreciate a course of instruction which is mainly based on the ancient languages, but which is pervaded with a modern spirit, and includes most of the subjects generally considered indispensable in an English education. It can scarcely be doubted that the confidence already felt throughout the district in the excellence of this school will be increased as the plan on which it is founded becomes more fully understood and carried out.

Reference is made in my General Report to the English or commercial department here. It is under the care of one master, a clergyman, who receives assistance at certain hours from the teacher of writing and arithmetic. The fees paid in this department are only half of those charged in the upper school, and the two departments are entirely distinct. The trustees do not desire to develop this department into a large school, and have fixed fifty for the present as its numerical limit. I examined some of the scholars, and found them to be making fair progress in general English subjects, in elementary Latin, and in French. It is too early to pronounce with any confidence as to the ultimate success of this experiment, or to determine how far the general objections to the establishment of two departments for scholars of different social grades in one school are met by the plan pursued here. It will be observed that the upper department, containing less than four times the number of scholars, commands the entire services of seven masters; whereas the lower school, comprising boys of very various ages, has only one master, and cannot therefore be completely organized or effectively classified.

The accommodation for boarders is extremely good, but the number is limited to 25, since the trustees believe that the requirements of Leeds are more likely to be met by an efficient day school than by encouraging the admission of a large proportion of boarders from a distance.

The income of the school is chargeable with some heavy annual deductions, amounting to about £800, in respect of the debt on the new school buildings. This encumbrance will be wholly removed in about 30 years.

The scheme provides four exhibitions of £50 each, tenable for four years each, at Oxford, Cambridge, or Durham. Three of these are paid from the general funds of the school, and the fourth or 'Beckett' exhibition from a special fund bequeathed for the purpose by two ladies bearing that name. There is one vacancy each Midsummer, and this is filled up by the governors, on the recommendation of the examiner for the year. The school is one of those entitled to send competitors for Dr. Milner's scholarships at Magdalen College, Cambridge, the others being Halifax and Haversham. It is also one of the twelve entitled to compete for the exhibitions of Lady E. Hastings at Queen's College, Oxford. Within the two years preceding this inquiry, both of these valuable prizes had been won in competition by boys from Leeds Grammar School; and the list of distinctions obtained during the year 1864–5 includes four university scholarships, four places in the honour list at Cambridge, two in the second-class moderations at Oxford, besides a divinity studentship at St. John's, Cambridge, and a high place in the competition and a Pollock medal at Woolwich.

The scheme reserves to foundationers, i.e. to boys born in Leeds, or sons of residents in the town, the right of admission on lower terms than other scholars. The rates of payment have been increased since the time of my visit, and are now (1866) fixed at ten guineas a year in the upper school, and five in the lower. Non-foundationers pay fourteen guineas if under fourteen years of age, and sixteen guineas if above that age. The only extra charge is for drawing, and this amounts to £1. 10s. per annum.

4. Six Unreformed Grammar Schools, 1868

The contrast between schools where some reform had been undertaken and those where the personal interests of trustees or schoolmaster continued to predominate may be seen by comparing the last extract on Leeds Grammar School with Fitch's account of the six endowed schools lying to the North West of that city. The account of Bradford Grammar School may also be compared with that given of the school in 1895 in the subsequent extract.

SOURCE: Report of the Schools Inquiry Commission, Vol. IX, 1868, pp. 110–13.

In one part of this district there are on or near a single line of railway six towns in succession which will furnish illustrations of the general statement I have made. If we start from Leeds and proceed up the valley of the Aire in a N.W. direction towards Lancaster, we pass in succession Bradford, Bingley, Keighley, Skipton, Giggleswick and Sedbergh. The united annual revenue of the grammar schools in these towns exceeds £4,000, and if the rent of the buildings, &c., be taken into account, it nearly approaches £5,000. By reference to 'Carlisle' to the 'Liber Scholasticus' and to the first Charity Commission report it is evident that every one of these schools has in old times sustained a high character, has turned out respectable, if not eminent scholars, and has been the centre of civilization and of knowledge to the neighbourhood in which it was placed. Yet at this moment it cannot be said that the whole six schools are imparting to twenty boys preparation for university life, or are giving in any sense classical education to fifty scholars. It will be fairer, however, to speak of them in detail.

BRADFORD. Bradford Grammar School has an endowment estimated by the trustees at £900 per annum. It is situated in a spirited and prosperous town, which, in 1821 contained 26,307 inhabitants, and in 1861, 106,218. Thus the population has increased more than fourfold in 40 years. One would expect, therefore, that the demand for a higher education has not diminished. There are good premises, built in 1819, capable of accommodating at least 120 scholars. I found in this school 42 pupils, of whom two were reading a Greek play, and otherwise studying with a view to admission into one of the universities. Eight only were able to translate a simple passage from a Latin author. The elements of Latin are learned lower down in the school, but imperfectly. The staff consists of two clergymen, and one assistant master, who holds a Government certificate of merit. There are no boarders in the house of the head master. The school is entitled to send a candidate for the valuable exhibition of Lady Elizabeth Hastings, with £75 per annum, tenable for five years at Queen's College, Oxford. But since the regulation which made that exhibition obtainable by competitive examination has been in force, the school has never sent up a candidate, and it will probably forfeit its privilege ere long.

BINGLEY. At Bingley is a new and commodious school, well adapted for the reception of from 80 to 100 scholars. I found 18 pupils present; the number belonging to the school being 25, of whom six are boarders in the head master's house. There is a clergyman at the head, and a junior master, who is himself reading for the university. Of the elder boys, two are reading Virgil and the Hecuba of Euripides, and two others are reading Cornelius Nepos and the Greek delectus. Below this the knowledge of Latin, and, indeed of all else, is very elementary. Of the five boys at the head of the school two are the sons of the master, two of the vicar of the parish, and one of a neighbouring clergyman. Thus the extent to which the grammar school contributes to the general education of the town is very limited, and all my inquiries led me to fear that it is diminishing. Yet in this town also there has been a large increase of population within 40 years; for in 1821 the number residing in the parish was 7,375, while at the last census it was found to be 15,367.

KEIGHLEY. Keighley is the next town in order, and here the increase of population is also very marked. It has risen in the course of 40 years from 9,223 to 18,819. The grammar school is a handsome building, well adapted for 100 scholars. The endowment amounts to £246. 14. 6d. I found 42 pupils here, of whom nine board in the master's house. Though called a grammar school, it has long ceased to deserve the name. No boy learns Greek, or can read the simplest passage from a Latin author; only two can parse or interpret an easy sentence in one of Arnold's early exercises. With these exceptions the general organization and instruction of the school are those of an average national school; and it is filled for the most part with the same class of children.

SKIPTON. At Skipton there is an endowment which at present realizes £758. 10. 5d per annum, but the estates are notoriously let for less than their true value, and if properly managed would, according to the admission of the trustees, easily realize more than £1,000 per annum. Here are good premises and an excellent ground. The head master is a clergyman, and has two assistants, his own son and nephew. Thirty-six boys were present on the day of my visit. The organization of the school is so confused that it was difficult to ascertain what was learned by the various classes; but the general average of instruction is very low. Fifteen of the boys profess to learn the Latin accidence, but of them ten are quite unable to write down the conjugation of a simple verb. The five boys at the head of the school are nominally reading Ovid, but only two of them could parse or translate with tolerable accuracy a line in the epistle which they had just read with the master. None are able to scan a line, and none are learning Greek; none learn Euclid, and I could find no evidence of mathematical knowledge even of the humblest kind. It is a free school, but its status may be estimated from the fact that scarcely any parents above the rank of the poor avail themselves of it; and it is not an uncommon thing for a child to be sent to the Grammar School for a time and then transferred to the National School, for the last year of his education, to finish.

GIGGLESWICK. The village of Giggleswick by Settle gives its name to the rich foundation school whose condition has so often been before the public. This school has a controversial and historic literature of its own, into the merits of which I do not here enter. It is but fair to say that its present condition is rather the result of past mistakes and weakness than of any defect in its present teaching arrangements. It possesses excellent school premises, an annual revenue of £1,200, besides houses for the head and second masters, who are clergymen of high scholastic distinction and great experience. There is a third master who holds a government certificate of merit. Thus the institution is well equipped with the means of instruction. Yet there are only 37 boys in the school, and of these only 22 in the higher classes are learning Latin. The sixth form is at present represented by one boy only, and about eight scholars in all are able to read a simple passage from a Latin author. I cannot doubt that ere long confidence will be felt by the people of the neighbourhood in the excellence of the teaching arrangements, and in the un-questionable ability and earnestness of the three masters. There are other circumstances to which I will hereafter draw attention, and which make me very hopeful about the future of this im-portant school; which once held a high rank, and in which Archdeacon Paley received his education. But there can be no doubt that at present it is under a cloud. With premises adapted for six times the present number, with so splendid an income, and so efficient a staff of teachers, it is a great scandal that there should be only 37 boys, of whom four only are boarders.

SEDBERGH. The last school in the group is at Sedbergh, a small town finely situated in the hill country, and at the edge of Westmoreland. Here there is an endowment producing £660 per annum, and good premises adapted for the reception of more than 100 scholars. There are two masters, both of whom are clergymen. The number in the school is 13, of whom ten are in the upper and three in the lower school. The house of the head master is a large mansion, with accommodation for 45 resident pupils. There are, however, no boarders, except three in the house of the second master. The ten pupils of the upper school are lads of about 17, who are, as it seems to me, perform-ing the ceremony of a nominal attendance in order to entitle themselves to the very valuable exhibitions in which this school is so rich.* When these boys shall have left, I do not see how, under the present regime, the school can remain open. No new scholar has been admitted for more than a year past, and at the time of my visit none were expected.

GENERAL RESULTS IN THESE SIX CASES. It will be seen that the total number of scholars in these six schools is 195, and that the number of masters is 15, giving an average of 13 pupils to each teacher. Eight of the masters are in holy orders. With the single exception of Giggleswick, in which six boys are reading French with the head master, no modern languages are learned in any one of these schools. There is no teaching of physical science, and scarcely any attempt at drawing. The number of boys who have done anything deserving the name of mathematics is much smaller than of those who profess to read Latin. As to the reading, arithmetic, English grammar, geography, and history, and the power to explain the meanings of the words which occur in a reading lesson; the attainments of the boys are (I must again except Giggleswick from this general statement) far inferior to those of ordinary elementary schools receiving the parliamentary grant. The methods of instruction are less intelligent, the organization and management less methodical, and the results in the way of instruction and of general culture appear to me inferior both as to quality and extent.

These schools have not been arbitrarily selected as the worst in the district, but because they happen to form a group possessing a sort of geographical unity, and easily visited in succession in the course of a single official tour. They furnish, therefore, a convenient and striking illustration of the general state of the grammar schools in one part of the district. Not one of these

---

* This school possess a claim for eight exhibitions, viz.:

One in gift of the governors of the school, of about £50 per annum for three years, at St. John's College, Cambridge, for boys born in the township and parish of Sedbergh.

Six exhibitions to St. John's College, Cambridge, £33. 6. 8d. Two elected from Sedbergh School every year if qualified; tenable for three years.

One at Christ's College, Cambridge, £20 per annum, with preference to Kirkby Lonsdale and Sedbergh schools, for scholars of two years' standing previous to election.

Sedbergh also shares with eleven other schools the right to send candidates for the Hastings Exhibition at Queen's College, Oxford.

schools is at this moment improving, and only one is in a state which justifies any hope of improvement. Yet no new public schools in the neighbourhood have superseded them; there has been no drifting of the population away from them. On the contrary, the six towns in which they are situated are the educational and social centres of an extensive and populous region, about 50 miles in length, covering the whole N.W. of the riding, and at least one-fifth of the district assigned to me. It is exactly to these points that the children of the vast population inhabiting the valley of the Aire and the district of Craven would naturally be drawn if the schools possessed the public confidence.

5. Bradford Grammar School, 1895

The often drastic changes brought about as a consequence of the Schools Inquiry and the Endowed Schools Commissions is well illustrated by this extract from the Report on Secondary Education in the West Riding by A. P. Laurie. The complete re-organization of the Bradford Grammar School and the introduction of a sizeable contingent of able but less well-off boys through scholarships supported by the City Council and by the West Riding County Council combined to make unrecognizable the description in the last extract written a quarter of a century earlier.

SOURCE: Report of the Royal Commission on Secondary Education, Vol. VII, 1895, pp. 178–81.

Bradford

Bradford is specially interesting from an educational point of view, as it can claim to have a fairly complete organisation for Secondary Education, which with a few developments and improvements might be made completely satisfactory. After describing the schools in Bradford I shall show how they fit one into another, and how little would be required to complete the present system. The first school which we must consider is the Bradford Grammar School which is certainly the leading day grammar school of the West Riding. Like so many other Yorkshire manufacturing towns, the working part of Bradford is down in the valley, the residential part is up on the hills, and the big secondary schools lie between the two. But Bradford is a much smaller town than Sheffield, and the distances are not so great, while the grammar school occupies a position which is

9

fairly midway between the two districts and within reach of boys of all classes. The school is situated in good buildings, with large airy class-rooms, a fairly good playground, and a good gymnasium, and though not examples of the latest designs in school buildings, and not well arranged with a view to easy supervision by the headmaster, the rooms are sufficiently good for their purpose. There is a well-appointed chemical laboratory, a small physical laboratory and a good chemical lecture-room, so that fittings and appliances for science teaching are quite up to the mark. The school has a remarkably good staff of assistant masters, most of whom are honours men, and impress one as thoroughly good men who quite understand their work; in fact, I have seen no staff of grammar school masters in the West Riding who impressed me so favourably on the whole. The secret of this is to be found in the wisdom of the headmaster and the governors, who are prepared to pay well, as such things go, and to obtain, as far as possible, the best men available. One sometimes, in going round a school staffed by university men, begins to doubt whether there is anything in university culture after all. There are so many men at present teaching in the country, who, while having the outward stamp of the university, as represented by a degree, seem to have imbibed little or nothing of the general culture of the university, or to have lost what little they had in the drudgery of teaching the same round of elementary subjects in a school situated in a provincial manufacturing town. This is not the case at Bradford. One feels at once that the boys are gaining more, as they ought to gain, than the mere lesson before them, and are benefiting every day from being in the company, and under the influence, of highly educated men. This is, perhaps, most striking in the English classes, and I could not help being amused at noticing the contrast between the English literature as taught in the Grammar School and as taught in the Belle Vue School, which will be shortly described. At the Belle Vue School the ignorance of English literature was well illustrated by the fact that the teachers apparently knew nothing better to give children of 12 or 13 than Shakespeare, and, in selecting a play of Shakespeare, could be content with nothing simpler than Lear, while, at the Grammar School, boys of the same age were reading Washington Irving. One is repeatedly impressed by the fact, both in elementary and secondary schools, that teachers seem to be totally ignorant of the vast literature that exists in the English language, and do not know that it is possible to select from these stores portions which will be perfectly intelligible and interesting to young children, and which, as beautiful examples of style, will train them in a nice and accurate use of their own language. Other men besides Shakespeare, they may be assured, have written good English, both as poetry and prose.

The number of boys in the school is 420, and their ages vary from 8 to 19, while the fees vary from 10l. up to 16l. a year. There is a preparatory school for little boys, and the upper school is divided into two departments, classical and modern. The modern side is an organised science school, and takes the ordinary Science and Art subjects. The classical side is strong, and a fair number of boys are sent on every year to the universities. On the modern side, the sixth form takes theoretical chemistry, honours and advanced, and practical chemistry, honours and advanced, and advanced organic chemistry, advanced sound, light, and heat, advanced electricity, and have four hours a week of practical physics. The science side begins on the third form with elementary theoretical chemistry, and elementary sound, light, and heat, or elementary electricity. The boys are put through a laboratory course, but are not sent in for examination. In the fourth form they take the same course and are sent in for practical chemistry, while in the fifth form they begin at the advanced stage of these subjects, and, as already stated, the sixth form take either honours or advanced. It will be seen from this that the practice here is very similar to the practice in the higher grade school at Leeds, where a boy of average ability requires four years to take his advanced certificate. The headmaster has now divided the upper school into three instead of two, distinguishing the commercial from the science side. The science side will now take six hours' science, six hours' mathematics, and six hours of drawing; the rest of the time being occupied by modern languages, English, and geography.

In order to explain Mr. Keeling's method of working the school, we must now say a little about the sources from which the boys are obtained. Two-thirds of the boys come in young and pass through the whole course of the school, but besides these there are 15 West Riding County Council scholarship boys and 40 boys who hold scholarships giving free education granted by the Bradford County Council from the technical instruction grant. These boys enter at about 13 years of age, and are selected from the five higher board schools which I shall have shortly to describe. In the last examination there were 110 candidates for 13 of these scholarships, so that the competition is pretty severe. Mr. Keeling has, therefore, to supply, on the one side, the wants of these boys, who, along with the others who are already in the school, wish for a commercial or scientific education, and on the other hand he has to keep up the reputation of the school as a classical school in direct touch with the universities. Of course the difficulty to be met is, that these large numbers of scholarship boys coming in at the age of 13 do not fit readily into the school work, as they may be very advanced in some subjects and not so advanced in others as boys of their own age already in the school; but this is not a serious difficulty in the case of a school so large as the Grammar School, and in which so many scholarship boys are being received at a time. It is merely, as Mr. Keeling says, a matter of organisation, and after a few months of special treatment these boys can fit into the ordinary work of the school. The success with which this is done is well shown by the fact that the strength of the upper forms, on the modern side, is made up very largely of these scholarship boys; they form at least one-third of the number of all the top boys in the school, and more than hold their own in the gaining of scholarships to the universities. Mr. Keeling's views on this question are of considerable interest. He considers that the development of higher grade schools must ultimately seriously affect the position of the grammar schools, if they are not put on a thoroughly popular footing, and would even propose not only putting them under control of such a body as the town council, but also making them free, like the elementary and many of the higher grade schools. He considers that in the case of his own school he has been able to meet the new conditions of things successfully, for the time, by means of the town and county scholarships, which practically means freeing the school to a considerable number of boys of poor parentage. By these means he has been able to take the cream of the boys each year from the higher board schools, and so, to a great extent, diminish the danger of their competition, while, at the same time strengthening his own school with a new and valuable element.

With reference to the science teaching as a whole, though too much under the influence of the examinations of the Science and Art Department, it is better than one finds in the ordinary grammar school. This is largely due to the fact that there is a physical laboratory and lecture-room, and that the boys are put through a course of practical physics, beginning with Worthington's book, and going on to Shaw and Glazebrook. There is a carpentering workshop, and two hours a week carpentering is compulsory in the junior school, but it is a voluntary subject in the upper school. The Bradford Grammar School as a whole impresses one as being the best of the day grammar schools in the West Riding of Yorkshire, and it shows that a thoroughly good grammar school, which is ready to adapt itself to the new conditions and take its proper place, need not fear the competition of the new educational forces coming into play. The Bradford Grammar School has had to face in recent years the development of five higher board schools of the town and of a day technical school, and in spite of this has 420 boys, while the maximum number ever reached was 450. As showing how successfully the school, while supplying the wants of the boys from the elementary schools, has kept in touch with the universities, I may mention that in the last 10 years, 108 boys have proceeded to the universities from this school, 73 scholarships have been gained at the universities, and 44 have obtained first classes in honours at Oxford, Cambridge, and London. The school has 718l. a year income from endowment, apart from 680l. a year for scholarships. This money is spent on leaving scholarships, there being no scholarships for boys within the school.

6. The Education of the Commercial Classes in Manchester, 1868

The well-known public schools and the endowed grammar schools have both survived and flourished so that they are today both pacesetters and objects of envy. Private secondary education in day schools has dwindled in the face of increasing state provision and no longer makes any vital contribution in meeting the educational needs of the community. A hundred years ago it made an important contribution and some knowledge of what these vanished schools undertook is necessary to an understanding of nineteenth century education. This extract is from a report on Manchester by Mr Bryce, then Assistant Commissioner.

SOURCE: Report of the Schools Inquiry Commission, Vol. IX, 1868, pp. 713–18.

... having regard solely to the education given in the non-elementary schools of Manchester itself, there are three questions to be asked respecting it.

Firstly. What sort of an education do Manchester parents, business men, desire for their sons?

Secondly. Where do they receive that education?

Thirdly. What is the range and quality of that education as now actually given?

First. The great majority of persons in Manchester above the rank of labourers are engaged in business, and it is for business that the great majority of their sons are destined. Now it need not be said that the Manchester man has none of that stolid indifference to 'school learning' which distinguishes the British farmer. He desires his son to get an education and is willing to pay a fair price for it. But his notion of what education should be is far more negative than positive, and is in all respects vague. The boy is to go into a warehouse at 14 or 15; and the father's views are necessarily governed by the thought of what it is he will have to do there. Hence he objects to Greek and Latin as useless, or at best tolerates them as established by custom, but destitute of intrinsic value. He has less direct hostility to mathematics, but quite as little inclination to favour them. Sometimes he talks of French or German. More rarely, and only when he desires it for professional purposes, he mentions natural science—chemistry, or physics—and mechanical drawing. But his feeling, when it attains to a conscious expression is in nine cases out of ten simply this, 'I want my boy to write a good clear hand, and to add up figures quickly. I want him to spell correctly, and to know enough about history, geography, and all that sort of thing, not to seem ignorant in society. As for other matters, I suppose he must learn what the school teaches while he stays there, but it is by his own shrewdness and activity that I expect him to get on; and none of these ornamental things that he learns will make any difference to that. Too much schooling oftener mars a man of business than it makes him.' This is in substance to say that the practical value of education is confined to writing, reckoning, and so much skill in composition as a business letter requires. Manchester people are too shrewd not to recognise the value of thorough literary or scientific training when carried on up to the age of 18 or 20. But in Manchester, as in Liverpool and I suppose in all commercial towns, it is an axiom that not only is a boy as fit for business at 15 as he will ever be, but that he will not take kindly to an office if he goes to it a year or two older. Secondly. The next question is, in what local institutions is the desired education given? These institutions (excluding of course the Privy Council schools) fall under three heads.

1. The Owens College, giving a collegiate or quasi-university course, i.e., a general education in the higher branches of literature, history, and science.

2. The Grammar School, giving a mainly classical, and to some extent also mathematical, education, preparatory to the Universities.

3. The private adventure (and other quasi-private)*schools, giving either a classical and commercial, or, more frequently, a wholly commercial education.

Of these three, it is the last that are of the greatest practical importance to the present inquiry, since it is they which give its general character to the education of the city. Among them there is of course great diversity in cost, in pretensions, in size, in substantial excellence. Still there is a sufficient similarity to make it possible to characterise in general terms the instruction which they give. It is of this, then, the commercial education, that it will be necessary in the first place to speak, reserving for subsequent description the classical teaching of the Grammar school and the collegiate course of Owens College.

* By quasi-private schools I mean those which, though not absolutely the property of the teacher, are managed by him for his sole benefit. Such are for the most part the schools held in buildings belonging to congregations. Such, too, is a large school called the 'Manchester Commercial School,' established by the Manchester Church Education Society.

Thirdly. What is the range and what the quality of the education given?

It must be remembered that the education of a Manchester boy is usually a short one, not extending beyond 14 or 15. In the private schools which have made returns to the questions of the Commission, only 12 per cent. of the scholars were over 14 years of age; and less than 2 per cent. over 16. It is also, considered as a systematic training, of a somewhat loose and fluctuating character. The parent, having in most cases no special reason to prefer one private school to another, since he has no means of ascertaining the real merits of any, is apt to take fancies, and make frequent changes. Boys are removed from school to school losing more, it may be, by the change of books and system, than they gain by passing even from a worse school to a better. According to the report of teachers themselves, the average duration of a boy's stay at one school does not exceed three years. These are disturbing influences, but the aim and general character of the teaching in all these schools is substantially the same. They profess it their chief object to give 'a thorough commercial education.' If ever a phrase can do mischief by intensifying an error which lurked vaguely in the mind till words gave it a definite shape and confidence in itself, the phrase 'commercial education' may be thought to have done it.

There are two different senses in which it may be taken. It may mean the education best suited for a man who is to live by commerce, that is to say, one whose schooling (according to Manchester custom) ends at 15 or 16; the education which shall leave him at that age in the completest state of preparation for active mercantile life with his faculties trained, his tastes cultivated, his moral and social feelings strengthened and wisely directed to the right objects. Or it may mean the education which is most likely to give him an immediate success in trade, i.e., which will enable him to get money most quickly. In either sense the phrase has a rational meaning; it is from the confusion of the two that so much mischief has arisen. Parents who, if the question were put to them, would prefer to choose the former, practically follow the latter. The schoolmaster, whose zeal and sense of duty would lead him to strive to carry out the wider and more liberal view, finds his interests driving him into the more narrow and selfish one. In practice he makes a sort of compromise between the two. The subjects which tradition has established as part of a liberal education are not wholly discarded, but being supposed to be of little practical use, they are taught in a languid, careless way. Both boys and teacher are aware that the parent neither knows nor cares what progress is made in them; and the strength of the teaching is expended on the commercial subjects, with what result it may be proper to state. I will first take the case of a merchant or well-to-do shopkeeper, with an income of from £700 a year up to £1,500. The son of such an one, if he is not sent to a distant boarding school, has most probably the following career: When he has learnt his letters he goes for a year or two to some small preparatory school, kept by a lady, where he learns to read correctly, to spell a little, to say the multiplication table, and to know that English grammar has four parts, orthography, etymology, syntax, and prosody. At nine his father takes him to a boys' school in the neighbourhood; the head master receives him, and places him in one of the smaller rooms, if it be a big school, and in one of the corners of the room, if it be a small one, under the charge of an assistant. The assistant is possibly ignorant, and probably a dull and unskilful teacher. He has little interest in the progress of his pupils being a hireling, and knowing that if their performances redound to anyone's credit, it will not be to his. Moreover, as he takes them (usually, though not quite invariably) in all branches of instruction, any special gift that he may have for teaching one branch goes for little. At first the boy is taught reading, spelling, writing, English grammar, arithmetic; then geography is added, then history; in the course of another year French, and possibly Latin; by the time he is 13, Euclid, algebra, and it may even be some little German and drawing. These subjects, to the number of a dozen or more, are worked in by means of an elaborate time table, according to which five hours a week are spent on one subject, let us say arithmetic; four on another—writing; three on another—French, geography, mathematics; two on others—Latin, history, dictation; one on English composition, German, and drawing, or on some branch of natural science. If the boy stays long enough at the school he passes in time, perhaps when he is 13 or 14, from assistants up to the head master, and then his horizon grows brighter. The head masters of some six or seven of these schools are able and painstaking men, and under them the boy, now in some measure delivered from the thraldom of his time table, and allowed to concentrate his attention on a few subjects, may make good progress in mathematics or Latin. But not one-eighth part of the whole number remain to this stage, and even those who do have in the previous weary years under the handling of the assistants suffered evils and contracted habits which it is now too late to cure.*

The desire for knowledge, which is surely when properly fostered a strong passion in the minds of most children, even those whose volatility makes them troublesome to deal with, has been checked by the listless monotony of the teaching, and has found no extraneous stimulus to take its place. The classes are too small to rouse emulation, or that other and better feeling which is sometimes confounded with emulation, the sympathy of numbers. At home there has been little to rouse or encourage the boy's diligence. The father is away at business all day, and sees him only for an hour or two in the evening. He may sometimes glance through the lately finished copybook, or perhaps give him a sum to do, or ask where Pernambuco is. 'What, you don't know this, and I pay three guineas every quarter to Mr. Smith for teaching you it.' In his other studies he shows no interest; it is well if he does not openly sneer at his Latin and Euclid, and threaten to forbid him to work any longer at them, a threat which it may be supposed is seldom heard with alarm.

Then at 15 the father declares he will wait no longer. A place has been found in a warehouse, and the merchant doubts whether the boy is not already too old to rough it as a boy ought, to run errands, carry letters to the post, and make himself generally useful at the beck of others. The father is not a rich man, and began life himself even younger. Education is all very well, but his sons must learn to look out for themselves. Thus the boy goes and leaves most of what he learnt behind him. He is a pretty good arithmetician, so long as he knows which of his rules to apply to a sum, and is not required to think

---

* I need hardly say that I do not speak of every school, since, as has been said already, some two or three of the Manchester private schools which I visited were conducted by really able and philosophical teachers and seemed to deserve high commendation in many points. Even in them, however, faults similar in kind as those mentioned above might be discerned, faults which were no doubt due not to the men, but to their position.

about its meaning. He spells sufficiently well, and writes neatly, seldom quickly; he knows some English history and geography, and can translate an ordinary French book with tolerable ease, although he cannot write a letter in French, much less speak it.* His Latin has probably done him good, but it has not gone far enough to enable him to translate at sight an easy piece of Cicero. Mathematics have taken no hold on his mind at all. He is in most cases, although not in all, ignorant of natural history and natural science.

This is the result in the more expensive schools, where a boy remains, on the average, until he is 15. But these schools educate perhaps only one-fifth or so of the middle-class population of Manchester, and the education of the other four-fifths is there-fore much more limited. If the warehouseman with a salary of £200 per annum sends his son to a National or British school, he probably learns nothing but reading, writing, arithmetic, and some little English grammar and geography. If he goes to one of the cheap private schools that abound in the less genteel suburbs, schools charging from £3 to £6 annually, the instruc-tion he receives is nominally wider in its compass, but really not more thorough in its substance. There he learns no Latin, no mathematics, little or no French, no natural science, no English composition, no drawing. He is not to so great an extent taught by assistants, but he is taught by a head master who has seldom any competence for his work, either in point of knowledge or of talent. Coming from such a school at the age of 13 or 14, the boy will have done well if he can write a letter of three pages with only six blunders in spelling, if his arithmetic goes as far as fractions and compound proportion, if he can repeat the capitals of European countries and English counties, if he knows the difference between a common and a proper noun, between Magna Charta and the Habeas Corpus Act.

It is not, however, in respect of what he knows, or does not know, that the chief defect lies, it is rather in the condition of his mind. He has been taught a certain number of facts and rules,

* In one of the best private schools which I visited I found that the highest class had been at French for three years; and had for the sake of it almost entirely neglected mathematics and Latin. Yet, when I proposed that they should give some small specimen of their powers of composing in French, the headmaster said it would be quite useless for them to try to do so.

not the relations of the facts nor the meaning of the rules. Little or nothing has been done to give him the power of applying principles, of grasping distinctions, of fixing his attention upon any one subject. His judgment has not been strengthened, nor has the habit been formed in him of seeking for a reason in the facts he observes. His attention has never been called to the natural laws under which he must live in the world. What is perhaps worse, he has not been made to like any subject. His interests, if he have any, are dormant: he is sent out into life at an age when education must necessarily be incomplete, without any desire to preserve and extend his knowledge. To give this training and implant these tastes is hard enough, and no one who knows boys will be surprised by frequent disappointments. But an education which never makes the attempt stands self-condemned. The cheap schools, with very rare exceptions, do not make the attempt. The more expensive ones sometimes do, but their teaching staff is not strong enough, and the support of parents not assured enough, to make the attempt vigorous or the results often successful.

7. A School Board Secondary School, 1895

The strong demand for secondary education in the last two decades of the nineteenth century encouraged the school boards of some of the larger industrial cities to set up 'higher grade' schools. These were, in fact, secondary schools—as the Bryce Commission recognised. Yet in establishing them the school boards exceeded their legal powers which confined them to providing elementary education only. The confusion of authorities in the secondary field was one of the main reasons for the establishment of local education authorities with general educational powers in 1902. The Leeds Higher Grade School was probably the most widely acclaimed of school board secondary schools.

SOURCE: Report of the Royal Commission on Secondary Education, Vol. VIII, 1895, pp. 159–63.

The Leeds Higher Grade School

This school is the most interesting in Leeds in many ways, representing as it does the entering of a new power into the existing system of Secondary Education. It is situated in the same part of Leeds as the other secondary schools, in an enormous block of building which, while laying no claims to architectural beauty, has an attraction of its own, owing to its completeness and efficiency for the work for which it is intended. The building is divided into two halves, the one for boys and the other for girls, with a central double staircase which opens into long corridors separated from the class-rooms by glass partitions. These corridors are lined with white bricks and are lofty, bright, and airy, and have cases in them containing apparatus, geological specimens, many of them collected by the children themselves, and other articles of value for illustrating the different subjects taught. The classrooms which open from these corridors are large and airy, well-lighted, clean, and bright, and are perfectly equipped.

Many of the secondary schools, while displaying some architectural pretensions on the outside, are vastly inferior to the modern elementary schools inside in cleanliness, brightness, light, and air, while they are so arranged that the headmaster has the maximum of difficulty in supervising the school. This school is a direct contrast to these buildings. The headmaster's room is situated in the centre of the building, and in moving along the corridors he can glance into the class-rooms on either side so that no teacher can have an unruly class, or fall into the mistake of too much laxness, or too much severity without the headmaster's knowledge. Everything in the school is directly under his eye, and he can exercise real supervision over the work and discipline for which he is personally responsible. The brightness and cheerfulness of the school-rooms is another matter of the greatest importance, as it must add to the pleasure of the children in their work and lighten the task of the teachers. The ventilation of the rooms is provided for by a large fan driven by a gas engine, so that the close atmosphere which one associates with so many class-rooms, and which is so depressing mentally and physically, is unknown to the Leeds Higher Grade School. Nearly every room has a certain character of its own, owing to the drawings and diagrams of the children, which are placed up on the walls, and which vary according to the interests of the master who has charge of that room. In one place they may be little drawings and paintings of flowers, and in another prettily executed maps, diagrams of scientific apparatus, or geological sections, all assisting in diminishing the monotony of the work, and stimulating the children to the production, in their leisure time, of work requiring accuracy and neatness. The school has two playgrounds, the one for boys situated at the back of the building, and the other for girls on the roof. There is a fine chemical lecture-room, with seats rising one above another and perfectly equipped, and a large and well-appointed chemical laboratory with an accommodation for 120 students. The reason for this immense size is the necessity of examining large numbers at a time for the Science and Art Department, only a portion of this room being used for class-work. There is also a small physical laboratory, and the chemical laboratory is ventilated by a separate fan, so as to ensure its being fresh and free from bad odours. It is situated in a large and lofty room with plenty of space between the benches, and is well designed for teaching purposes. Across the boys' playground there is a large workshop very well fitted up for manual instruction, and in the main building there is a very large gymnasium, lofty and airy, and beautifully appointed with everything that can be required for ordinary gymnastic instruction. Everything in this building is so perfectly arranged, and so clean and bright, that it is a pleasure to wander through it from class-room to class-room. The number of children under instruction is about 2,200, of whom about 1,200 are either in or above the Seventh Standard.

There are 60 free entrance scholarships offered each year, and there are 62 West Riding free scholars at the school. There are also 30 £18 scholarships in the school from the City Technical Institute grant, 20 Bray scholarships of £9 first year, £12 second year, £15 third year, the exact analysis will be found in the appendix. The school can be considered as consisting of two parts, the elementary school and the secondary school. The secondary school beginning at the end of Standard VI. The children throughout the school pay a fee of ninepence a week, so that the lower part of the school is entirely fee-paying; but the upper part of the school contains a large number of free scholars holding either board school scholarships, or West Riding scholarships, or town council scholarships. The larger number of children enter the school in Standards V., VI., and VII. The upper part of the school is an organised science school under the Science and Art Department. The boys in the

Seventh Standard devote most of their time to English subjects, while doing some chemistry and physiography and Euclid. After having passed the Seventh Standard they then begin the work of the organised science school with a certain amount of preliminary knowledge of science.

Dr. Forsyth, the headmaster, is very much impressed with the importance of not beginning the science work seriously until the Seventh Standard has been passed, so as to ground the boys as thoroughly as possible in English. French is selected as the language for the upper school and is taught throughout. Of course, the larger number of boys, who leave the school comparatively young, go to work, but the school now contains 16 boys above 17 years of age although it is only five years old. Of these top boys, three have obtained Yorkshire College scholarships, two of the value of £40 and one of the value of £20 a year, seven have passed the London Matriculation Examination, and three the Victoria preliminary. Of these 16 boys, all except four are going on ultimately to Yorkshire College, and Mr. Forsyth expects, in a short time, to send 20 boys every year direct from the higher grade school to Yorkshire College. It is therefore obvious from these results that the Leeds Higher Grade School can claim to be a modern second grade secondary school, as it is keeping boys till they are quite as old as those in the ordinary grammar schools in the West Riding, is passing them through the same examinations, is carrying off in competition with them the same scholarships, and is sending them direct to Yorkshire College.

Latin of course is taught in the school, as it is necessary for some of these examinations, but it is taken only by certain boys and is not universal throughout the upper school. The masters are all men who have been trained as elementary schoolmasters, and who have obtained, or are on the way to obtain, university degrees.

Under the headmaster there are at present among the assistant masters, one London B.A., one London M.A., one London B.Sc., one Glasgow M.A., and five who have passed the intermediate science examination of London University. Dr. Forsyth's method is to get young men who are ambitious as his assistant masters, for though the salaries paid are not large, he has been able to place his assistant masters as headmasters in other higher grade schools, so that an assistant mastership at the Leeds Higher Grade School has considerable attractions. A young man entering there comes to improve himself both as a teacher and as a learner, and if he is not prepared to do both, he will not suit Dr. Forsyth. With the complete system of organisation in the school, Dr. Forsyth is able to devote a good deal of time to teaching his masters how to teach, and he is one of those men who can inspire others, so that his staff are keen and hardworking, and the influence of the headmaster is a living force throughout the school. There are to be found among the assistant masters at this and other higher grade schools a new type of teacher, young, brilliant, and enthusiastic, students of the best methods of teaching, with an ardent belief in their profession, and devoting their spare hours to their own education—a type which, though suffering from the absence of culture which belongs to the older universities, yet replaces this by such complete knowledge of their work, and enthusiasm for their subject, that they bid fair to take the scholastic world by storm and to sweep out of the profession the man who has taken a degree at Oxford or Cambridge, and who takes to teaching with no special aptitude or training, either because he can find nothing better to do, or with a view to preferment in the Church.

It is hardly necessary to say that the most perfect discipline reigns throughout the school, that the classes all impress one as bright, alert, and intelligent, and that everywhere one sees examples of the perfection of method in teaching.

The school, however, is suffering from two grave defects, both of which are an inheritance from bad traditions, and are likely soon to disappear. In the first place, the school having been organised by the school board, has necessarily suffered from the traditions of elementary schools as to the size of classes, and we consequently find that the classes are much too large, sometimes numbering as many as 60 children, and though the trained teacher can do a great deal to overcome this defect, and though the custom of grammar schools in this respect errs on the other side of having the classes too small, yet, large classes are objectionable, and in all cases tend to make the teaching mechanical, especially in the subject of languages. The other serious defect is due to the fact that the school is depending for its income very largely on the grants it earns from the Science and Art Department. The result of this is, in the first place, to give an undue bias to science as opposed to other subjects on which grants can be earned; in the second place, to require the children to store up an undue amount of information upon scientific subjects which they are too young to digest and which are necessary if grants are to be earned. This evil is, however, reduced to a minimum at the higher grade school, a boy taking four years to obtain his advanced certificates, while there are many schools in which he is expected to obtain them in two. Then the courses of instruction in science have no organic connexion one with another, and have been devised with a view to evening-class work, and are not at all adapted to forming part of a general scheme of education. And since the grants are made on the results of examination papers and not on inspection, the school is exposed to all the evils from which the elementary education of the country, after a long period of agitation, has escaped, and the proper use of laboratories for training in experimental science is almost impossible. These evils of the present system of supporting organised science schools must be discussed at greater length, but are of importance to mention here as they peculiarly affect a school of this character.

I heard a lesson being given on 'potential' to the older boys, which was admirably done, and I also heard a lecture on the elements of chemistry which was very fair and well illustrated, though not an example of the very best lecturing to boys on this subject. I think we may say that while Dr. Forsyth has made the best of a bad system, he is working under a bad system, and consequently he has been able to do little to raise the science teaching out of the ordinary routine, and put it on lines educationally sound. Similarly, while the art teaching is thorough and efficient, and adapted to the requirements of the Department, there is here little indication of the development of any originality in colour, form, or design; in fact, we may say that while the higher grade school at Leeds is a marvel of complete organisation, sound discipline, and sound teaching yet both in science and art it has been unable to take advantage of the latest methods of teaching these subjects, and will be unable to do so until its bonds are loosened, and this great giant is set free from the system of payment on the results of paper examination. In conclusion it is impossible to convey in a report the impression which this school makes upon one of efficiency, energy, and vitality, and I think no one who has spent some time inside it can fail to realise that we are here in the presence of a new educational force which has already developed to a vigorous and lusty youth and that it is impossible to say what may be the limit of its growth, or how soon, to quote Dr. Forsyth himself, 'the organisation which was originally devised for the elementary education of the country, passing with great strides across the realms of Secondary Education, may soon be battering at the doors of the ancient universities themselves.'

That this higher grade school represents a new educational movement from below, and a demand from new classes of the population for Secondary Education, which has sprung up in a few years, is easily shown by the actual numbers attending the school; for even if we credit the higher grade school with the 100 boys which the grammar school has lost, and with the 200 boys which the Church middle class school has lost, we still have left close upon 1,000 boys who are in the higher grade school, and who formerly were receiving secondary instruction.

5 The Growth of Scientific and Technical Studies in Schools and Colleges

There was probably more change in this area of education than in any other in the nineteenth century. The actual methods of teaching varied from the 'catechism' approach at the beginning of the period to the heuristic method a hundred years later. At the same time scientific and technical subjects came to be studied much more widely, their study being encouraged in later years by financial aid from the Science and Art Department and from the Technical Instruction Committees. Indeed, the Bryce Commission in its Report in 1895 complained that the curriculum of some secondary schools was too much dominated by science and that literary studies were being neglected.

1. Science as an 'Accomplishment'

There was very little attempt at teaching science in the early nineteenth century and much of what there was consisted of imparting facts which were felt to be matters of casual interest or curiosity for the educated person. Much of such instruction took the form of learning short catechisms by heart.

SOURCE: C. Irving, *A Catechism of Botany*, London, 1821, pp. 20–23. Chapter IX.

CLASS I MONANDRIA

Q. What plants are comprehended in the first class?

A. The class Monandria consists of such plants as have only one stamen in each flower.

T. Mention the most remarkable.

P. The plants of this class are very few, and chiefly found in tropical countries; but we have the hippuris-vulgaris or common mare's tail, and the jointed glass-wort or marsh-samphire, the former of which will serve to exemplify the class.

T. Describe the hippuris-vulgaris.

P. The hippuris-vulgaris grows in the muddy ponds and ditches of most parts of Britain, and flowers in the month of June:

the stem is straight, with the leaves growing out of the joints, and the flowers at the base of each leaf.

Q. What is the form of the flower?

A. The flower, which is very small, has no blossom; its single stamen and pistil growing upon the receptacle.

Q. What is the jointed glass-wort?

A. The jointed glass-wort, or marsh-samphire, is a very useful plant, found in marshes near the sea: when dried and burnt, its ashes are called kelp, and are used in the manufacture of glass and soap.

Q. What foreign plants belong to this class?

A. In monandria are found the beautiful exotic plants which produce ginger, turmeric, arrow-root, and cardamoms.

T. Describe the ginger plant.

P. The ginger plant is a native of the East Indies, and rises in round stalks, about four feet high: it withers about the close of the year; and the roots, which are the only valuable part, are then dug up, scraped and dried with great care, and packed in bags for exportation.

Q. What are the properties of arrow-root, turmeric, and cardamoms?

A. Arrow-root is a powder made from the root of an American plant, affording a wholesome and palatable food for children; turmeric is a root extensively used for dyeing yellow; and cardamoms are seeds valuable for their aromatic and medicinal qualities.

Chapter X.

Class ii   Diandria

Q. What plants are of the second class?

A. To the class Diandria belong all the plants which have two stamens in each flower.

Q. What native plants are there of this class?

A. The privet, butterwort, meadow-sage, brook-lime speedwell, and others are common in Britain; and the last of these may be chosen to illustrate the class.

T. Describe the plant.

P. Veronica beccabunga, or brook-lime speedwell, is very common in ditches and shallow streams: the stem is jointed, and about a foot in height; the leaves are oval, of a pale green colour, and growing out of the stem in pairs: the flowers, which rise in bunches from the base of the leaves, are of a faint blue colour, and divided into four small roundish leaves.

Q. How is it known to belong to the second class?

A. Brook-lime may be known to belong to the class diandria, by its having two stamens; and to the order monogynia, because there is but one pistil.

Q. Has this plant any medicinal qualities?

A. Brook-lime was formerly considered of much use in several diseases, and was applied externally to wounds and ulcers: it has a bitterish taste, and is considered very beneficial, if the fresh plant be eaten as food.

Q. What useful exotics belong to this class?

A. In the second class are found the different kinds of pepper-plants, which grow in the East and West Indies; and the olive-tree, cultivated in the South of Europe for the sake of its fruit, from which olive-oil is extracted by pressing it in a mill.

Q. Are there not also some that delight us with their fragrance?

A. The common lilac, that perfumes the air in the summer evenings; the elegant and odiferous jasmine; the rosemary and sage, cultivated in our gardens, but which grow spontaneously in warmer climates; are all in the second class, and display its characters.

2. Science at Rugby in the Middle Years of the Nineteenth Century

An Account by Canon J. M. Wilson.

> SOURCE: Board of Education. Pamphlet No. 17, 1909, Report on Science Teaching in Public Schools represented on the Association of Public School Science Masters.

Dr. Arnold, in some year about 1840, invited the Rugby boys to bring back after the summer holidays specimens of the rocks and road materials of their own neighbourhood. These formed the nucleus of a geological museum.

Lectures on Natural Philosophy were first given to the School in 1849 by Dr. Sharp, an eminent local physician. These were entirely optional. The Rev. Henry Highton was soon afterwards appointed as a master to teach Science.

I was appointed Science Master by Dr. Temple in January 1859, to succeed Highton (who was appointed Head Master of Cheltenham College), and I began work there in August of that year. Rather less than fifty boys took up Science; and their fees, £5. 5. 0. per annum, formed my salary. I also taught mathematics and took private pupils. There was no laboratory, and no Science School. I taught in the cloakroom on the ground floor of the Town Hall, which was furnished with tables and chairs, and a cupboard containing apparatus for illustrating elementary optics, hydrostatics, mechanics, heat, and some good electrical apparatus, a subject in which Mr. Highton was an expert.

No system or progressive course was followed, nor was it possible under the circumstances. New boys joined the classes every term. At first each class lasted a term. I was free to teach any subject, and I taught a great variety of subjects.

My only training in Science, apart from Mathematics, had been three months' work in the Birkbeck Laboratory under Williamson and Carey Foster; a slight practical acquaintance with Astronomy gained under Professor Chevallier in his observatory near Durham; and some knowledge of Geology in which books and maps and the hammer had been my only teachers. It was a slender equipment: but I never professed omniscience with the boys; we worked together, on a genuine 'heuristic' method; we had no examinations to check discursiveness; textbooks were kept in their right place, and used after, not before, some knowledge of the subject was acquired. My recollection of the lessons is that the boys were really interested in the matter, in the method, and in the logic of the method. I remember, for example, that a number of the older boys took up, as a 'Science Extra', Mill's Logic, Book III., 'On Induction', which I had recommended and used in a lecture on dew. Dr. Temple was much struck by this result of Science teaching, and with their mastery of the book.

In 1860 a Science School and a small chemical laboratory with six benches was built. I had spent my first Christmas holiday in the Edinburgh University laboratory under Playfair, and I fitted the laboratory on that model. . . .

In 1864 the position of Science in Rugby was completely changed by Dr. Temple, in deference to the recommendations of the Royal Commission on the nine public schools, published late in 1863.

They recommended that all boys should, at any rate during part of their school life, learn some branch of Natural Science; and that there should be two principal branches, one consisting of Chemistry and Physics, and the other consisting of Physiology and Natural History. New Science Schools were built, very humble indeed compared with the palace in which chemistry is now housed at Rugby, but sufficient for our needs at that time. Dr. Temple was anxious to adopt the recommendations of the Commission in the autumn term of 1864, though the difficulties were great. Two hundred and fifty boys would be beginning Science at once, and my old fifty would be going on with it. He could not get the man he wanted, the Rev. T. N. Hutchinson, to come to take charge of Chemistry and Physics, till January 1865. I decided that it was possible to carry out his wish if I had the assistance of one man, and if we taught during that term one subject only, and that not an experimental subject. Dr. Temple therefore asked Mr. Kitchener—afterwards Head Master of the Grammar School at Newcastle-under-Lyne, now a leading spirit of the Staffordshire County Council—to co-operate with me, and advised us to learn Botany.

We set to work at once with immense enthusiasm under Dr. Hooker's advice, and worked through the summer term; and we spent the summer holidays delightfully at Barmouth, with Professor George Henslow as our tutor; and with the aid of a party of ladies made collections, and a large series of diagrams for teaching. The spirit of our teaching was unquestionably derived from the brilliant Leçons Élémentaires de Botanique fondés sur l'analyse de 50 Plantes Vulgaires par M. Emm. le Maout. That book is a model of what the teaching of such a science ought to be. Its spirit is well shown in Mrs. Kitchener's 'A Year's Botany'.

In January 1865 Mr. Hutchinson came and took entire charge of the Chemistry. I taught Geology and some other subjects to middle school boys, and higher Physics with the Fifth and Sixth. Mr. Kitchener taught Botany. Mr. Kitchener and I also taught Mathematics. Perhaps I ought to add that

Rugby was exceptionally suited for teaching Geology, from its Lias quarries, with curved and faulted strata, and numerous interesting fossils; and its very complex drifts, sand and boulder clay, at which we all worked. Our results as to the drifts are shown in a paper in the Quarterly Journal of the Geological Society for May 1870. The Annual reports of the Rugby School Natural History Society are valuable. Arthur Sidgwick was the inspirer of the study of entomology, F. C. Selous of the study of birds. . . .

In September 1867, at the meeting of the British Association in Dundee, the report of the Committee appointed in the previous summer 'to consider the best means of promoting Scientific Education in schools' was received and widely circulated. The Committee consisted of Dean Farrar, Professor Huxley, Professor Tyndall, and myself. . . .

I cannot forbear relating an incident at one of our meetings, held at Professor Huxley's house. I had been asked at our first meeting to prepare and submit in print a draft report on the lines we agreed on. The draft contained some resolutions, of which the last two had reference to the importance of our gaining the co-operation of the Universities. My next sentence was: 'With reference to the last two recommendations we would observe that schools are so much influenced by the Universities that reform in the subjects of teaching at schools must come from above'. Huxley gravely demurred, and said he was not prepared to adopt a report containing a statement which appeared to have a theological signification.

3. Practical Work at Uppingham

Edward Thring was Head Master from 1852 to 1887 and his work in broadening the curriculum is of particular interest because of the recognition he accorded to aesthetic and practical subjects. Afternoons were devoted to Music and optional subjects of which every boy had to take one or two, these included carpentry, turning, drawing, chemistry and modern languages. The workshops were the first of their kind in any English public school.

SOURCE: Second Report of the Royal Commission on Technical Education, Vol. V, Appendix HH, Workshops in Uppingham School by the Revd E. Thring.

The carpentry at Uppingham School was opened in October, 1862, and put in the hands of a very clever man, recommended by the late Mr. G. E. Street. A payment of £1. 10. 0. p.a. gave a boy the right of admission to the workshop as a learner, and at first tools were found for beginners. From 50 to 80 boys, year by year, were carpentry pupils, and from time to time very good work was done, but little need be said of this period, as no true system was followed, and the teacher, clever as he was, failed to work the thing in a satisfactory manner. Individuals did well, and profited, but there was no real effective description, or definite plan. Matters continued in this state until the year 1882.

In the autumn of 1882 a class was formed for the purpose of giving greater reality to the science teaching. The boys who joined were taught to make scientific apparatus of a simple kind, and then to experiment with it.

A small room was fitted up as a workshop, with a lathe and a couple of benches. The class was not a part of the regular school work, but was taken up voluntarily by the pupils. Attendance, when a boy had joined, was compulsory.

During the first term various instruments were made: a barometer, an acoustic bridge, several galvanometers, etc.

As the numbers promised to increase, it was considered advisable to engage an assistant to be constantly at work under the superintendence of the science master. A first-class mechanic was found, who had considerable experience in scientific instrument making. A larger room was fitted up and the classes grew in size.

In the Spring of 1883 the carpenter's workshop was thrown under the same direction as the new scientific workshop. All the mechanical branches are now under the superintendence of the science master.

A forge was established by the head-master, who also defrayed the expenses of fitting up a new carpenter's shop. But, apart from this, no pecuniary assistance has been received from without for the works.

The Carpenter's Workshop

There are two departments, a lower shop and an upper. In the lower shop the boys begin with (1) tenon and mortice, (2) tool

box, dovetailed, (3) cabinet door panelled, and so on. There is a
certain amount set for each term, boys who have completed
this are allowed to submit a design to the teacher, and to work
at it if approved of. Drawing is not obligatory.

There are two times of attendance in the week for each boy,
during which he receives lessons. If he wants to work out of his
regular time, he applies for a bench, and if there is one vacant it
is allotted to him. There are a number of small benches, at
which pupils are allowed to occupy themselves with fretwork
etc. But this is not allowed in the regular time. It is considered
advisable to provide an opportunity for amusement in a
mechanical pursuit for the boys who have an inclination; but
this is quite separate from regular work in the shop.

In the upper workshop, at stated times, lessons are given in
cabinet making. But, except for these, attendance is not obligatory. Drawings are required. There are only a limited number
in this shop, and there is always room for those who are promoted to it. In this manner, a boy who has won his promotion
has full opportunity for getting through a great deal of work.

The wood-turning lathes stand in this shop.

Terms:

Carpentry   1os. ⎱
Turning   5s. ⎰ a term

The cost of an outfit is about 30s. All materials are charged
for, and the work done belongs to the pupils.

Number of pupils   70
Men employed: Carpenters—foreman, man and boy; cabinet
maker and assistant   .   .   .   .   .   5 hands

The Forge

At the forge pupils make nails, brackets, hammer-heads etc.
Forgings are made for the metal workshop; boys make their
turning tools. When some familiarity with the work has been
acquired, pupils are taught to make horseshoes, and to fit them
on the dead hoof, and when they can do this they are allowed,
under careful supervision, to shoe horses brought into the forge.

Number of boys   12
Fee   .   .   .   .   £1 a term

The forge teaching is partly undertaken by the mechanical
teacher from the metal shop, partly by a local blacksmith.

Metal Workshop

This workshop was started for the purpose of making scientific apparatus, but it has grown into a mechanical workshop for all kinds of work.

Boys do not pass into it from the carpenter's shop, but can enter it without previous training.

The work commences with the forging and filing of a set of turning tools. Then an electric bell is made, which affords a variety of work, none of it of too difficult a nature. Opportunity is taken to interest the boys in the scientific facts connected with everything which they make, or see being made, and no trivial work is allowed, except by special permission out of work hours.

When the bell is completed, which generally takes more than one term, various pieces of apparatus are chosen to be made, such as a scribing block, a pump, an electric motor, or an induction coil.

Stress is laid on the boys learning to make and sharpen their own tools. They are required to make a drawing of the machine to be made.

In this shop a set of scientific instruments is being made for the use of the school.

Work is also being turned out for outside orders, and in every way the pupils are given to understand that they are admitted to a place in which real work is turned out, not to a place in which they can play with metal and tools.

A room is set apart for experiments with the instruments made. The boys are led as much as possible to take an intelligent interest in science. But the workshops are distinct from the scientific teaching of the school, although boys working at physics are often sent to the workshops for special purposes, and the facilities of the mechanical department are always ready for scientific requirements.

Boys who intend to take up the engineering profession are allowed more time at practical work, drawing, and mathematics during the last year of their stay than is laid down in the ordinary school course.

Also, after leaving school, boys occasionally stay in the workshops for a special training to fit them for their further education in technical work.

The times of attendance are twice a week, an hour and a half each time. But many boys come six and more hours a week. The fee is £1. 10. 8d. a term. There are 23 boys in the workshop. Every boy buys a set of necessary tools and castings. The work turned out belongs to the boy.

A foreman, a man and a boy are employed in this shop.

The machinery consists of two Whitworth screw-cutting lathes, eight 5-inch lathes, one planing machine, vices, benches etc.

(Signed)   EDWARD THRING
Uppingham, March, 1884.

4. Introduction of Science Teaching in Elementary Schools

Only after the establishment of school boards under the Education Act of 1870 was much systematic teaching of science introduced into elementary schools. The programme adopted by the London School Board is given here.

One of the difficulties which faced any elementary school authority which might want to introduce science teaching was the inability of the teachers to give it. Some of the larger boards, such as Birmingham and Liverpool, overcame this difficulty by employing peripatetic demonstrators who proceeded from school to school with a hand cart containing their apparatus.

(a) SOURCE: Report of the Royal Commission on Technical Instruction 1884, Vol. I, Part III, pp. 393–4.

LONDON

London School Board—Instruction in Elementary Science.— Before passing on to the institutions for scientific, art, and technical instruction, it may be well to state briefly the steps which have been taken by the School Board for London for introducing instruction in elementary science into their schools.

In addition to the object lessons given in the infant schools, the School Management Committee have decided that elementary science shall be taught throughout the boys' and girls' departments, in place of the object lessons hitherto given, and their instructions to the teachers, on object lessons, have been modified accordingly.

The following is suggested by the School Management Department as a model scheme, but teachers have full liberty to vary it according to their tastes and acquirements:

Standard I	Standard II	Standard III	Standard IV
Extension of the object lessons in the infant school, with simple illustrative experiments.	Comparison of different plants or animals. Ordinary phenomena of the earth and atmosphere. Substances of domestic use.	Simple principles of classification of plants and animals. Further phenomena of the earth and atmosphere. Substances used in the arts and manufactures.	More complete classification of plants and animals, with typical examples. The three forms of matter familiarly illustrated.

Standard V	Standard VI	Standard VII
(a) Animal and plant life, with the most useful products; or, (b) More definite notions of matter and force, illustrated by simple machinery or apparatus.	(a) Animal and plant life, with special reference to the laws of health; or, (b) The commonest elements, and their compounds. The mechanical powers.	(a) Distribution of plants and animals, and the races of mankind; or, (b) Light, heat, and electricity, and their applications.

A more detailed description of the courses on physics, mechanics, chemistry, and physiology, has also been prepared by the Board.

Moreover, courses of instruction in elementary science, have been established by the Board for the central instruction of pupil teachers.

(b) SOURCE: Second Report of the Royal Commission on Technical Instruction, Vol. V, 1884, pp. 201-2, Appendix 33, Introduction of the Teaching of Science in the Elementary Schools of Liverpool.

With a view to the provision in the curriculum of their schools of some subject especially calculated to awaken and exercise the observing faculties of the children, the Liverpool School Board, acting on the advice of several eminent scientific gentlemen, in March 1877, resolved to introduce the systematic teaching of elementary science into their schools. The branches of instruction were selected from the limited number of science subjects included in the fourth schedule of the New Code of that date, viz., mechanics (or the principles of natural philosophy) for boys, and domestic economy for girls. The instruction given is necessarily based on the syllabus of each subject as set out in the schedule, in order to qualify the scholars to earn grants under the Education Department; but in each case the subject, as arranged in the Code, has been modified and extended so as to enable it the more readily to be taught by experimental demonstration to large classes of children.

The method of teaching the subjects, which has been found by experience to be capable of producing very beneficial results to the scholars, is to combine ordinary lessons by the teachers of the school, with a system of experimental demonstrations given by means of specially appointed demonstrators. The apparatus required for the demonstrations is kept at a central laboratory, and is transferred from school to school as required, by means of a light hand cart. In this way each demonstrator is able to give from 18 to 20 demonstrations per week. And in order to simplify the arrangements for demonstrations as much as possible, by providing for the same demonstration to be given in several schools in succession, the Education Department were, at the commencement of the scheme, requested to provide for the school years of the different schools to end as nearly as possible at the same time; and this was carried out so far as to admit of the schools being arranged in two groups, the annual examinations of which fall in the autumn and spring respectively. In the case of domestic economy, the demonstrations are given only every alternate week, and the same is the case in the second stage of mechanics (taken by the fifth standard), but to the fourth standard, just commencing the subject of mechanics, one demonstration is given every week. In the intervals between the demonstration, the teachers of the respective classes, who are required to be present at the demonstrations, are expected to go over with the children the subject of the demonstration; and in many instances their lessons are illustrated by simple experiments. And in order to enable the teachers (the large number of whom have unfortunately had no special training for the subject) to perform their portion of the work more satisfactorily, a simple textbook has been specially prepared, containing reading lessons on the subjects of the demonstrations, and exercises to be worked by the scholars. The demonstrations have been given in several of the other elementary schools of the town, not under the board, on payment by the managers of the schools, of a proportion of the expenses.

At the present time there is one chief demonstrator, who has also to organise the instruction, and two assistants.

The cost of the apparatus used in the school demonstrations for the five years during which the scheme has been in operation amounts to about £120., many of the articles having been provided in duplicate in consequence of the large number of classes.

5. The Work of the Science and Art Department, South Kensington

The Science and Art Department came into existence under the aegis of the Board of Trade after the Great Exhibition of 1851 and its original purpose was to encourage the study of those branches of science and art which would be of value in fostering the competitive position of British industry. Its influence became very widespread by the end of the nineteenth century when it was paying grants to the majority of secondary and higher grade schools for their work in the much enlarged list of subjects it had taken under its wing. It would be difficult to overestimate the importance of the Department's grants in gaining a major place for science in the grammar schools of this country; the grants were also important in helping to finance technical colleges, polytechnics and the new civic universities.

SOURCE: Second Report of the Royal Commission on Technical Instruction, Vol. 1, 1884, p. 400. Examinations under the Science and Art Department, South Kensington.

Examinations in Art, in connection with the Science and Art Department, date back to 1853, though the existing comprehensive plan of annual examinations was not established until 1857. In that year 12,509 students were instructed in local schools of art, and 396 in the Central Training School, and through the various agencies connected with the Department, 43,212 children in elementary and other schools were taught drawing. No general system of examinations in science was formulated until 1859, when the number of subjects, on which payment could be obtained, was limited to six. In May 1861 when the first general and simultaneous science examination was held, there were 38 classes with 1,330 pupils, besides some 800 pupils in classes not under certificated teachers.

In the year 1882, there were in all 909,206 persons receiving art instruction in connection with the Department and 68,581 students in science, in 1,403 science schools, with 4,881 classes.

The Examinations in Art are of three grades, the first grade being intended for children attending the elementary school, the second grade for the pupils of secondary schools and the students of art classes and schools of art, and the third grade is applicable for teachers or art masters.

Science examinations are held in 25 subjects; the examinations take place in May, and are divided into three stages; the 'elementary', 'advanced' and 'honours'. In each stage there are two grades of success.

On receipt of proper demands from local authorities, papers, both for the science and art examinations, are forwarded from South Kensington to the centres where the examinations are conducted. The worked papers are sealed up directly after the examination, and forwarded to London. On the result of these examinations, prizes and scholarships are awarded to the successful students, and money payments are made to the local committee, which vary in accordance with the degree of success attained by the students, and with the nature of the subject. The total payments in the year 1882–3, on account of science schools and classes, grants, prizes, etc. was £45,376. 0. 6. and for success in art the amount was £67,354. 10. 6.

The total expense of the Science and Art Schools is returned at £155,367. 5. 4. for the year 1882–3, exclusive of the staff of the Department, who received £8,898. 4. 10.

6. Manchester School Board Central School

School boards in some of the larger cities attempted to meet the demand for scientific and technical instruction by developing higher grade schools which shed their junior classes and provided science courses earning grants from the Science and Art Department. The Central School at Manchester developed in this way. It was established in 1827 as Manchester New Jerusalem School, an elementary school for the poor. Much later it became a board school and flourished so that it became necessary to exclude junior standards in order to make more room for higher work and by 1883 it accepted only those pupils who had already passed Standard IV.

SOURCE: Report of the Royal Commission on Technical Instruction, Vol. V, 1884, Appendix 33, Educational Work in Manchester, Liverpool and Oldham.

The position thus gradually assumed by these schools led to their being regarded more and more as a kind of higher elementary school, and a large number of boys remained at school after passing Standard VI. The Science and Art Department in South Kensington make grants for instruction in Science, and boys and girls who have passed Standard VI may be engaged in studying various science subjects during the ordinary school hours. The managers were thus enabled to introduce science teaching as part of the general work of the schools. In February 1880, the schools were handed over by the managers to the Manchester School Board, and were adopted by them as their higher grade school. One of the rooms was fitted up for science teaching, a good laboratory for 24 scholars was made, and a master engaged to devote the whole of his time to teaching science to boys who had passed Standard VI. The schools would not now, under these arrangements, accommodate more than 320 boys and 150 girls. At present they are full, and out of the 320 boys, over 200 have passed Standard VI., and are taught during the day, mathematics, physiology, chemistry (practical and theoretical), sound, light, and heat, magnetism and electricity, physical geography, and mechanics. French is taught throughout the school. The pupils are examined in physical geography, mechanics, and French by the Government inspector of schools, and in the other science subjects by the Science and Art Department at South Kensington. During the past year the following classes have been formed, and the pupils were examined May 1882:

Mathematics, Stage II.	25
⎧ A.	30
,, ,, I. ⎨ B.	50
⎩ C.	45
Physiology, elementary stage	50
,, advanced stage	20
Chemistry, Practical, class A., advanced	20
,, ,, ,, A., elementary	30
,, ,, ,, B. ,,	50
,, ,, ,, C. ,,	50
,, Theoretical, class A., advanced	20
,, ,, ,, A., elementary	30
,, ,, ,, B. ,,	50
,, ,, ,, C. ,,	50
Sound, light, and heat, class A., advanced	20
,, ,, ,, A., elementary	30
,, ,, ,, B. ,,	50
,, ,, ,, C. ,,	50
Magnetism and electricity, class A., advanced	20
,, ,, ,, A., elementary	30
,, ,, ,, B. ,,	50
,, ,, ,, C. ,,	50

The following are the results of the examination held by the Science and Art Department in May 1881:

	1st Class	2nd Class
Mathematics	8	19
Physiology	11	42
Practical Inorganic Chemistry	17	49
Theoretical Inorganic Chemistry	15	44
Magnetism and Electricity	8	60
Acoustics, Light and Heat	19	38
First Grade Freehand Drawing	11	43
,, Geometrical Drawing	8	20
,, Model Drawing	0	10
Second Grade Freehand Drawing	0	14
,, Geometrical Drawing	3	25
,, Model Drawing	0	2

The following time table, for the scholars who remain at school after passing Standard VI, shows the number of hours devoted to each subject from October 1st to the middle of May.

The school is open in the morning from 9 o'clock to 12 o'clock, and in the afternoon from 2 o'clock to 5 o'clock. The first half-hour each day is occupied with religious exercises and scripture history.

		Each Week			Each Week
		hrs.			hrs.
1	Scripture	2½	9	French	3
2	Practical Chemistry	1½	10	Geography	2
3	Theoretical Chemistry	1	11	Arithmetic	2
4	Magnetism and Electricity	1	12	Physical Geography	2
5	Acoustics, Light etc.	1	13	Mechanics	2
6	Physiology	1½	14	Drawing	3
7	Mathematics	3	15	Preparation	2½
8	Grammar and Composition	2			

The home lessons of the scholars include general and scientific subjects.

Rough notes are taken at each science lecture, and these are carefully re-written at home. This home-work will take on the average one hour each night for four nights in the week, besides the half hour each day mentioned in the above table under the head of preparation.

In connection with these schools, the Manchester School Board has established elementary school scholarships, which are open for competition to all the elementary schools in the city, both board and voluntary. Various gentlemen subscribe £5, and for each subscription of £5 the Science and Art Department at South Kensington, London, give another £5, provided the successful candidates attend the school regularly for 12 months, and pass in one or more of the science subjects named in the Science Directory. The sum of £10 is given to the parents of the pupils to enable them to pay the school fees, and to keep their children longer at school than they would otherwise be able to do. The scholars who gain scholarships continue their education in these schools, and at the present time there are 16 boys and 7 girls who hold them. There is also another kind of scholarship, called a science and art scholarship, of the annual value of £15. These are competed for by the scholars who during the previous year held a £10 elementary science scholarship, the award being decided by the result of the May examination in science and art.

The following is a copy of a report received from H. E. Oakeley Esq., H.M. Senior Inspector of Schools, this year (1882).

Peter Street Boys' School
'This well-known school continues to maintain its reputation for first-rate teaching and organization. The results in the 4th Schedule subjects are excellent.'

The Commissioners, in inspecting this school, were impressed by the high character of the teaching, and the enthusiasm which animated both teachers and scholars.

The accommodation was inefficient, several classes being crowded in one room, and the fullest concentration was required to sustain the attention of the scholars to the particular work of their own class. The head master did not consider the system of several classes being taught in one room as a serious waste of power or drawback to the general efficiency of the school, and it was also pointed out by Mr. Hughes that the Board favoured the open school system rather than a general adoption of the class-room system, on the ground that in addition to the open school enabling the head master to take a general surveillance of the work of the whole school, it also promoted a very useful discipline in inculcating a habit of concentration in the children at an early age. At any rate the school clearly illustrated the fact that a number of classes being taught in one room, under separate teachers, is not inconsistent with thorough teaching and very high results at the examinations.

All the boys in the Sixth and Extra Sixth Standards take a number of the science subjects of the Science and Art Department. A class of 20 were engaged in the second stage of mathematics, another in 'sound' experimentally illustrated, and a large class in practical chemistry. Professor Roscoe questioned the boys on chemistry and other subjects, and their answers showed evidence of practical knowledge and intelligent training.

The Commissioners were informed that new premises for this school, with complete arrangements for secondary and scientific teaching, are about to be erected in Deansgate, one of the leading thoroughfares of Manchester.

Table III
Results of Examinations

Year	Qualified for Examination*	Presented	Reading	Passes in Writing	Arithmetic	Percentage of Passes
1876	259	235	221	224	203	92
1877	241	226	214	215	207	94
1878	254	240	237	233	232	97·5
1879	248	244	240	240	238	98
1880	283	274	271	269	267	98·1
1881	298	290	290	286	287	99·1
1882	315	299	299	297	298	99·6

Table IV
Grants Earned

Year	£. s. d.		s. d.		
1876†	189 13 0	or	13 0¼	per head on average attendance, including infants	
1877	244 6 0	,,	17 4	,,	,, ,,
1878	263 14 0	,,	17 4	,,	,, ,,
1879	270 16 0	,,	17 5	,,	,, ,,
1880	288 19 0	,,	17 8½	,,	,, ,,
1881	294 2 0	,,	18 0	,,	,, ,,
1882	298 16 0	,,	17 9¼	,,	,, ,,

The last official Report (Mr. H. E. Oakeley's) received from the Education Department is as follows:

'The results of the Examination in elementary subjects are

* Children under seven excluded.
† The grant actually earned was £222. 2s., or 15s. 3d. per head; but £32. 9. 0. was deducted under a regulation of the committee of council, a regulation which is now abolished.

again excellent. The number of sums given was 1,106 of which
985 were worked correctly. The 299 boys examined made only
109 mistakes in spelling altogether. Grammar and Geography
were most satisfactory. Thoroughness of work, intelligence, neatness, and accuracy were conspicuous in all the classes.'

In the blue book just issued by the Educational Department,
Mr. Oakeley, Her Majesty's Senior Inspector for the Northern
Division, gives a list of the Manchester Schools which have
passed the best examinations, and in the list the 'Manchester
Free School' takes the best mark (E) and ranks in the foremost
place. This notice ought not to be concluded without mentioning that the success of this remarkable school and the extraordinary attendance of the scholars (not to be found in any
other school in the kingdom) is mainly, if not entirely, due to
the present excellent head master, Mr. George E. Mellor,
whose attention to his duties is most exemplary.

Much of the management and organization is in the hands of
Mr. H. J. Leppoc, to whom the school is much indebted.

Mr. Mellor stated that he was aided by four assistant masters
and two assistant mistresses, but that he had no pupil teachers.
Few boys stayed at the school after the age of employment, and
in the case of the few who did remain they were children of
better class parents who knew the value of education. In some
cases, however, the boys are kept at school because they are too
little to obtain employment. The proportion of boys in the
upper standards (4, 5 and 6) is about 32 per cent; in the two
upper Standards (5 and 6) about 13 per cent. There are only
two boys in the Sixth Standard out of 330. The School Board
inspection has been found to be of very considerable service.

7. The Regent Street Polytechnic

In 1882 Quintin Hogg, a philanthropic man of business, founded the
Regent Street Polytechnic. This was the first of the London Polytechnics and it sought to offer a mixture of technical instruction,
adult education and recreation to young working people. The term
'polytechnic' used in this context did not indicate an institution for
advanced technological studies.

SOURCE: Second Report of the Royal Commission on Technical
Instruction, Vol. I, 1884, pp. 411–3.

VIII—The Polytechnic Young Men's Christian Institute
Regent Street, London

The Commissioners were received by Mr. Quintin Hogg and Mr. Mitchell, the secretary. Mr. Hooper, a member of the committee, also accompanied them. They were conducted by these gentlemen through the various class-rooms, and Mr. Hogg explained to them briefly the origin of the Institute. The work was started many years ago as a philanthropic effort, and in its first form took the shape of a ragged school, which ultimately developed into the Young Men's Christian Institute, and the building in which the lectures and classes were now being carried on had been purchased by Mr. Hogg for the purpose. The Institute numbers 2,000 members, which is the maximum number admitted, but there are 1,200 applicants awaiting the opportunity of admission. Youths between the age of 16 and 23 are eligible for election, but as the Institute is principally intended for apprentices and young artisans, only 20 per cent of persons not belonging to the artisan class are admitted at any one election. The subscription is 3s. 6d. per quarter, and a small fee on joining the various classes. In certain cases outsiders are admitted to the classes on payment of double fee, but, practically, three-fourths of those attending the classes are members of the Institute. Special efforts are made by the Committee to provide the members with the opportunity of acquiring a sound theoretical and practical knowledge of their various trades, and care has been taken that the instruction should not be too difficult to be understood by the average mechanic. The following is a list of the systematic trade courses given, with the syllabus of subjects taught, but there are also practical classes for other trades as will be seen from the account. Nearly all these classes are in connection with the City and Guilds of London Institute, their teachers being registered by the Institute and receiving payment on results.

*Classes at the Polytechnic Young Men's
Christian Institute*

Bricklaying—Practical, Plane, and Solid Geometry, Building Construction, Practical Mensuration, Elementary Sanitary Engineering, Practical Bricklaying.

Metal Place Work—Freehand and Model Drawing, Practical, Plane, and Solid Geometry, Theoretical and Applied Mechanics, Metallurgy, Metal Plate Pattern Cutting, Metal Plate Work.

Electrical Engineering—Geometry, Machine Drawing, Mathematics, Magnetism and Electricity, Applied Mechanics, Acoustics, Light, and Heat; Telegraphy Electric Lighting, Electric Instrument Making.

Engineering—Geometry, Mathematics, Machine Construction, Theoretical and Applied Mechanics, Pattern Making, Steam, Mechanical Engineering.

Plumbing—Geometry, Building Construction, Elementary Chemistry, Sanitary Engineering, Applied Mechanics, Plumbing.

Watch and Clock Making—Practical, Plane, and Solid Geometry, Machine Construction and Drawing, Mathematics, Theoretical Mechanics, Applied Mechanics, Watch and Clock Making.

Carriage Building—Freehand and Model Drawing, Practical, Plane, and Solid Geometry, Mathematics, Theoretical and Applied Mechanics, Carriage Building.

The Commissioners first visited the class, numerously attended, for electric lighting. We then inspected the class for photography, in which practical demonstrations were being given. We next proceeded to a large class for tailors' pattern cutting, the work being done in chalk on cloth strained over tables, and the cut patterns being made in brown paper. The teacher, Mr. Humphreys, a self-trained cutter, stated that he had himself invented the methods by which he worked, after carefully studying all the plans adopted in America, Germany, and elsewhere. After having been many years practically engaged in the trade as a foreman cutter, he now entirely devoted himself to literary work, editing a trade paper with fashion plates and patterns, which appears monthly, and teaching classes in the evening. So numerous had been the applications for membership of this class that upwards of 100 students had to be turned away. The next class was one for printing. Here the teacher was explaining the composition of printers' rollers, and giving practical instruction for their preparation. Thence a visit was paid to the class for shorthand writing, and next the workshops were inspected. The class actually at work at the time of the visit was that for plumbers' work, the making of all kinds of lead joints was in progress, and practical plumbing of every kind was going on under the teaching of Mr. Davies, the foreman of a large firm in the trade. Various other classes for practical work are held on different evenings; thus, for instance, metal turning and wood turning, cabinet-making, carpentry, etc. In the class for tinplate working, which was next visited, Mr. Millis, the teacher, stated to the Commissioners that his instruction was chiefly theoretical, and that he did not consider it necessary to include practical work, as is done in the plumbing class. The drawing and modelling classes, which seemed almost over-crowded, were next visited. The drawing was chiefly outline and shading from cases, but some few of the students were attempting to apply their knowledge to designing, and work of a more advanced character. A theoretical class was also inspected by the Commissioners, in which instruction was being given in watchmaking by Mr. Herrmann.

After a brief inspection of the library and reading rooms, the recreation room, and the arrangements in the basement for lavatories, cloak rooms etc. the Commissioners adjourned to the large hall and witnessed a display of fencing and gymnastics by some of the more proficient members of the association. Mr. Hogg explained that one of the great attractions of the Institute was the gymnasium, which was largely patronised, and for which members paid an additional fee of sixpence per quarter. He encouraged them to come in their working clothes directly after leaving work, and to spend the whole of the evening at the Institute, refreshments being provided at a moderate cost, and recreation and teaching being jointly cared for. In addition to the teaching on the week-days, the largest adult Bible class in the world (Mr. Hogg believed) is held on the Sunday, when he has an average attendance of 650 young men in one class. In order to give them a sufficient amount of outdoor exercise, he had leased a field of 13 acres at Barnes, for cricket, lawn tennis, football, etc. and he made a practice of inviting all the members of the Institute to stay with him in the country for a week every summer. He could arrange to receive fifty at a time.

The Commissioners understand that Mr. Hogg has expended £80,000 in the purchase, fitting, and endowment, of the Institute.

8. The Heuristic Approach to the Teaching of Science

During the nineteenth century the teaching of science took many forms from learning a catechism by heart to seeking to get each pupil to find out for himself. One of the best known advocates of the heuristic method was Professor Armstrong who at different times served as President of both the Chemical and Educational Sections of the British Association.

> SOURCE: Education Department, Special Reports on Educational Subjects, Vol. II, 1898, H. E. Armstrong, *The Heuristic Method of Teaching*, pp. 390, 400–1.

Heuristic methods of teaching are methods which involve our placing students as far as possible in the attitude of the discoverer—methods which involve their *finding out* instead of being merely told about things. It should not be necessary to justify such a policy in education. Unfortunately, however, our conceptions are blunted by early training or rather by want of training. Few realise that neither is discovery limited to those who explore Dark Continents or Polar Regions nor to those who seek to unravel the wonders of Nature; that invention is not confined to those who take out patents for new devices; but that, on the contrary, discovery and invention are divine prerogatives, in some degree granted to all, meet for daily usage: consequently, that it is of importance that we be taught the rules of the game of discovery and learn to play it skilfully. The value of mere knowledge is immensely over-rated and its possession over-praised and over-rewarded; action, although appreciated when its effects are noted, is treated as the outcome of innate faculties and the extent to which it can be developed by teaching scarcely considered. . . .

. . . It is in no sense mere opinion on my part but a conviction gradually forced upon me and established beyond all doubt by actual trial and observation during many years past, that the beginner not only may but must be put absolutely in the position of an original discoverer; and all who properly study the question practically are coming to the same opinion, I find. Young children are delighted to be so regarded, to be told that they are to act as a band of young detectives. For example, in studying the rusting of iron, they at once fall in with the idea that a crime, as it were, is committed when the valuable, strong iron is changed into useless, brittle rust; with the greatest interest they set about finding out whether it is a case of murder or of suicide, as it were—whether something outside the iron is concerned in the change or whether it changes of its own accord.

A lady teacher who has thus presented the case to a class of young girls told me recently that she had been greatly amused and pleased to hear one of the girls who was sitting at the balance, weighing some iron that had been allowed to rust, suddenly and excitedly cry out, '*Murder!*' This is the very attitude we desire to engender; we wish to create lively interest in the work and to encourage it to come to expression as often, as emphatically, as freely as possible.

It is of no use for the teacher merely to follow an imaginary research path: the object must ever be to train children to work out problems themselves and to acquire the utmost facility in doing so. Of course, the problems must be carefully graduated to the powers of the scholars and they must be insensibly led; but do not let us spoil them by telling them definitely in advance what to look for and how to look for it: such action is simply criminal.

My experience teaches me also that it is the grossest libel on young scholars to say that it is useless to expect them to reason for themselves in the way necessary to follow out the simplest research; but, unfortunately, if you substitute teachers for scholars this is too often a true statement and here the supreme difficulty of properly carrying out heuristic teaching comes in. It is the teachers who are preventing advance. Let us teachers recognise this; but do not let us overlook and misrate the powers of young children. Let us try what we can do and if we do not at first succeed let us try and try again; we shall surely succeed if only we can adopt this attitude. But if we fail, let us give up the work as soon as possible and leave it to others to succeed where we have failed. No other policy is an honest one—for the teaching of young children should never be regarded as a perfunctory task but as a sacred office. The whole policy of the teacher's duty is summed up in one little word, yet the most expressive in the

English language: it is to train pupils to *do*. On this it is easy to base a simple test of competency.

It is needless to say, young scholars cannot be expected to find out everything themselves; but the facts must always be so presented to them that the process by which results are obtained is made sufficiently clear as well as the methods by which any conclusions based on the facts are deduced. And before didactic teaching is entered upon to any considerable extent, a thorough course of heuristic training must have been gone through in order that a full understanding of method may have been arrived at and the power of using it acquired; scientific habits of mind, scientific ways of working, must become ingrained habits from which it is impossible to escape. As a necessary corollary, subjects must be taught in such an order that mainly those which can be treated heuristically shall be attended to in the first instance.

6 The Education of Women in the Nineteenth Century

1. A Girls' School in the 1830s

The 'problem' of women's education in the nineteenth century was essentially an upper or middle class one; in the elementary schools, girls and boys usually followed much the same curriculum. During the first half of the century there was hardly anything recognisable as secondary education for girls; the activities of the finishing schools, boarding schools and smaller local, private schools were aimed not at educating girls but at imparting a veneer of accomplishments. Brighton, as a fashionable watering place, was a noted centre for girls' finishing schools.

SOURCE: *The Life of Frances Power Cobbe as told by Herself*, Swan Sonnenschien, 1904, pp. 60–9.

... it was not in London but in Brighton that the ladies' schools most in estimation were to be found. There were even then (about 1836) not less than a hundred such establishments in the town, but that at No. 32, Brunswick Terrace, of which Miss Runciman and Miss Roberts were mistresses, and which had been founded some time before by a celebrated Miss Poggie was supposed to be nec pluribus impar. It was, at all events, the most outrageously expensive, the nominal tariff of £120 or £130 per annum representing scarcely a fourth of the charges for 'extras' which appeared in the bills of many of the pupils. My own, I know, amounted to £1,000 for two years' schooling.

Profane persons were apt to describe our school as a convent, and to refer to the back door of our garden, whence we issued on our dismal walks, as the 'postern.' If we in any degree resembled nuns, however, it was assuredly not those of either a Contemplative or Silent Order. The din of our large double schoolrooms was something frightful. Sitting in either of them, four pianos might be heard going at once in rooms above and around us, while at numerous tables scattered about the rooms were girls reading aloud to the governesses and reciting lessons in English, French, German and Italian. This hideous clatter continued the entire day till we went to bed at night, there being no time whatever allowed for recreation, unless the dreary hour of walking with our teachers (when we recited our verbs), could be so described by a fantastic imagination. In the midst of the uproar we were obliged to write our exercises, to compose our themes, and to commit to memory whole pages of prose. On Saturday afternoons, instead of play, there was a terrible ordeal generally known as the 'Judgement Day'. The two school-mistresses sat side by side, solemn and stern, at the head of the long table. Behind them sat all the governesses as Assessors. On the table were the books wherein our evil deeds of the week were recorded; and round the room against the wall, seated on stools of penitential discomfort, we sat, five-and-twenty 'damosels', anything but 'Blessed,' expecting our sentences according to our ill-deserts. It must be explained that the fiendish ingenuity of some teacher had invented for our torment a system of imaginary 'cards', which we were supposed to 'lose' (though we never gained any) whenever we had not finished all our various lessons and practisings every night before bed-time, or whenever we had been given the mark for 'stooping', or had been impertinent, or had been 'turned' in our lessons, or had been marked 'P' by the music master, or had been convicted of 'disorder' (e.g., having our long shoe-strings untied), or, lastly, had told lies! Any one crime in this heterogeneous list entailed the same penalty, namely, the sentence, 'You have lost your card, Miss So-and-so, for such and such a thing;' and when Saturday came round, if three cards had been lost in the week, the law wreaked its justice on the unhappy sinner's head! Her confession having been wrung from her at the awful judgement-seat above described, and the books having been consulted, she was solemnly scolded and told to sit in the corner for the rest of the evening! Anything more ridiculous than the scene which followed can hardly be conceived. I have seen (after a week in which a sort of feminine barring-out had taken place) no less than nine young ladies obliged to sit for hours in the angles of the three rooms, like naughty babies, with their faces to the wall; half of them being quite of marriageable age, and all dressed, as was de rigueur with us every day, in full evening attire of silk or muslin, with gloves and kid slippers. Naturally, Saturday evenings, instead of affording some relief to the incessant overstrain of the week, were looked upon with terror as the worst time of all. Those who escaped the fell destiny of the corner were allowed, if they chose, to write to their parents, but our letters were perforce committed at night to the school-mistress to seal, and were not as may be imagined, exactly the natural outpouring of our sentiments as regarded those ladies and their school.

Our household was a large one. It consisted of the two school-mistresses and joint proprietors, of the sister of one of them and another English governess; of a French, an Italian, and a German lady teacher; of a considerable staff of respectable servants; and finally of twenty-five or twenty-six pupils, varying in age from nine to nineteen. All the pupils were daughters of men of some standing, mostly country gentlemen, members of Parliament, and offshoots of the peerage. There were several heiresses amongst us, and one girl whom we all liked and recognised as the beauty of the school, the daughter of Horace Smith, author of Rejected Addresses. On the whole, looking back after the long interval, it seems to me that the young creatures there assembled were full of capabilities for widely extended usefulness and influence. Many were decidedly clever and nearly all were well disposed. There was very little malice or any other vicious ideas or feelings, and no worldliness at all amongst us. I make this last remark because the novel of Rose, Blanch and Violet, by the late Mr. G. H. Lewes, is evidently intended in sundry details to describe this particular school, and yet most falsely represents the girls as thinking a great deal of each other's wealth or comparative poverty. Nothing was further from the fact. One of our heiresses, I well remember, and another damsel of high degree, the granddaughter of a duke, were our constant butts for their ignorance and stupidity, rather than the objects of any preferential flattery. Of vulgarity of feeling of the kind imagined by Mr. Lewes, I cannot recall a trace.

But all this fine human material was deplorably wasted. Nobody dreamed that any one of us could in later life be more or less than an 'Ornament of Society.' That a pupil in that school should ever become an artist, or authoress, would have been looked upon by both Miss Runciman and Miss Roberts as a

deplorable dereliction. Not that which was good in itself or useful to the community, or even that which would be delightful to
ourselves, but that which would make us admired in society,
was the raison d'etre of each acquirement. Everything was
taught us in the inverse ratio of its true importance. At the
bottom of the scale were Morals and Religion, and at the top
were Music and Dancing; miserably poor music, too, of the
Italian school then in vogue, and generally performed in a
showy and tasteless manner on harp or piano. I can recall an
amusing instance in which the order of precedence above described was naively betrayed by one of our schoolmistresses
when she was admonishing one of the girls who had been detected in a lie. 'Don't you know, you naughty girl,' said Miss R.
impressively, before the whole school; 'don't you know we had
almost rather find you have a P—' (the mark of Pretty Well)
'in your music, than tell such falsehoods?'

It mattered nothing whether we had any 'music in our souls'
or any voices in our throats, equally we were driven through
the dreary course of practising daily for a couple of hours under
a German teacher, and then receiving lessons twice or three
times a week from a music master (Griesbach by name) and a
singing master. Many of us, myself in particular, in addition to
these had a harp master, a Frenchman named Labarre, who
gave us lessons at a guinea apiece, while we could only play with
one hand at a time. Lastly there were a few young ladies who
took instructions in the new instruments, the concertina and the
accordion!

The waste of money involved in all this, the piles of useless
music, and songs never to be sung, for which our parents had to
pay, and the loss of priceless time for ourselves, were truly
deplorable; and the result of course in many cases (as in my own)
complete failure. One day I said to the good little German
teacher, who nourished a hopeless attachment for Schiller's
Marquis Posa, and was altogether a sympathetic person, 'My
dear Fraulein, I mean to practise this piece of Beethoven's till
I conquer it.' 'My dear,' responded the honest Fraulein, 'you
do practice that piece for seex hours a day, and you do live till
you are seexty, at the end you will not play it!' Yet so hopeless a
pupil was compelled to learn for years, not only the piano, but
the harp and singing!

Next to music in importance in our curriculum came dancing. The famous old Madame Michaud and her husband both
attended us constantly, and we danced to their direction in our
large play-room (lucus a non lucendo), till we had learned not
only all the dances in use in England in that ante-polka epoch,
but almost every national dance in Europe, the Minuet, the
Gavotte, the Cachucha, the Bolero, the Mazurka, and the
Tarantella. To see the stout old lady in her heavy green velvet
dress, with furbelow a foot deep of sable, going through the
latter cheerful performance for our ensample, was a sight not to
be forgotten. Beside the dancing we had 'calisthenic' lessons
every week from a 'Capitaine' Somebody, who put through
manifold exercises with poles and dumbbells. How much better
a few good country scrambles would have been than all these
calisthenics it is needless to say, but our dismal walks were confined to parading the esplanade and neighbouring terraces. Our
parties never exceeded six, a governess being one of the number,
and we looked down from an immeasurable height of superiority
on the processions of twenty and thirty girls belonging to other
schools. The governess who accompanied us had enough to do
with her small party, for it was her duty to utilise these brief
hours of bodily exercise by hearing us repeat our French, Italian
or German verbs, according to her own nationality.

Next to Music and Dancing and Deportment, came Drawing,
but that was not a sufficiently voyant accomplishment, and no
great attention was paid to it; the instruction also being of a
second-rate kind, except that it included lessons in perspective
which have been useful to me ever since. Then followed Modern
Languages. No Greek or Latin were heard of at the school, but
French, Italian and German were chattered all day long, our
tongues being only set at liberty at six o'clock to speak English.
Such French, such Italian, and such German as we actually
spoke may be more easily imagined than described. We had bad
'Marks' for speaking wrong languages, e.g., French when we
were bound to speak Italian or German, and a dreadful mark for
bad French, which was transferred from one to another all day
long, and was a fertile source of tears and quarrels, involving as it
did a heavy lesson out of Noel et Chapsal's Grammar on the last
holder at night. We also read in each language every day to the
French, Italian and German ladies, recited lessons to them, and

wrote exercises for the respective masters who attended every week. One of these foreign masters, by the way, was the patriot Berchet; a sad, grim-looking man of whom I am afraid we rather made fun; and on one occasion, when he had gone back to Italy, a compatriot, whom we were told was a very great personage indeed, took his classes to prevent them from being transferred to any other of the Brighton teachers of Italian. If my memory have not played me a trick, this illustrious substitute for Berchet was Manzoni, the author of the Promessi Sposi; a distinguished-looking middle-aged man, who won all our hearts by pronouncing everything we did admirable, even, I think, on the occasion when one young lady freely translated Tasso,—

'Fama e terre acquistasse,'

into French as follows:

'Il acquit la femme et la terre'!

Naturally after (a very long way after) foreign languages came the study of English. We had a writing and arithmetic master (whom we unanimously abhorred and despised, though one and all of us grievously needed his instructions) and an 'English master,' who taught us to write 'themes,' and to whom I, for one, feel that I owe, perhaps, more than to any other teacher in that school, few as were the hours which we were permitted to waste on so insignificant an art as composition in our native tongue!

Beyond all this, our English studies embraced one long, awful lesson each week to be repeated to the schoolmistress herself by a class, in history one week, in geography the week following. Our first class, I remember, had once to commit to memory— Heaven alone knows how—no less than thirteen pages of Wood-houselee's Universal History!

Lastly, as I have said, in point of importance, came our religious instruction. Our well-meaning schoolmistresses thought it was obligatory on them to teach us something of the kind, but, being very obviously altogether worldly women themselves, they were puzzled how to carry out their intentions. They marched us to church every Sunday when it did not rain, and they made us on Sunday mornings repeat the Collect and Catechism; but beyond these exercises of body and mind, it was hard for them to see what to do for our spiritual welfare. One Ash Wednesday,

I remember, they provided us with a dish of salt-fish, and when this was removed to make room for the roast mutton, they addressed us in a short discourse, setting forth the merits of fasting, and ending by the remark that they left us free to take meat or not as we pleased, but that they hoped we should fast; 'it would be good for our souls and our figures!'

Each morning we were bound publicly to repeat a text out of certain little books, called Daily Bread, left in our bedrooms, and always scanned in frantic haste while 'doing-up' our hair at the glass, or gabbled aloud by one damsel so occupied while her room-fellow (there were never more than two in each bed-chamber) was splashing about behind the screen in her bath. Down, when the prayer-bell rang, both were obliged to hurry and breathlessly to await the chance of being called on first to repeat the text of the day, the penalty for oblivion being the loss of a 'card.' Then came a chapter of the Bible, read verse by verse amongst us, and then our books were shut and a solemn question was asked. On one occasion I remember it was: 'What have you just been reading, Miss S——?' Miss S—— (now a lady of high rank and fashion, whose small wits had been wool-gathering) peeped surreptitiously into her Bible again, and then responded with just confidence, 'The First Epistle, Ma'am, of General Peter.'

It is almost needless to add, in concluding these reminiscences, that the heterogeneous studies pursued in this helter-skelter fashion were of the smallest possible utility in later life; each acquirement being of the shallowest and most imperfect kind, and all real education worthy of the name having to be begun on our return home, after we had been pronounced 'finished.' Meanwhile the strain on our mental powers of getting through daily, for six months at a time, this mass of ill-arranged and miscellaneous lessons, was extremely great and trying.

One droll reminiscence must not be forgotten. The pupils at Miss Runciman's and Miss Roberts' were all supposed to have obtained the fullest instruction in Science by attending a course of Nine Lectures delivered by a gentleman named Walker in a public room in Brighton. The course comprised one Lecture on Electricity, another on Galvanism, another on Optics, others I think, on Hydrostatics, Mechanics, and Pneumatics, and finally three, which gave me infinite satisfaction, on Astronomy.

If true education be the instilling into the mind, not so much Knowledge, as the desire for Knowledge, mine at school certainly proved a notable failure. I was brought home (no girl could travel in those days alone) from Brighton by a coach called the Red Rover, which performed, as a species of miracle, in one day the journey to Bristol, from whence I embarked for Ireland. My convoy-brother naturally mounted the box, and left me to enjoy the interior all day by myself; and the reflections of those solitary hours of first emancipation remain with me as lively as if they had taken place yesterday. 'What a delightful thing it is,' so ran my thoughts 'to have done with study! Now I may really enjoy myself! I know as much as any girl in our school, and since it is the best school in England, I must know all that it can ever be necessary for a lady to know. I will not trouble my head ever again with learning anything; but read novels and amuse myself for the rest of my life.'

This noble resolve lasted I fancy a few months, and then, depth below depth of my ignorance revealed itself very unpleasantly! I tried to supply first one deficiency and then another, till after a year or two, I began to educate myself in earnest.

2. Arithmetic for Females

The following extract is taken from a book which presented Arithmetic to girls as a 'useful accomplishment among the female sex.' It was intended for use in schools such as that described in the last extract.

SOURCE: John Grieg, *The Young Ladies' New Guide to Arithmetic.* London, 1835.

The first idea of the following selection was suggested in the course of professional practice. The author having been employed for many years in the instruction of youth of both sexes, had sufficient opportunity of being convinced, by experience, that among the numerous Treatises of Arithmetic already published, not one was to be found where a judicious and necessary attention had been paid to the subject, considered as a branch of FEMALE education. He was induced, therefore, to attempt the present selection, one step towards a more improved system, and better calculated for the attainment of this useful accomplishment among the Female Sex, than any hitherto published.

On a subject where so much has already been written, it will hardly be expected to find originality. It is chiefly on the Model of Arrangement, and the Usefulness of the matter selected, that any claim to approbation, in the present instance, can be founded. . . .

ARITHMETIC is the art of computing by figures, as 1, 2, 3, 4, 5, 6, 7, 8, 9, 0, and consists of five principal rules, viz. NOTATION or NUMERATION, ADDITION, SUBTRACTION, MULTIPLICATION, and DIVISION.

NOTATION

Or NUMERATION, is the art of expressing any number in figures, and teaches also to read figures, according to their true value, as in the following:

Table

Units	1
Tens	1 2
Hundreds	1 2 3
Thousands	1 2 3 4
Tens of thousands	1 2 3 4 5
Hundreds of thousands	1 2 3 4 5 6
Millions	1 2 3 4 5 6 7
Tens of millions	1 2 3 4 5 6 7 8
Hundreds of millions	1 2 3 4 5 6 7 8 9
Thousands of millions	1 2 3 4 5 6 7 8 9 0

Note: This table extends only to ten figures, which in common use may be sufficient; yet as instances sometimes occur where the figures run much higher, an example is here subjoined, which exhibits the method of numerating figures to any extent.

15,431,204,367,043,206,039,860,734,246,075,000,000

Sextillions   Quintillions   Quadrillions   Trillions   Billions   Millions   Units

Septillions, Octillions, etc.

Read thus fifteen sextillions, four hundred and thirty-one thousand two hundred and four quintillions, three hundred sixty-seven thousand and forty-three quadrillions, two hundred six thousand and thirty-nine trillions, eight hundred sixty thousand seven hundred and thirty-four billions, two hundred forty-six thousand and seventy-five millions.

Write down in words at length the following numbers:
33. 49. 102. 111. 363. 1243. 4910. 39614. 156490. 364943. 7196801. 6936950. 1943670. 43160000. and 238565825.

3. A Girl's Letter to her Mother, 1818

This letter gives some idea of the thoughts and attitude which a girl attending school should have had. It is taken from a short book setting out a number of letters expressing the correct sentiments on the part of both mother and daughter.

SOURCE: Mrs and Jane Taylor, *Correspondence between a Mother and her Daughter at School*, 1818.

LETTER III

I could not have believed, my dear mamma, that I should so soon have become reconciled to my absence from home. But, I assure you, I have so many things to do and to think of here, and in the short intervals of employment there is so much to interest me, that, though I find plenty of time for affectionate thoughts, I have none for melancholy reflections.

You must not expect, in these few weeks, to hear of my having made any particular progress. I find however, already, the great advantage, to my volatile temper, of being obliged to apply with so much regularity. And I do hope that you and papa will not have to lament, that your kindness in sending me here has been quite thrown away.

I am often reminded of your cautions on the subject of emulation. Mrs. W. I am certain, is exactly of your opinion about it. She takes great pains to check in us a spirit of emulation and rivalry; while she endeavours to inspire us with the genuine love of knowledge, and with a true taste for our acquirements; urging us to be more ambitious to excel ourselves, than to excel each other. Do you know, she has so much penetration, that she has found out a great many of my faults already. The other day, when speaking of emulation, she told me that although her admonitions on that subject were not so applicable to me as to some others, she could not compliment me on my superior magnanimity. 'My dear,' she said, 'it would gratify you, would it not, to surpass your companions? and yet, rather than submit to the toil of competition, or hazard the mortification of being outdone, you are ready to stand still and let them all get the start of you.' When she said this, I knew that she could see into every corner of my heart.

I hope I shall not forget your advice with regard to my conduct to Mrs. W. She is, indeed, very kind and considerate; though I am sure she has much to try her patience, in our various dispositions.

I expected to have a great deal to tell you, when I had seen all my new companions. But really I am disappointed to find so few out of the whole number, with whom I could form anything like a friendship. Many of them, to be sure, are such little things that they are quite out of the question; and as to the rest, they are most of them so uninteresting! There are, however, some exceptions; and I must tell you, that there are five of us great girls who take the lead in everything. At the top of all is Grace Dacre; and, though as I told you before, I think I could never be very confidential with her, yet it is impossible not to admire and esteem her very much. She is uncommonly clever; but so superior to any littleness and vanity, that although she does everything best, no one seems envious of her superiority. Next to her is a Miss Raymond: I don't believe Mrs. W. thinks she has a great deal of taste; and she is certainly not what one would call bright, she is too grave and solid for that; but she has such indefatigable application and industry, that there seems to be nothing but what she can accomplish. Though not at all ill-natured, she is very reserved; and perhaps a little high, she is obliging to us all; but not intimate with anyone. Fanny Fielding, the next I shall mention, is, I think, in most things equal to Miss Raymond; but they are completely different in their dispositions. There is not one of us who has half so much emulation, nor that applies with so much avidity. You never saw anything like her anxiety, when we are at our lessons together. In drawing, for instance, for which she has certainly no particular taste (indeed she acknowledges that she never liked it much), yet the idea of being outdone in anything is so terrible to her, that she makes the greatest exertions to excel in it. I often see her casting envious glances at my drawing-book, and then redoubling her own efforts; and it is the same with music, Italian, and everything she does; she seems to succeed only because she is determined that she will. Yet she is extremely amiable and affectionate, and most of the girls love her very much; but some, who are less good-natured, take advantage of her temper, and tease her sadly. The fourth on my list is Phillis Parker, a sharp, clever little thing, rather plain and odd-looking; who, though she is but lately come, and has had few advantages at home, seems likely soon to surpass us all. She is not vain in the least, but very droll; and often says smart witty things, which makes poor Fanny Fielding very angry; for she dreads being laughed at beyond everything.

You see I have included myself in this distinguished five: but I am well aware that this must be attributed to my age, and the great advantages I have enjoyed at home, rather than to my own quickness or industry; in both which respects I am much surpassed by many who are younger than myself. You will be surprised to find that my friend Jessy is not one of the number: the reason is, that although she is so pleasant and affectionate as a friend, and has been and indeed continues to be, particularly kind to me, she is not so anxious about the cultivation of her mind as could be wished.

I had much more to say, particularly in answer to your letter; but must now only add, with kind love to all, that I am your affectionate

LAURA.

4. Schools for Girls of the Lower Middle Class

The Assistant Commissioners of the Schools Inquiry Commission found themselves confronted with an unreformed situation in girls' education in the 1860s. This passage gives some idea of the education given to their daughters by those who could not afford the more expensive boarding establishments.

    SOURCE: Report of the Schools Inquiry Commission, Vol. IX, 1868, pp. 826–9, Report by Mr Bryce, Assistant Commissioner.

The education received by girls of what is called the lower

middle class, daughters of persons whose incomes range from £150 to £600 per annum (excluding the professional men) is considerably shorter, stopping at 14 or 15 instead of 17 or 18, and turns rather less upon accomplishments. The great majority of people of this class—the clerks, warehousemen, and shop-keepers, with the highest grade of artisans—live in towns and send their children to day schools; it is chiefly by the richer farmers (who are few in Lancashire) and by the petty manu-facturers, mine managers, and so forth, who live scattered through the country, that the cheap boarding schools are sup-ported. I will suppose, therefore, that the typical girl of this class, daughter of a clerk with 200 l. per annum, or of a grocer in one of the manufacturing towns, goes to a day school. She is nearly ten years old when she goes, and has learnt at home little but reading and how to hold a needle, that being pretty nearly all her mother or elder sister can teach her. In the school, which is a small one, she is perfected in reading, learns spelling from a book, of which she repeats half a column daily; learns geography and English grammar—both by rote; does sums out of an arith-metical text-book twice or thrice a week, and reads in Gold-smith's History of England. After two or three years this course is extended to include chronology, geology, and mythology, with other branches of science and general information, which she learns by committing to memory the answers in Mangnall's Questions, or some one of the numerous catechisms already mentioned. An hour or two in the afternoon is also devoted to needlework, plain and ornamental, the latter being especially precious in the eyes of farmers' wives. And if her parents are rather more ambitious than their neighbours she is also taught French, and takes lessons on the pianoforte, spending, however, far less time in practising than is spent by pupils in the genteel schools. This course of study—interrupted, of course, by fre-quent absences from school when the day is wet, or she is wanted to mind the baby—continues till the girl is 14 or 15. Everything, except perhaps the music and in rare cases the French, is taught by the mistress, either single-handed, or with the assistance of a younger sister or a governess, who gets 15 l. or 20 l. a year and her board. The classes consist of four or five children each, who stand round the mistress to repeat their lesson; while the rest of the school (which seldom exceeds 20 or

25 in number) sits here and there sewing, or doing sums, or learning the Mangnall which is to be repeated immediately afterwards. The rooms are those of a small private house, low-roofed and stifling; the playground is a back yard surrounded by houses.

How little a girl can manage to learn during five years spent in such a school will hardly be believed by those who have not had ocular proof of it. So far as I could discover most girls in these private schools carry nothing away but reading (which is generally good), an angular and scratchy handwriting, and a very indifferent skill with the needle, much less, that is to say, than they would have got in a well-conducted National or British school. I remember to have gone into a ladies' school* in one of the chief towns of the county, where there were some 25 girls, daughters of professional men and shopkeepers, paying £6 or £8 per annum. The list of the school-books which they used—mostly catechisms upon all subjects, including Greek and Roman history and geography and nearly every branch of science—would fill a page, yet not one could do the simplest sum in the addition of money, or answer any question in English grammar except in the words of the book which she had got by rote. Further examination of the pupils would no doubt have disclosed equal ignorance in other subjects, but the mistress seemed so much distressed by the children's performances that I gave over questioning them. She was a well meaning and may have been a painstaking woman, a widow who had started a school to support herself, engaged a master for music and dancing, and then gone on teaching the other subjects, without the least notion of her own incapacity. Happening to enter another school—in a great manufacturing town,—where there were some 25 girls (fees £5. 5s. to £6. 6s. per annum) I found a lesson in geography going on. The chief mistress, an elderly person and rather deaf, was sitting knitting with a geography book open on her knee, the children stood round, and she questioned them from it thus; 'What is separated from Scandinavia by the narrow sea called the Sound?' 'What island in the South of England is remarkable for its beauty?' When I

---

* In this school, a typical one in its way, music was learnt by one-fourth of the girls, and French by about one-eighth. There was a master for music and dancing.

asked her whether grammar was taught, she answered 'Yes, they learn a verb every day.' As to teaching them what grammar meant, they might as well have said their lessons to the arm-chair as to her. I might describe a dozen such schools in all of which it was evident that the teaching had effected nothing; the pupil's mind at the end of five years was just where it had been; no more knowledge, no more taste, no more aptitude for any useful occupation.

A Lancashire parent of the lower middle class is usually satisfied with this education for his daughter, and takes her from it at 14 or 15. Sometimes, however, it is desired to put on a finer polish, and the girl is therefore sent for a year to a boarding school 'to finish.' No one could blame the boarding school if it did but little in one year for a mind already dwarfed and distorted by bad teaching. But the boarding-school (assuming it, as one may do, to belong socially to the same class) follows (in all probability) the same vicious system as the day-school, and the only difference that it makes to the girl is to take away some of the primitive roughness or simplicity of her manner and give it an air of affectation and constraint. Then at 16 she goes home 'for good'. She displays the two or three pieces of ornamental needlework, each of which has occupied her three months,* and some drawings, copies from the flat of figures and landscapes, whose high finish betrays the drawing master's hand. A neighbour drops in, conversation turns upon Jane's return from school, and the mother bids her play one of the pieces she learnt there. For two or three weeks this exhibition of skill is repeated at intervals, and then it ceases, the piano is no more touched, the dates of inventions, the relationships of the heathen gods, the number of houses burnt in the fire of London, and other interesting facts contained in Mangnall are soon forgotten, and the girl is as though she had never been to school at all. There are few books on her father's shelves, perhaps two or three green and yellow novels, some back numbers of the Family Herald, Mr. Tupper's Proverbial Philosophy, Cowper's poems with gilt edges, dusted more often than opened, 'Enquire within upon Everything,' and one or two religious biographies. It is not this want of material, however, that quenches her taste for reading,

---

* The farmers are fond of framing these works of art, and hanging them up in the state parlour.

for school gave her no such taste; her life henceforth till marriage
is listless and purposeless, some of it spent in petty occupation,
more of it in pettier gossip; and when at last she is called upon to
manage a household she finds that her education has neither
taught her anything that can be of practical service, nor made
her any fitter than nature made her at first to educate and
govern her children. In point of knowledge and refinement she
is just where her mother was, and her sons and daughters suffer
for it.

5. Secondary Schools for Girls—a Comparison of the position in Lancashire in 1894 with that thirty years earlier

The last thirty years of the nineteenth century saw a revolution in
the education of girls which reflected both the modernisation of
secondary education for boys and the growth in influence of the
feminist movement. The extent of this revolution can be seen by
comparing the findings of the Assistant Commissioners of the Bryce
Commission in 1895 with the situation described by the Taunton
Commissioners Report in 1868.

> SOURCE: Report of the Royal Commission on Secondary Educa-
> tion, Vol. VI, 1895, pp. 257–61, from the Report by Mrs
> Kitchen, Assistant Commissioner.

In reading the Blue Books of the 1864–68 Commission with
their melancholy account of County after County in which all
the girls schools from the highest to the lowest were spending
their days, and the minds of their pupils, in handing on to yet
another generation the frivolous and mischievous traditions of
the last; when even the most enlightened headmistresses wrote
their regrets at being obliged to see the children entrusted to
their charge waste nine hours a week on music, regardless of
whether they had sufficient musical ability to give themselves or
their friends the faintest pleasure as the result; when it was
seriously doubted whether a girl's brains were able to grapple
with the difficulties of vulgar fractions, and when it was generally considered that her physical and moral delicacy was so
frail, that both would be injured by a written examination to be
looked over by a strange man; in reading all this, and much
more to the same effect, one's feeling is one of unmixed and
thankful satisfaction.

Bad schools still exist, but they are driven into holes and corners instead of boasting of their shame. We have endowed schools for girls, as good as those for their brothers; we have 35 prosperous high schools, belonging to a single company, managed by a council composed of both men and women, who bring enthusiasm and experience to the task, and in these schools alone 7,111 girls are receiving an excellent education. Other companies, of which the Church School Company is the largest, have followed their example, while in many towns wealthy people have joined to establish one much-needed high school in their own locality; so that there is a net-work of day schools all over the country, with the immense advantage, as they are proprietary, of their being permanently established. There are also many private day-schools founded on the same lines, and hardly, if at all, inferior to these, in the character of the education given in them.

Public examinations, so often, and on the whole, so timidly discussed in the pages of the Blue Books, have long been open to girls, and the healthy competition with boys' work, with the attendant assimilation of the curriculum of boys' schools has done much to raise the tone of the work in girls' schools, from the lowest classes to the top. This has been specially useful in the case of private schools in country districts which still suffer from the isolation of their mistresses, though to a less extent than in the days of the Schools Inquiry Commission.

The oldest universities have opened their doors (though not quite wide), to women, while new universities, offering the same advantages to them as to men, have sprung up as centres of learning and culture in the busy stir of the great manufacturing cities; these and other agencies have done even more than was prophesied by the Commissioners from 'the opportunity of higher liberal education' for the teachers in girls' schools. Indeed, the whole race of assistant mistresses is so changed that it is difficult to believe that many are sisters and daughters of the ignorant and oppressed women on whom so much slightly contemptuous pity was bestowed less than 30 years ago.

If, however, one turns to Mr. Bryce's report of Lancashire, and takes his division of girls schools (Vol. IX. Schools Inquiry Commission, page 793) into 'the cheap day-school and the 'genteel school in which, although day-scholars are not excluded, 'the chief objects of the mistress is to procure boarders,' one finds that the satisfaction has to be pretty much confined to what he calls 'genteel schools,' and which I have incidentally described in the chapter on 'Relations of Secondary Education to Life Career,' under the head of Private Schools charging High Fees.—The improvement in these, with which I will couple the high schools and large day-schools (which were practically non-existent 25 years ago), as compared with the descriptions of every one of the reports contained in the 'Public Schools Inquiry' Blue Books, is really marvellous; far greater, I should think, than was contemplated at the time of the inquiry. The boarding schools, now as then, are chiefly concerned with the more lucrative portion of their pupils, but it is found that a certain number of day-girls brings in a wholesome whiff of outer life. These schools are usually situated, either in the suburbs of large towns, or quite away from them in places recommended by their healthiness, as Southport, which may well be called the 'Brighton of Lancashire'; one part of it seems made of nothing but schools, judging from the brass plates. Thanks to these, I was able to form some opinion of the buildings of numbers which I was unable to visit. They are generally large private houses, standing in their own grounds and looking well adapted for their purpose, though few seem to have been built expressly as schools. In those which I went over, the rooms were large and airy, the bedrooms comfortable though very simply furnished, and in none did there seem too many beds for health; if the numbers were large, there was often a difficulty in finding a suitable assembly room; in some cases, the entrance hall has been successfully arranged for this purpose; in one instance the wide staircase was also pressed into the service, and the girls rose, tier after tier, on the different steps.

In boarding schools, the provision for games and exercise of various kinds is usually sufficient, but some of the purely day-schools, especially if they are in a town, are sadly wanting in this respect. One or two schools boast of a private golf link, all have tennis courts; in some places the barn or stables of the former occupants have been turned into excellent gymnasiums or play-rooms for wet weather. One school which I visited in Southport has a boating club with an annual regatta, and a champion cup for the best rowing; a tennis club with champion belt won at the summer tournament; and a hockey club is just established to ensure interest in winter games. This is evidently a most popular school and the long list of examination honours shows that the lessons are by no means sacrificed to the games.

It was pleasant to see the zest with which some of the younger mistresses entered into the play; on inquiry, I usually found that they had been at Oxford, Cambridge, or Holloway. Several headmistresses spoke of the value of this phase of university training for teachers in secondary schools. One, who had been the principal of a rather old-fashioned school for many years told me how a bright young mistress from Newnham had brought new life into the place, 'I always wanted my girls to have real games, and play them with spirit; but somehow they never seemed to care for anything I proposed; just a few played tennis, and that was all, but since Miss X. came, we have cricket, in which they all join, and next year they are to play matches against other schools. The tennis has become quite a different thing; they even play hockey in the winter, and I thought it dreadfully rough at first,' the old lady said, 'but they enjoy it, and no one has been hurt, so I suppose it is all right; all the games are managed by a committee of girls, chosen by the rest of the school, so I hope the games would go on, even if we lost Miss X.; the girls' work is as much improved as their play.' I quote this as a strong evidence of the alteration in public opinion, for this school is one of the least affected by modern ways of any which I visited, and I have no doubt that if it existed at the time of the 'Schools Inquiry Commission' it would have been fairly described as one in which 'girls suffer very much from the want of good games. A girl of 16 looks upon the skipping rope and similar diversions very much as a boy of 16 looks upon marbles. Hence at a day-school there is hardly anything that can be called genuine hearty play; and a boarding school has to fall back upon the dreary two-and-two walk along the dusty highway, or the dull suburban street.' Vol. IX., page 818.

The education is quite as much altered as the recreation; after the above comparison it is difficult to put the case more strongly.

The former state of things all over England is summed up by the Commissioners in Vol. I., page 548. 'It cannot be denied that the picture brought before us of the state of middle-class female education is, on the whole, unfavourable.

The general deficiency in girls' education is stated with the utmost confidence, and with entire agreement, with whatever difference of words, by many witnesses of authority. Want of thoroughness and foundation; want of system; slovenliness and showy superficiality; inattention to rudiments: undue time given to accomplishments, and those not taught intelligently or in any scientific manner; want of organization,—these may sufficiently indicate the character of the complaints we have received in their most general aspect.'

I have not seen a single school, of the class which we are now considering, to which this description could be truly applied now, and according to the different reports of the Assistant Commissioners, Lancashire was not the county in which the most rapid improvement was to be expected.

The excessive amount of time given to music is one of the commonest complaints in the reports of all the districts: Mr. Bryce has made an elaborate calculation by which he shows that an average girl of the upper-middle class would have 'sat before her piano during 5,520 hours, at a cost to her parents of at least 100 l.' by the time she left school at 18. In all the more expensive day-schools which I visited I found that while class-singing was learnt by all without extra charge, instrumental music had become almost entirely dislocated from the regular course of education; thus at a large high school of 250 girls, only 10 per cent. learnt music. The headmistress explained that this only meant that they did not learn from the teachers who attended that school, she did not know how many might have lessons at their own homes, but it seemed probable that a large number did not learn it at all; in fact, those who give extra time to drawing (which is exceptionally well taught at the school in question) could not have given the necessary time to it. This treating of music as a separate subject, to be taught out of the regular school hours, has done much towards bringing it down from its old perniciously important position. There is, however, one danger connected with it; most of the headmistresses of high schools with whom I conversed were fully alive to the danger of over-work on the part of the cleverer girls, and had invented time-tables of home work with other ingenious devices, to en-

sure that they did not spend too long hours over their preparation; but while the headmistress 'does not know which of the
girls learn music at home' there is always the possibility of this
care being made useless by long hours of music practice, exacted
by independent teachers, and allowed by unwise parents. This
is, however, a danger affecting few, while the gain of checking
unmusical music is universal. The ladies to whom I pointed out
this risk recognised it as one, but said, 'After all, one must leave
some things to the common sense of the parents.'

Obviously, the same musical arrangement cannot hold good
with girls in boarding schools; the importance of the question
had not occurred to me at the time of my visits to these schools,
and I now regret that I did not find out in each school what proportion of the pupils were learning music. I can only hope that
the same reformation has taken place there also, from the fact
that music was hardly mentioned among the many matters
discussed between private headmistresses and myself.

The distribution of time allowed to each subject, and even
the subjects taken, vary considerably in different schools, but
the time tables of boys' and girls' schools are far more alike than
30 years ago, when indeed, most of the latter do not seem to
have worked by time-tables at all. The similarity is greatest in
the case of girls' high schools, where the public examinations,
Oxford and Cambridge locals and others, have most influence.
I have taken the tables of the Manchester High School, Bury
High School, and of one of the Girls' Public Day School Company's schools, as illustrative of the best day school education of
this kind.

6. The Curriculum in Secondary Schools for Girls, 1868–1900

SOURCE: Report of the Consultative Committee on the Differentiation of the Curriculum for Boys and Girls, 1923, pp. 31–3.

The idea constantly recurs in the writings and work of the
pioneers of women's education in the sixties that it was necessary to show by identity of curriculum and examinations that
women could do as well as men if they were to secure opportunities of earning a living in professional work. It is noticeable that

13

even at the present time there seems to be considerable apprehension among many friends of the women's cause at any suggestion of differentiation in curriculum, lest women should find the doors closed which have only just begun to open the way to economic independence.

Development of Girls' Education after 1868. The High Schools (21) The serious defects of girls' education in general as described by the Commissioners of 1868 go far to explain how it came about that the pioneers, such as Miss Buss and Miss Beale, infused the ideal of thoroughness and accuracy, and advocated the study of Latin and Mathematics to this end. For example, Miss Todd, in her work on 'the Education of Girls of the Middle Classes' (1874), writes, 'Mathematics offers peculiar advantages for the correction of the mental errors to which the neglect of real culture has made women liable.' The chapter on girls' education in the Commissioners' Report (1868) produced a profound impression on public opinion. The Endowed Schools Act, 1869, made it possible to apply part of the funds of Educational Trusts to girls' education. In 1869 the Cambridge Higher Local Examination was instituted, and the need of preparing women for it led to the foundation of Newnham College (1871).*
In 1869 London University established a general Examination for women with more advanced special papers. In 1870 girls were admitted to the Oxford Local Examination. In 1871 the National Union for the Improvement of the Education of Women of all Classes was founded, whose chief aims were to promote the foundation of cheap day schools for girls and to raise the status of women teachers by giving them a liberal education and a good training in the art of teaching. To this end the National Union in 1872 formed the Girls' Public Day School Company, whose purpose was 'to supply for girls the best education possible, corresponding with the education given to boys in the great Public Schools.' The Company established, first in London and later in other large towns, a number of excellent schools whose curriculum was largely modelled on that of the North London Collegiate School.

The growing recognition of the claims of Natural Science, to which public attention was directed by the Report of the Royal

* Girton College, founded at Hitchin in 1869, was removed to Girton in 1873.

Commission on Scientific Instruction (1875), led to the gradual introduction of Natural Science, especially Botany, into Girls' Schools; and the increasing attention to questions of health and physical development aided the introduction of Physical Training into these schools. Head mistresses were therefore, even in the seventies, compelled to consider the congestion of studies; and the more liberal education which they themselves had received in the Women's Colleges, fortified by the professional spirit which from the first marked their activities, enabled them to arrive at a working solution of the problems involved. The curriculum was made more educative and more manageable by the recognition of diversity of aptitudes in the pupils and by a corresponding arrangement of studies, while a common basis of indispensable subjects was retained in the lower part of the school. The high schools were unfettered by the traditions and prejudices which obsessed the older endowed schools, and the mistresses were more receptive to new ideas, more critical and more ready to adapt themselves to changing circumstances. Reforms in curriculum and in methods of teaching were readily accepted. Manual work was introduced at a relatively early date, and mistresses were quicker than masters to recognise the claims of less gifted pupils. The rapid development in girls' education in the seventies is marked by the permission, accorded in 1876, for girls to take the examinations of the Oxford and Cambridge Joint Board, established in 1873. The Maria Grey Training College for women teachers in Secondary Schools was founded in 1878; London University opened all its examinations and degrees to women in 1878; Cambridge opened its Triposes to them in 1881, and in 1884 Oxford allowed women to sit for examinations in certain of its schools. The earliest Colleges for women at Oxford date from 1879. The new Universities from the first made no distinction of sex in respect of teaching, emoluments, or degrees.

The curriculum in high schools and Endowed Schools for Girls up to about 1900

The curriculum in use in 1878 at the Manchester High School (founded in 1872) may be taken as typical of a good High School at that period. Girls in the sixth form studied English Grammar and Literature, French, Geography, History, Latin, Mathematics, and German (from which a few girls were exempted), and Drawing and Harmony were taken by most girls. Singing, Pianoforte playing, and Political Economy were each taken by a few pupils. Greek was probably as a rule only studied by those who were going to Oxford or Cambridge, and a custom early grew up in Girls' High Schools of making German alternative to Latin. There was always also a considerable number of girls who did not take Mathematics. At the North London Collegiate School a short intensive course on Political Economy, was given at a special period of the year. In the teaching of Natural Science girls' schools up to 1904 were as a rule behind boys' schools, as the ordinary High School had no funds to provide expensive laboratories. Moreover girls at that time had not the same practical reason for studying Natural Science as boys had, nor did the influence of the grants of the Science and Art Department to the Organised Science Schools affect girls' education in the same way. In some schools, however, such as the North London Collegiate School, and the King Edward VI. High School at Birmingham, much time and attention were devoted to Science towards the end of the century. Botany was popular in many schools and was considered suitable for girls, the more so as it did not involve any expensive equipment. At the Manchester High School in 1898 Chemistry and Physics were taught but not to any great extent as the head mistress was doubtful of their value and especially of the 'heuristic' method of teaching which was then fashionable. At that time Botany and Latin were alternatives in the middle forms of the School, and Physical Geography was included among the Sciences.

7 Experimental Schools

It is commonplace to say that many of the accepted ideas of today concerning schools have their origins in scholastic establishments regarded by contemporaries as wildly experimental. In this sense freedom to experiment has played an important part in the evolution of pedagogy. It might also be salutary to remember that all experiments do not succeed, not even in education, and the unsuccessful experiments have tended to slide into a merciful oblivion.

1. Hazelwood School

This very remarkable experimental school was opened in 1819 by the Hill family at Hazelwood, near Birmingham. The most striking features of the school were the degree of self-government accorded to the pupils, the breadth of the curriculum and the organisation of students for teaching purposes into sets based on aptitude and attainment in each subject. The school contained about 120 boys.

> SOURCE: *Plans for the Government and Liberal Instruction of Boys, in large numbers, as practised at Hazelwood School*, Anon, 1825.

The two great departments of education are government and instruction. We shall first speak of the government of our school. The principle on which we have acted has been to leave as much as possible all power in the hands of the boys themselves. To this end we permit them to elect a committee from their own body, in which the laws of the school are prepared, discussed and erected. The teachers having the regulation only of the routine of exercises, and the boys appointed for their performance; and these powers are not exercised individually, but by acts of the whole body, meeting in conference.

Our judicial establishment consists of a Jury-Court, over which a Judge presides. Slight offences are disposed of by a Magistrate, who is at the head of a small but vigorous police. The executive department consists of various officers, who, with the judge and magistrate, are appointed from time to time by the Committee. These officers are treasurers of various funds raised in the school; one for charitable purposes, another for the purchase of books and instruments, and a third for the purchase and repair of gymnastic apparatus. Each of these little institutions has its President, Secretary, and Committee. We have also conservators of the school property, who have the care of the books, drawings, and instruments, belonging to the general body. We have many officers for the preservation of order. Each dormitory has its *prefect*, and during school hours, and at meals, *silentiories* are employed.

In the choice of our rewards and punishments, we have aimed at making them as slight as is consistent with their being effective. Under the conviction that all such artificial excitements are objectionable, inasmuch as they interfere with the great principle of self-government, and are therefore only to be justified by necessity.

Our rewards consist of a few prizes, given at the end of each half-year, to those whose exertions have obtained for them the highest rank in the school; and of certain marks, which are gained by superiority in the classes, by fulfilling the duties of the various offices, and by the performance of *voluntary labour* during the pupils' leisure hours. These marks are of two kinds: the most valuable, called *personal marks*, can only be obtained by successful exertions of a high order; these will purchase holiday. The others, called *transferable marks*, may be obtained by performances less perfect. These have their value, in being the general medium for the discharge of penalties. The transferable marks consist of counters of various denominations, while the personal works exist only in record. Our punishments are fines, and sometimes, though very rarely, short imprisonment. Impositions, public disgrace, and corporal pain, have been for many years discarded.

To obtain rank is an object of great ambition among the boys; with us it is entirely dependent on their conduct and acquirements; and our arrangements according to excellence are so frequent, that no one can maintain a respectable station, without constant exertion, and watchfulness.

The employments of the pupils in the acquisition of knowledge may be arranged under two general heads. Those which are merely instrumental to an ulterior object, as writing copies and parsings; and those which are not only useful as a means, but valuable as an end; such as taking reports of lectures—in which, while the pupil is exercised in penmanship, orthography, and composition, he is laying up a store of knowledge valuable in itself. To these divisions of employment, a third must in most schools be added, comprehending such acts as are necessary to order and discipline; as calling a roll, recording the names of absentees, etc. Considered as exercises, these latter duties, as usually performed, contribute but little, if at all, to forward the pupils' education. Our aim has been to diminish the first head, increase the second, and annihilate the third; this last object has been effected, by taking care that all the acts here contemplated shall be performed with so much precision, and shall employ so many of the pupils as to become useful occupations, and thereby to range fairly under one of the former heads. Almost all our movements are made to military step, and several of them to the sound of music. Thus the boys learn to march with precision, and become attentive to the word of command, while many of them learn to play very respectably on various instruments.

The whole business of our government, complex as it necessarily is, must of course be replete with occupation of this kind; so that even those who, differing from us, may think our regulations are unnecessarily numerous and minute, considered merely as laws, will perhaps be of the opinion that as furnishing the means of useful exercise, they are capable of justification.

We consider it important that instruction should as much as possible, be social: we have, therefore, divided the school into classes; by which the teacher may be enabled to afford time for copious explanation. The principle upon which a class is formed is, that it should contain no student who is not on a par, or nearly so, with his fellows; consequently a different division has been made for each branch of study; since a boy as a linguist may hold a very different rank to what he may justly claim as a mathematician.

Economy of time is a matter of importance to us: we look upon all restraint as an evil, and, to young persons, a very serious evil; we are, therefore, constantly in search of means for ensuring the effective employment of every minute which is spent in the school-room, that the boys may have ample time for exercise in the open air. The middle state between work and play is extremely unfavourable to the formation of good habits;

we have succeeded, by great attention to order and regularity, in reducing it almost to nothing.

In early youth the power of applying to one task for any great length of time, or of remaining with comfort in one position, is very limited; we, therefore, change the place and occupation of our pupils much more frequently than is generally done: but at the same time, as it is important to them to acquire the habit of continued application, we have so arranged our exercises that the upper classes remain stationary for a much longer period than their juniors.

We are careful to lose no opportunity of providing maxims and means for self-instruction; thoroughly convinced that the great maxim of education ought to be—'It is better to learn than to be taught'. One maxim for voluntary employment has already been pointed out. No fair occasion is overlooked for exemplifying and insisting upon the advantages of possessing knowledge; and we are careful that no obstacle shall be thrown in the way of any boy who is anxious to avail himself of his opportunities for private study. The library of the school is of some extent, and is constantly increasing: partly from the fund already adverted to, and partly from the presents which are made, from time to time, by the friends of the system. We have literally hidden the walls of several of our largest rooms with maps, plans and prints of various descriptions. We are collecting busts, we are adding largely to our philosophical apparatus; and we hope our modellers and handicraft men will soon be able to construct models of buildings and machines, ancient and modern.

We have a printing press, which we find a great auxiliary, as it furnishes a pleasant and useful employment for many boys. If any one is peculiarly deficient in his knowledge of orthography or punctuation, he may soon be induced to cure himself by a course of printing. A little magazine is written and printed in the school, which is now and then embellished by etchings executed among the pupils.

The improvement of the bodily powers is not forgotten. Gymnastics form a regular part of school exercises. Our playgrounds are extensive, and supplied with gymnastic apparatus, and we have a swimming bath.

From the foregoing sketch the reader, we hope, will perceive that we have taken some pains to render the life of a schoolboy as happy in progress as it generally is in recollection; and if our evidence can be admitted, we shall have no hesitation in saying, that our endeavours to this effect have been rewarded with a degree of success beyond our most sanguine expectations.

2. Kings Somborne School

Kings Somborne in Hampshire had a population of 1,125 in 1847 and the inhabitants were entirely dependent on agriculture for their living. Just over 200 children attended the remarkable village school which, through its success, gained the active support of the local people and was patronised by children of farmers, labourers and local tradespeople, all of whom paid fees adequate to meet the cost of running the school. Perhaps the most noteworthy feature of the school was that it attempted so to organise the pupils' studies as to build upon the day-to-day experiences of village children—quite the reverse of the general practice in contemporary schools.

> SOURCE: Report of the Committee of Council on Education for 1847–8, Vol. I, pp. 12–18, Report by the Rev H. Moseley, H.M.I.
> Attainments of the Children in the Kings Somborne School.

The school is distinguished from most others in this district by the use of the Scriptures for the instruction of the children in the subject-matter of Scripture only, and the use of secular books, exclusively, for their instruction in reading.

At my first inspection, I examined all the classes minutely; 160 children were then present in the two schools, of whom I found 64 (being 2 in 5) capable of reading with tolerable ease and correctness. In other schools I have found this proportion 1 in 6.

Here, then, where so many other things are taught besides reading, the children are found in advance, in reading, of others, in the majority of which scarcely anything else is taught.

And this is always the case, and a fact which seems to point to the expediency, if not the necessity, of teaching children something else besides reading, that we may be able to teach them to read.

To emancipate them now and then from the drudgery of reading cannot but make the task a less irksome one to them, and it is impossible that the instruction they receive in other things, awakening the intelligence and strengthening the memory, should not aid them in learning to read. . . .

All the children in the school, except five write on slates; and all, except those of the lowest class, are accustomed to write, not only from copies and from dictation, but in some degree from their own thoughts.

Thus a child in the lowest class but one, when it can write words legibly upon a slate, is told to write the names of its brothers and sisters, of all things in the house where it lives, of all the birds, or trees, or plants that it knows and the like. Another stage in its instruction associates qualities with things. It is told, perhaps, to write down the names of all the white or black things that it knows, of all the ugly or handsome things, or the tall or short ones, or iron or wooden ones. And then, when the child can write sentences, on the uses of things familiar to its observation—it writes of things used for the food of man or of animals, used in building a cottage, or as implements of agriculture. Lastly, it is made to exhaust its knowledge of such things by being told to write down all it knows about them; all it knows, for instance, about sheep, or cows, or horses, wheat, iron, or copper, of the village of Kings Somborne, or the neighbouring downs and hills, of the farms and holdings in the parish, or the parish roads, of the river Teste which runs through it, of the neighbouring town of Stockbridge, of Hampshire, of the island of Great Britain, of the earth, or of the sun, moon, and stars.

To summon together the scattered elements of its knowledge of these familiar things, to combine them in a certain order, and to express them in a written language, is an exercise which may be adapted to each stage in a child's intellectual growth, and which seems well calculated at once to accustom it to think, and to give it the power of expressing its thoughts in appropriate words. Not the least advantage of commencing these exercises from the lowest classes in the school is, that they serve not only as a practice in thinking and writing, but in spelling, and that, probably, of the best kind; the subjects, and therefore language, of them being more familiar than those commonly found in books used for writing from dictation. I certainly never have examined little children who could spell so well; and that good spelling and good reading, and skill in the expression of written thoughts, go together, may be taken as an illustration of the fact that to achieve excellence in any one subject of instruction in an elementary school (even the simplest and most elementary), it is necessary to unite with it others; and that the singular slowness with which the children of our National schools learn to read (a fact to which all our reports have borne testimony) is, in some degree, to be attributed to the unwise concentration of the labours of the school on that single object. . . .

In all the classes of the school the children appear to have, according to their standing, a good knowledge of arithmetic; they are, moreover, taught English Grammar, geography, and English history. Mr Dawes [the head teacher] has adapted the teaching of these subjects to elementary education by a judicious selection and by various simple methods, the particulars of which are detailed in his work [Suggestive Hints].

Among the most interesting features of the girls' school is the needlework. The elder girls are taught not only to work, but, by paper patterns, to cut out work for themselves; and the dresses of the first class, on the day of my examination, were many of them thus cut out, and all made by themselves. There seems to be no reason why the economical cutting out of work should not thus enter, as a part, into the ordinary instruction in needle-work in our schools. The cost of paper for patterns would be little. The fitting of different articles of clothing to the children of the school would supply an inexhaustible variety of subjects for patterns; and for such an object the school might well afford a good many facilities. The exercises of the girls in *arithmetic* might even be associated with this useful object. It is, for instance, a good question in the Rule of Three, knowing what the length of the sleeve of a dress for a person of a given height is, to determine what that for a similar dress for a person of another height should be; or, knowing how many yards of cloth would be required to make the dress in the first case, to determine how many would make it in the other. There can be no reason why the girls should not know that this last proportion is as the square of the height in the one case to the square of the height in the other; that, for instance, the cloth in a dress for a person 4 feet high is to that in a similar dress for a person 5 feet, as 16 to 25.

When a girl has cut out for herself the dress she has made, she has associated her labour, in a natural relation, with the exercise of her judgement; she has taken one step towards her emancipation from a state of pupilage, and gratified an instinct which associates the growing independence of her actions with her progress towards womanhood.

Algebra is taught to 21 boys of the first class, including the two pupil teachers, and geometry to 11 of these. I examined into their knowledge of these subjects with much care, orally and on paper. Their written exercises are now before me. Nine of them have solved correctly a proposition in the first book of Euclid, beyond which book none have yet advanced. From my oral examination, I am convinced that they have been well taught the propositions they profess to know, and that they understand them. I have rarely, indeed, heard boys answer so well in Euclid as some of them did. . . .

That feature in the teaching of Kings Somborne which constitutes probably its greatest excellence, and to which Mr Dawes attributes chiefly its influence with the agricultural population around him, is the union of instruction—in a few simple principles of natural science, applicable to things familiar to the children's daily observation—with everything else usually taught in a National school. He thus speaks on this interesting subject.

'After the school had been opened rather more than two years, I began giving to the teachers, and the more advanced of the school children, short explanations of a philosophic kind, and in a common-sense sort of way, of the things almost daily passing before their eyes, but of the nature of which they had not the slightest conception; such as some of the peculiar properties of metals, glass, and other substances in common use; that the air had weight, and how the pressure of the atmosphere helped them to pump up water; enabled them to amuse themselves with squirts and pop-guns; to suck up water, as they called it, through a straw; why the kettle top jumped up when the water was boiling on the fire; why, when they wanted to know whether it boiled or not, they seized the poker, and placing one end on the lid and the other to their ear, in order to know whether it actually boiled; why a glass sometimes breaks when hot water is poured into it, explaining the reason of the unequal expansion of the two surfaces: these and similar things I found so excessively amusing to them, and at the same time so instructive, that I have scarcely missed a week explaining some principle of this nature, and in questioning them on what had been done before.

'In subjects of this kind, and to children, mere verbal explanations, as everyone will perceive, are of no use whatever; but when practically illustrated before their eyes by experiment, they become not only one of the most pleasing sources of instruction, but absolutely one of the most useful.

'For instance, a teacher may talk to them about a thermometer, and find, in the end, they just know as much about it as they did when he began; but if he shows them one, and then grasps it in his hand, telling them to look at the fluid as it rises, or plunge it into cold water, and let them see the effect, they then begin to open their eyes in a wonderful manner, light breaks in upon them, and information thus given leaves an impression which in after-life, they turn to a source of instruction, by the reasoning powers of their own minds.

'The teachers here, who at first knew but little of these matters, are now well qualified to give instruction in them; to teach the mechanical principles of the tools they use,—the spade, the axe, the plough; and to explain such things as the common pump, barometer, pair of bellows; metals varying in volume, according to the quantity of heat which is in them, or, as it is termed, expanding by heat and contracting by cold; why one substance feels colder to the hand than another; the way in which metals are separated from their ores; how water is converted into steam, and again condensed; how clothes are dried, and why they feel cold sitting in wet clothes; why one body floats in water and another sinks; how much in volume, and how much in weight, a floating body displaces of the fluid in which it floats; why, on going into the school on a cold morning, they sometimes see a quantity of water on the glass, and why it is on the inside and not on the outside; why, when their ink is dried up, does it leave a substance behind which does not go away; the substances water holds in solution; water of the springs taking up some of the soil through which it has fallen; chalk &c; equal volumes of water varying in weight according to its density.'

To the discussion of subjects of this class Mr Dawes brings a rare sagacity, and that quality which in education is above all others to be desired,—a great practical common sense.

The children, when they disperse, carry home with them their books, for the evening's lesson, in satchels. The sight was to me, as an Inspector, a new and a very gratifying one. My thoughts followed them to the cottage fireside; and I was not surprised when Mr Dawes repeated to me the following words of the mother of one of the children whom he had recently visited; 'You cannot think, Sir, how pleasantly we spend our evenings now, compared with what we used to do; the girls reading and getting their lessons while I am sewing, and their father working with them; and he so disappointed, Sir, if the task is above him, so that he cannot help in it.'

3. The Dalton Plan at Bedales

Bedales is well-known as a pioneer co-educational boarding school. It was founded in 1893 by J. H. Badley who was the first headmaster; Bedales was the name of the country house near Lindfield in Sussex where the school was housed until it moved to its present home at Petersfield. The school has a considerable reputation for its progressive approach and adopted the main features of the Dalton Plan as a basis for its teaching.

SOURCE: J. H. Badley, *An Educational Experiment at Bedales School*, Dalton Association, n.d.

. . . What it implies is letting the child use the classroom as he uses (or should be allowed to use) a laboratory, to obtain knowledge at first hand, under the guidance of the teacher, but by his own active research, instead of waiting passively with the other members of the class to have it put before them in fixed quantities only and at fixed times. We had long felt class-teaching on the usual lines to be unsatisfactory. In the first place there is the difficulty of proper grading by forms, in which a very small percentage of the children can be at anything like the same level; for even if they could be alike in ability they have most of them had a different previous training, with considerable gaps, probably, and these at different points in the earlier work. Then again, they do not all advance at the same pace: the quicker are necessarily kept back to the average rate of advance, and often in consequence lose interest in the work, while the slower must either be neglected or forced on faster than they can properly go, and so, finding that they cannot follow all that is done, are apt to lose heart and sometimes to give up the attempt altogether. Any but the most temporary absence from the class means an unfilled gap, as the rest cannot be kept waiting while the work is gone through again; and this often means a failure to understand the later work and the erection of a shaky superstructure on insecure foundations. . . .

Is there any way in which we can ensure that each can advance at his own pace and in the way most suitable for himself, yet without sacrificing the indisputable advantages of form organisation? It is this that the 'laboratory' method seeks to do.

The point last mentioned is one of some importance. Whether from the point of view of supervision of work or from that of companionship and healthy emulation, the form, not too large in numbers, and under the charge, for at least a part of each day, of a form master or mistress, is a convenient unit. This therefore, we have retained for all general purposes, but rather as a social unit than as a unit for class teaching. In the upper half of the school—at the age, that is, when the stage is reached of preparation for definite examinations—we have not this year made any change as we wanted to see the effect of the new method of work in the middle forms before judging of its applicability to those preparing to take the 'School Certificate' or Matriculation. What we did, therefore, was to group together for teaching purposes the forms that we call the middles, and in them the experiment has been tried on the lines now to be described.

The various subject-teachers, instead of taking each form in turn, at fixed hours, for a given lesson to the whole class at once, remain in the rooms allotted to the special subjects, ready to give help to any individuals who come there to work at the subject in question. Certain times have been reserved for group-lessons in each subject, but the groups taken at these times are not the same, either in numbers or in composition, as the forms, but consist of those drawn from any of the forms who happen to be at the same stage of progress in that subject and can conveniently, therefore, have a lesson together when new work has to be explained. In a subject in which the work must be mainly oral, as in French and the earlier stages of Latin, the whole of the time allotted to the subject could be taken for group-work, though not all of it was necessarily so used. In other subjects a comparatively small proportion of the time was reserved for work with groups, least of all in Science and Mathematics: but the rooms in which they are taken are open for 'individual work' for as large a part of each day as possible, so that all who wish may come in (those, of course, excepted who may have a group-lesson fixed in some other subject) and go on with their own work, either alone or with a partner as they find most helpful. To such individual work, however, certain conditions have been attached. All the working hours of the week, i.e. all those that by the old time-table were assigned to class work, must be spent upon some kind of school work; a certain number, more in some subjects, fewer in others, as above explained, are reserved for group lessons, the rest are given to individual work in any subject, according to the child's choice, in one of the subject rooms shown on the time-table to be open at the time. The room is open for such work when the subject teacher is there and free to attend to any who come in, whether to answer their questions, to explain difficulties, or to go through with them what they have previously done. Except for group lessons no times were fixed at which work in a particular subject must be done, any time when the room is open being available, and the choice of subjects taken on any given day, and the length of time given to each being left to the child. But a fixed minimum of hours is expected to be given to each subject during the week, and to prevent time being wasted on snippets of work it has not been allowed to give less than half an hour at a time to any subject, though anyone who wished could continue at the same work for two or more of these half-hour periods.

In each subject the work is mapped out into so many 'grades', a grade representing approximately a month's work for a child of average ability, so that normally it can be expected that three grades should be passed in each term. An outline of the work in each grade is posted in each subject-room, so that all can at once find out what work to start upon, according to the grade they have reached. A test has to be passed before the work of one grade can be left and that of the next begun. Normally the test should be taken at the end of each month's work; but a rapid worker who gets through the work in shorter time can take it earlier, and so get through more than the normal three

PLATE 17

A LET DOWN

Professor Blinkers. 'I hope you did not find my lecture too technical
Miss Baynes!'

Miss Baynes (with pride). 'Oh no, Professor. I was able to follow it all.'

Professor B. 'I am glad of that as I tried to make it intelligible to the
meanest comprehension.' (*Punch, 1902*).

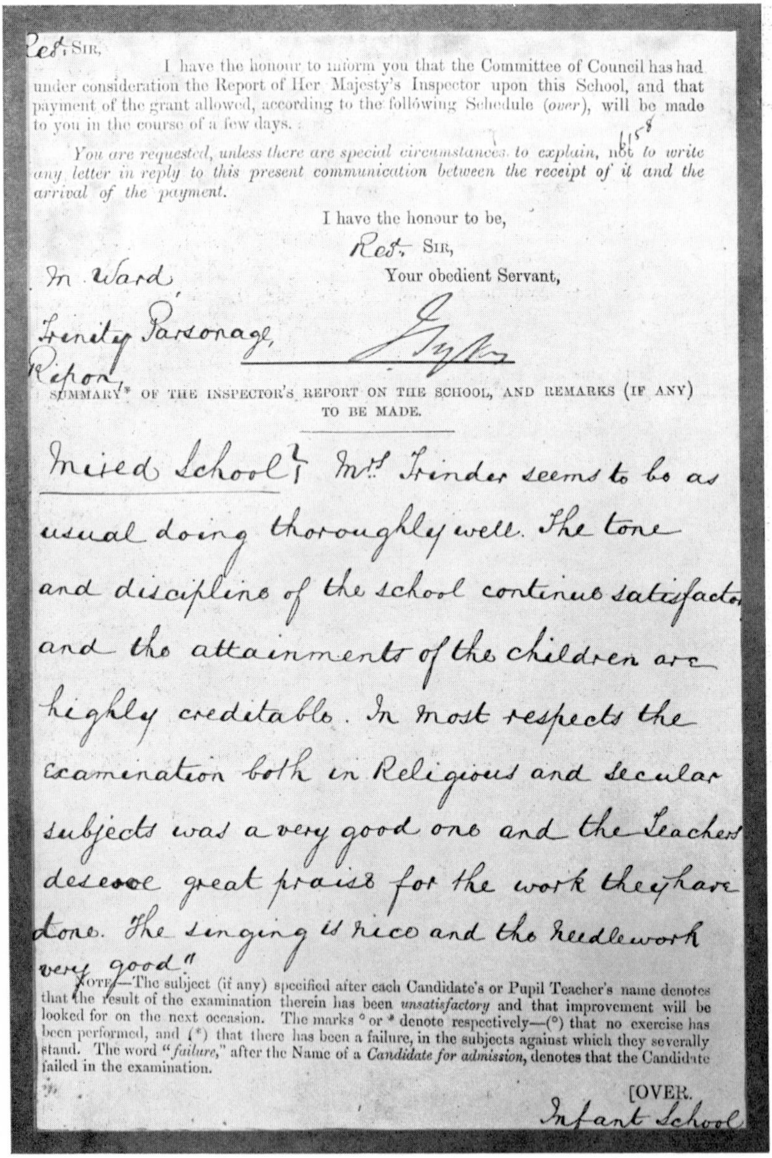

PLATE 18

Red. Sir,

I have the honour to inform you that the Committee of Council has had under consideration the Report of Her Majesty's Inspector upon this School, and that payment of the grant allowed, according to the following Schedule (*over*), will be made to you in the course of a few days.

You are requested, unless there are special circumstances, to explain, not to write any letter in reply to this present communication between the receipt of it and the arrival of the payment.

I have the honour to be,

Red. Sir,

Mr. Ward,   Your obedient Servant,

Trinity Parsonage,

Ripon,

SUMMARY* OF THE INSPECTOR'S REPORT ON THE SCHOOL, AND REMARKS (IF ANY)
TO BE MADE.

Mixed School "; Mrs. Trinder seems to be as usual doing thoroughly well. The tone and discipline of the school continue satisfactory and the attainments of the children are highly creditable. In most respects the examination both in Religious and secular subjects was a very good one and the Teachers deserve great praise for the work they have done. The singing is nice and the needlework very good "

NOTE.—The subject (if any) specified after each Candidate's or Pupil Teacher's name denotes that the result of the examination therein has been *unsatisfactory* and that improvement will be looked for on the next occasion. The marks ° or * denote respectively—(°) that no exercise has been performed, and (*) that there has been a failure, in the subjects against which they severally stand. The word "*failure*," after the Name of a *Candidate for admission*, denotes that the Candidate failed in the examination.

[OVER.

Infant School

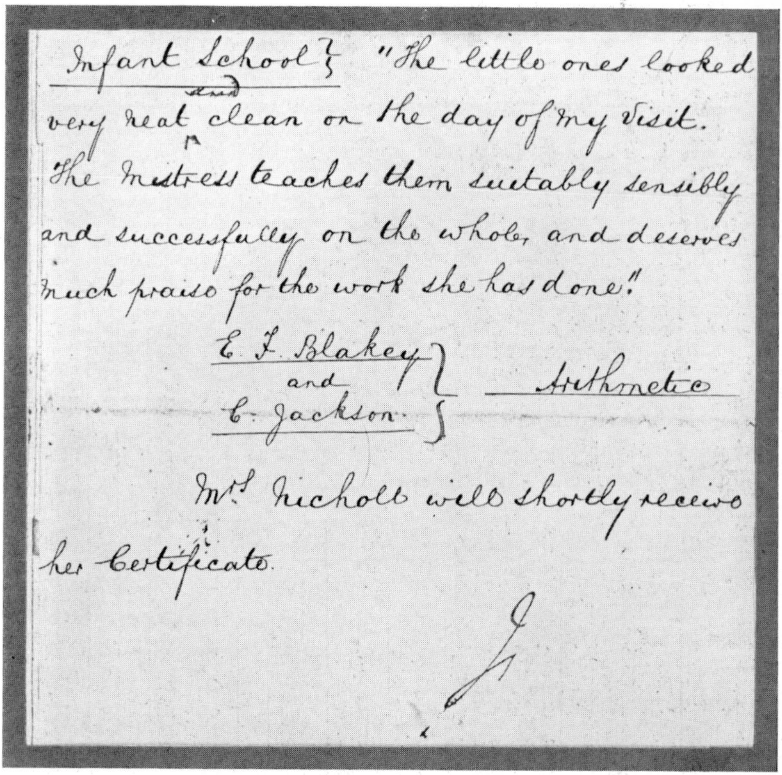

PLATE 19

Infant School } "The little ones looked very neat and clean on the day of my visit. The Mistress teaches them suitably sensibly and successfully on the whole, and deserves much praise for the work she has done."

E. F. Blakey
and } ————— Arithmetic
C. Jackson.

Mrs. Nicholl will shortly receive her Certificate.

Extracts from an Inspector's report, dated 1870.

PLATE 20

LANCASTERIAN SCHOOLS.

THE

Public Examination

OF THE

CHILDREN

Attending these Schools, Boys and Girls, and

ANNUAL MEETING

Of the friends of the Schools, will be held

IN THE TOWN-HALL,

On Friday Evening, 27th April Inst.,

Dr. MURRAY,

PRESIDENT OF THE SCHOOLS,

WILL TAKE THE CHAIR AT SIX O'CLOCK.

After the Examination is over, several Ministers and Friends will address the Meeting.

In the course of the Evening, Dr. MURRAY, according to his usual custom, will present a number of Bibles as Prizes, to the best Scholars in both Schools.

All interested in the cause of Education are invited to be present.

A COLLECTION WILL BE MADE ON BEHALF OF THE FUNDS OF THE SCHOOLS.

WILLIAM ROWNTREE, ⎫
RICHARD HUIE, Jun., ⎭ HON. SECS.

April 19th, 1860.

PRINTED FOR A. RUSSELL, BOOKSELLER, SCARBOROUGH.

'The Public Examination' was an oral examination of pupils by teachers from other schools in the presence of parents and friends.

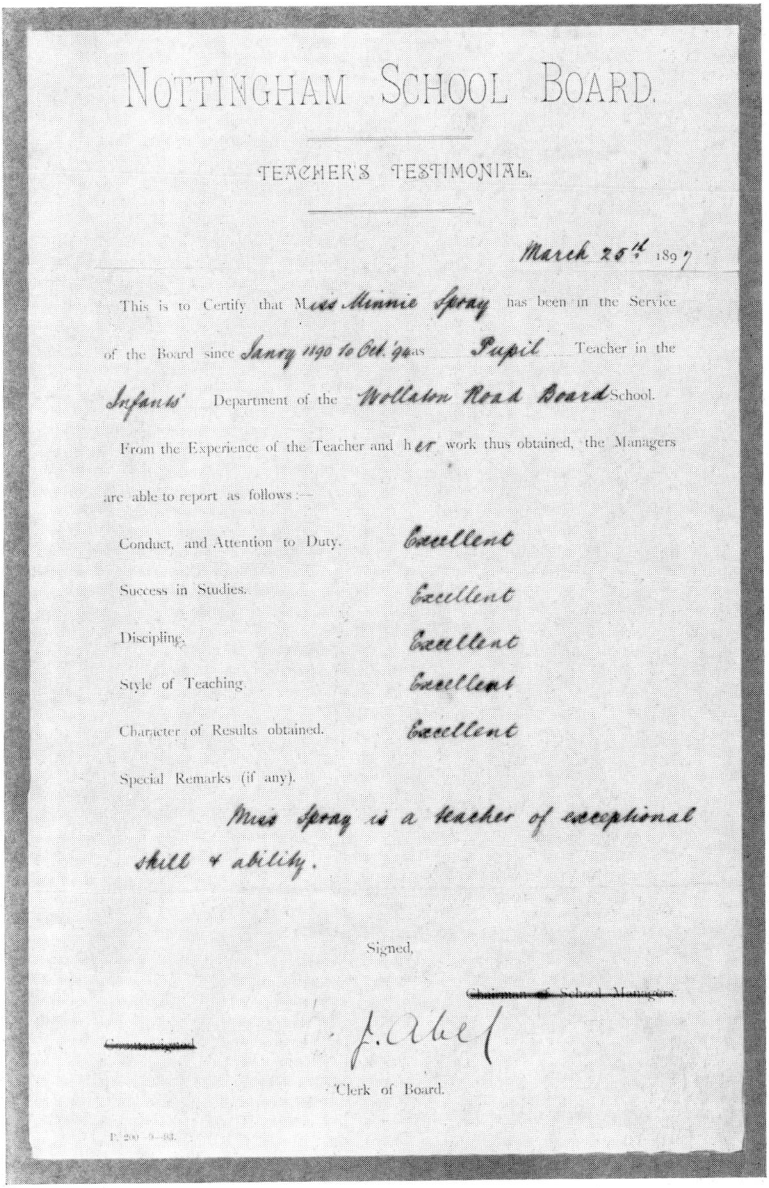

PLATE *21*

NOTTINGHAM SCHOOL BOARD.

TEACHER'S TESTIMONIAL.

March 25th 1897

This is to Certify that M*iss Minnie Spray* has been in the Service of the Board since *Jan'y 1890 to Oct. '94* as *Pupil* Teacher in the *Infants'* Department of the *Wollaton Road Board* School.

From the Experience of the Teacher and h*er* work thus obtained, the Managers are able to report as follows :—

Conduct, and Attention to Duty.   *Excellent*

Success in Studies.   *Excellent*

Discipline.   *Excellent*

Style of Teaching.   *Excellent*

Character of Results obtained.   *Excellent*

Special Remarks (if any).

Miss Spray is a teacher of exceptional skill & ability.

Signed,

~~Chairman of School Managers.~~

J. Abel

'Clerk of Board.

Printed forms for Teachers' testimonials were commonly used by the larger school boards.

PLATE 22

Frenchay Lodge,

FRENCHAY, near BRISTOL.

MISS ROBE AND MISS CRAMPTON

Receive a limited number of Pupils, whose education they personally superintend, assisted by an efficient staff of resident and visiting Teachers and Professors, and to whose Religious, Intellectual, and Physical well-being they devote earnest and careful attention.

The Course of Study includes the usual branches of English, as well as Euclid, Algebra, Science, Literature, Political Economy, French, German, Latin, Drawing, Painting, Harmony, Practical Music, Physical Training, and Class Singing.

TERMS (INCLUSIVE).

	PER TERM.
RESIDENT PUPILS	£24
NON-RESIDENT PUPILS	£6

ADVANCED MUSIC, DANCING, SOLO SINGING and VIOLIN LESSONS at Professor's Charges.

These terms are strictly inclusive—no extra charge being made for Stationery, Use of Books, &c.

Special arrangements are made for Pupils whose Parents are abroad.

Pupils are prepared for the Oxford and Cambridge, Locals, London Matriculation, Higher Cambridge, and all Musical Examinations.

A Term's Notice is required previous to the removal of a Pupil.

Each Pupil is requested to bring with her, Sheets, Towels, Serviettes, Spoon, and Fork.

A School Prospectus of the 1890s.

PLATE 23

REFERENCES.

Rev. F. PENLEY, Cam Vicarage, Dursley, Gloucester.

Rev. S. SKENE, Myton Vicarage, Helperby, Yorkshire.

Lady CAVE, Cleve Hill, Downend, Nr. Bristol.

Captain BELFIELD, Malmains, Frenchay, Nr. Bristol.

Colonel VERSTURME, 1, Portland Place, Bath.

Mrs. CORNER, Woodside, Portishead, Somerset.

Captain CONOR, Governor's House, H.M. Prison, Bristol.

Dr. ALCOCK, Riverside House, Innishannon, Co. Cork.

General CORBAN, Fermoy, Ireland.

Mrs. COLLETT, Highclere, Warberry Hill, Torquay.

Mrs. VINCENT, 109, Eaton Place, London.

H. LANGRIDGE LANE, Esq., Otterburn, Cranford Avenue, Exmouth.

Mrs. REID SHARMAN, Ivy Lodge, Wellingborough.

WALTER MILLER, Esq., The Firs, Barnfield, Exeter.

A list of 'References' was a common feature of the nineteenth century prospectus.

PLATE 24

TECHNICAL EDUCATION (What we are coming to)
'I've got a really excellent cook now. She develops all my photos for me!' (*Punch, 1902*).

PLATE 25

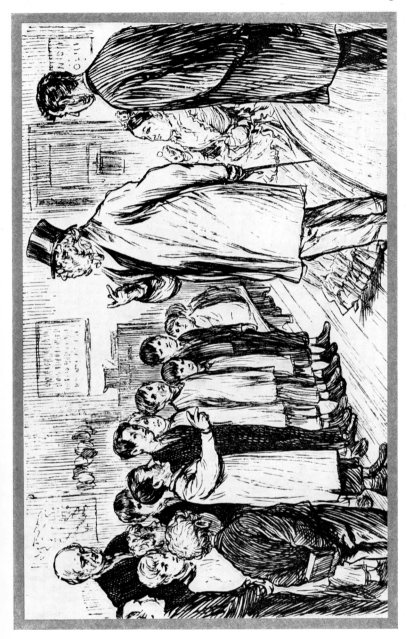

'Self-made Man' (examining school, of which he is a manager). 'Now, boy, what's the capital of 'olland?'

Boy. 'An "H", Sir.' (Punch, 1870).

PLATE 26

AN UNPOPULAR IDOL

How Billy and his Sunday-schoolmates intend to wreak their vengeance, if only a snowstorm be propitious, on the Embankment some Sunday afternoon about Christmas-time. (*Punch, 1902*).

PLATE 27

1. The pupil-teacher is engaged to serve under a certificated teacher during the usual school hours in keeping and teaching the *Huntington barwick and Towthorpe Board* school of the said Board, but so that the said pupil-teacher shall not serve therein less than three or more than six hours upon any one day, nor more than 25 hours in any one week. Sunday is expressly excluded from this engagement.

2. This engagement shall begin on the first day of *February* 189 *5*, and, subject to the proviso in paragraph 4, shall end on the last day of *January* 189 *9*, but if the pupil-teacher shall, with the consent of the other parties hereto, enter a Training College as a Queen's Scholar before the last-mentioned date, or such later date as shall be fixed by an extension of the engagement under paragraph 4, this engagement shall thereupon end.

3. The Board shall pay to the pupil-teacher as wages *£10-8-0 per year in the first year, £13 in the second year, £15-12-0 in the third year, and £20-16s-0d in the fourth year of the engagement, but such increase may be stopped at the discretion of the Board for the unexpired remainder of any year, after receipt of notice from the Education Department that the pupil-teacher has failed to pass the examination or to fulfil the other Conditions of a pupil teacher according to the Standard of the preceding year as prescribed in the Articles of the Code of the said Department applicable to the case.*

4. *Provided* always, that (1) if the pupil-teacher fails to pass the examination prescribed by the Code for any year, this engagement shall, with the consent of the Board and the Education Department, be extended so as to end on the last day of *January* 189 *1900* ; and (2) if the pupil-teacher defers the Queen's Scholarship Examination for a year in accordance with the Code, this engagement shall, with the consent of the Managers, be extended so as to end on the last day of the month in which such deferred examination takes place.

When this engagement is so extended, the course of study of the pupil-teacher in the remainder of the year succeeding that in respect of which the pupil-teacher failed shall be the same as in the last-mentioned year; and that year shall not be reckoned in calculating any payment to be made under paragraph 6 of this agreement.

A pupil-teacher's memorandum, April 1895.
A Memorandum of Agreement had to be drawn up between the pupil-teacher, one of his parents and the school managers before the period of apprentice could begin.

PLATE 28

Inspection of a pontoon bridge structure constructed by boys of Clifton College, 1896. The Training Corps came to play an increasingly important part in public school life about the turn of the century.

PLATE 29

This carpentry shop at Clifton College was constructed in 1875. The photograph was taken about 1900.

PLATE 30

Cheques Payable to Order must be endorsed . 7 . 8 . 1 .

Cheques Payable to Order must be endorsed 7 . 8 . 1 .

Cheques Payable to Order must be endorsed 7 . 8 . 1 .

Cheques Payable to Order must be endorsed 7 . 8 . 1 .

Cheques Payable to Order must be endorsed 7 . 8 . 1 .

Cheques Payable to Order must be endorsed 7 . 8 . 1 .

Cheques Payable to Order must be endorsed 7 . 8 . 1 .

Cheques Payable to Order must be endorsed 7 . 8 . 1 .

Cheques Payable to Order must be endorsed 7 . 8 . 1 .

Above. Pupil's Copy Book, 1901. Precepts of a moral or useful nature were frequently used as material for copybooks.

Below. School Signal, 1894. Used at Bubwith Board School, 1894–1904. These signals were manufactured by E. J. Arnold & Son, Leeds, until 1914. They were of two sizes, the smaller for assistant teachers and the larger one (shown here), which had a more pronounced click, for the headmaster.

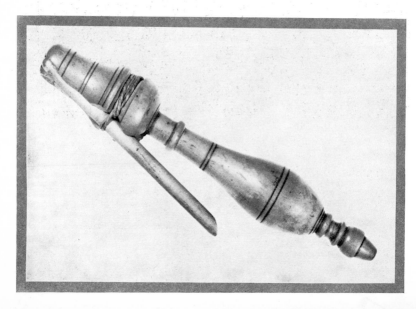

PLATE 31

Ragged class, *c* 1910.

PLATE *32*

The Evacuation of London Schoolchildren, 1939.

grades in a term, while a slow one can take a longer time than the month, and may even give the whole term to the work of a single grade in a subject in which he finds great difficulty. A record is kept of the grades passed and also a record of the number of hours spent each week on the different subjects. The form master can thus judge whether too much or too little time is being given to any subject, and whether progress in this or that subject is too slow. If less than the normal amount of time allotted to a subject is required, the time thus gained can be used for making up work, if this is required in a slower subject, or it may be given to a wider range of work in a good subject, or to some other kind of work, handwork for instance, in which the boy or girl is specially interested. If on the other hand progress proves to be so slow that even a single grade can hardly be passed in some particular subject after a term's work, even with the help of additional time gained from other things, it is then a question, if the form master is satisfied that reasonable effort has been made, whether it is worthwhile for that particular child to give time to work of this kind, at least for the present.

In this way, while much more is left to the work of the individual child and there is less risk of his remaining passive, as could so easily happen in the old system, whether from lack of interest or from discouragement, while the work of the class went on, he is not, under the 'laboratory' method, left entirely without guidance or stimulus; on the contrary, a more exact and complete measure of his progress is obtained, both for his teacher and himself, while at the same time he is neither hurried along beyond his capacity nor leaving gaps in the work behind him, and whatever advance he makes is real advance made by his own efforts, not merely apparent, due to the fact that the class as a whole has covered the ground.

This extract demonstrates the work of J. H. Badley as a headmaster and organiser of vision; the paragraph which follows gives a picture of him as a class teacher. The paragraph is taken from a Report on Bedales School following an inspection by Alfred Hughes, Professor of Education in the University of Birmingham, in 1908.

Of the many other lessons that I heard, there is at any rate one which calls for special mention. This is a scripture lesson given by Mr Badley himself. Two classes were put together— there must have been 30 boys and girls present. The chapters

15

taken were those leading up to and telling the story of Jael and Sisera. Every verse was made to yield up its contributory point—one point was collated with another—we threw back to a past verse and we threw forward to another verse—until, with suggestions from every child a consistent full story was gradually patched together, every phrase of the Bible being made to harmonize with it. The whole lesson was indeed a lesson in constructing a historical story out of original sources. More than that, it was a lesson in English literature; the beauty and poetry of the passages were implicitly brought out and made clear— and the whole thing was conducted in a spirit of beautiful reverence. To say that the thirty boys and girls attended well is to speak very mildly; every one felt himself a contributing party—and the utmost zest and keenness were shown throughout.

4. A Day in Summerhill

Mr A. S. Neill established Summerhill at Leiston in Suffolk in 1921; perhaps the chief characteristic of this well-known school has been the absence of any imposed pattern of discipline and the freedom given to individual pupils to satisfy their needs as and when they may desire to do so.

SOURCE: A. S. Neill, *That Dreadful School*, Herbert Jenkins, 1948, pp. 66–71.

Breakfast is from 8.15 to 9, and the staff and pupils fetch their breakfast from the kitchen hatch which is opposite to the dining-room. Beds are supposed to be made by 9.30 when lessons begin. At the beginning of each term a time-table is posted up. Children are divided into classes according to their age and interest; the classes being called by Greek letters. Thus Corkhill in the laboratory may have on Monday the Betas, on Tuesday the Gammas and so on. Max has a similar time-table for English, Cyril for Mathematics, Roger for Geography, my wife for history. The juniors usually stay with their own teacher most of the morning, but they also go to chemistry or the art-room. There is, of course, no compulsion to attend lessons, but if Jimmy comes to English on Monday and does not make an appearance again until the Friday of the following week, the others quite rightly object that he is keeping the work back, and they may throw him out.

Lessons go on until one, but the infants and juniors lunch at 12.30. The school has to be fed in three relays, and the staff and seniors sit down to lunch at 1.45. After-noons are completely free for everyone. What they all do in the afternoon I do not know. I garden, and seldom see youngsters about. I see the juniors playing gangsters, but some of the seniors busy them-selves with motors and radio and drawing and painting. In good weather they play games. Some tinker about in the work-shop, mending their cycles or making boats or revolvers.

Tea is at four, and at five various activities begin. The juniors like to be read to: the middle group likes work in the art room— painting, linoleum cuts, leather-work, basket making, and there is usually a busy group in the pottery; in fact the pottery seems to be a favourite haunt morning and evening. The Matricula-tion group works from five onwards. The wood and metal workshop is full every night.

There is no work, that is, no organised work, after six or six-thirty. On Monday nights the pupils go to the local cinema on their parents' bill, and when the programme changes on the Thursday those who have the money may go again. Pocket money is given out on Thursday for this reason.

On Tuesday night the staff and seniors have my psychological talk. The juniors have various reading groups then. Wednesday night is lounge night, that is dance night. Dance records are selected from a great pile . . . and as the lounge is next door to our sitting-room I dread Wednesday nights, for the tunes that the children like are to me simply a dreadful noise. Hot Rhythm is about the only thing in life that makes me feel murderous. They are all good dancers, and some visitors say that they feel inferior when they dance with them.

Thursday night has nothing special on for the seniors go to the cinema in Leiston or Aldeburgh, and Friday is left for any special event, such as play rehearsing. Saturday night is our most important one for it is General Meeting night. Dancing usually follows, and Sunday is our Theatre evening.

There is no distinct time-table for handwork. We have so far been handicapped by having only our stable loft as a wood and metalwork room, but with Shand's new workshop I hope to see more enthusiasm for handwork. Children make what they want to, and what they want to make is nearly always a toy revolver or gun or boat or kite. They are not much interested in elaborate joints of the dovetail variety; and even the older boys do not fancy elaborate joints. Not many of them take an interest in my own hobby, hammered brasswork, because you can't attach a phantasy to a brass bowl.

A workshop is a most troublesome department of a free school. In the early days the workshop was always open, and as a result every tool got lost or damaged, for a child of nine would use a fine chisel as a screwdriver, or take out a pair of pliers to mend his bike and leave them lying on the path. I had my own private workshop separated from the main workshop by a partition and locked door. My conscience kept pricking me; I felt that I was being selfish and a-social and at last I knocked down the partition. In six months there wasn't a good tool in what had been my division. One boy used up all the letter punches making cotter pins for his motor-cycle; another tried to put my lathe in screw-cutting gear when it was running. Polished planishing hammers for brass and silver work were used for breaking bricks. Tools disappeared and were never found. Worst of all the interest in handwork died away, for the elder pupils said: 'What's the good of going into the workshop? All the tools are rotten now.' And rotten they were. Planes had teeth in their blades; and saws had none. I proposed at a meeting that the workshop be locked again and the motion was carried. But in showing visitors round I had a feeling of shame when I had to unlock the workshop each time . . . What! Freedom . . . and locked doors? It looked bad indeed, and I decided to give the school an extra workshop which would remain open all the time. I got one fitted out with everything necessary—bench, vice, saws, chisels, planes, hammers, pliers, set squares, etc. One or two of the bigger lads sharpened up all the tools.

One day about four months later I was showing a party round the school. When I unlocked the workshop one of them said: 'This doesn't look like freedom, does it?'

'Well,' I said hurriedly, 'you see the children have another workshop which is open all day long. Come along, I'll show you it.'

There was nothing left in it except the bench. Even the vice had gone, and in what sundry corners of our twelve acres the chisels and hammers lay I never knew.

The workshop business continued to worry the staff, but myself most of all, because tools mean much to me. I concluded that what was wrong was that tools were communal. 'Now,' I said to myself, 'if we introduce the possessive element, if each child has his own kit of tools.' I brought it up at a meeting, and the idea was well received. Next term some of them brought back kits of tools, and in two months these also were kicking about the grounds. I had to conclude that children are not interested in tools. Possibly it is the range of ages that causes most of the trouble, for assuredly tools mean almost nothing to small boys and girls. The position to-day (Summer, 1936) is that Parsons, our handwork teacher, keeps the workshop locked when he isn't there, and I keep my own workshop locked ... I put the partition back some time ago. I graciously allow a few senior pupils to use my shop when they want to, and I admit that they do not abuse it, for they are at the stage when care of tools is a conscious necessity for good work.

Locking doors has increased recently at Summerhill. I brought the matter up one Saturday night.

'I don't like it,' I said. 'I took visitors round this morning and had to unlock the workshop, the laboratory, the pottery and the theatre. I propose that all public rooms be left open all day.'

There was a storm of dissent.

'The laboratory must be kept locked because of the poisons, and as the pottery is joined on to the laboratory it has to be kept locked too.'

'We won't have the workshop left open. Look what happened last time?'

'Well, then,' I pleaded, 'surely to goodness we can leave the theatre open. Nobody will run away with the stage.'

The playwrights, actors, actresses, stage-manager, lightsman—they all rose at once.

Said the lightsman: 'You left it open this morning and in the afternoon some idiot switched on all the lights, 3,000 watts at ninepence a unit.'

Another said: 'The small kids take out the costumes and dress up in them.' The upshot was that my proposal to leave doors unlocked was supported by two hands—my own and a girl of seven, who I discovered later, thought that we were still voting on the previous motion ... that children of seven be allowed to go to the cinema.

The hardest lesson we adults have had to learn is that children have no regard for property. They do not destroy it deliberately. They destroy it unconsciously. In our innocence we lined their bedrooms with beaverboard in order to make them warmer. Beaverboard is a kind of thick pasteboard, and a small child has only to see it to start picking holes in it. The beaverboard wall of the ping-pong room looks like Ypres after a bombardment. Boys seem to be more destructive than girls, possibly because they are less conscious, but destructiveness is seldom a senseless thing. The boring of beaverboard is similar to nose boring, and it is usually quite unconscious, but destruction often has a creative meaning and intention. If a boy needs a piece of metal for a boat keel he will take a nail if he can find one, but if he cannot find a nail he will use my precious Whitworth taps if one of them happens to be about the right size. A tap, like a nail, is to a child a chunk of metal. A bright lad once used a guinea white-wash brush for tarring a roof.

We have learned that children have values that are entirely different from adult values. If a school tries to uplift a child by giving it beautiful classical paintings on the walls and beautiful furniture in the rooms, it is beginning at the wrong end. Children are primitives, and until they ask for culture they should live in as primitive an environment as we can give them. Nine years ago when we came to our present house we had the agony of seeing primitive lads throwing knives at beautiful oak doors. We hastily bought two railway carriages and made them into a bungalow with a roof over all, and a sitting-room between, and a bathroom overhead. There our primitives could chuck their knives as much as they wanted to. Yet today the carriages are not in a bad state. They are inhabited by boys from twelve to eighteen, and the majority of them have reached the stage of caring for comfort and decorations. Some of them keep their compartments beautifully tidy and clean: others live in untidiness, and they are mostly boys who come from Public Schools. You can always tell the ex-Public School lads in Summerhill ... they are the most unwashed and wear the greasiest flannel bags.

8   Teachers and their Training

The systematic training of teachers for service in the elementary schools dates from about 1840 and the profession, as distinct from the occupation, of elementary school teacher dates from the same period.

1. Proposal to found St. Mark's College, Chelsea, 1839

The need for a much more thorough education for those who were to teach in their schools was fully understood by the two great societies, the National and the British and Foreign. The National Society in 1839 set on foot the project for a central Church training college in London. In the years that followed Colleges were also established for the training of teachers in many of the dioceses.

SOURCE: Report of the National Society for 1839, pp. 10 and 11.

'It has been resolved to adopt a measure which it is the special object of the Society to recommend to public attention on the present occasion, viz: The formation of a large boarding and training institution for Schoolmasters and mistresses in connection with the central school'.

'An opinion has long pervaded the Country, in which the Committee have fully concurred, that the moral and intellectual improvement of the teachers of schools was a principal object requiring attention . . . that the advancement of a system of teaching, however valuable, was of small account in comparison with this; that the minds and characters of the teachers must be carefully prepared and formed for the important office they were to fulfil; and that nothing could compensate for imperfect and defective education in those who were themselves to be the guides and instructors of the young'.

'With these views it is, that, the true purpose to found, without delay, an Institution for the boarding and training of young persons, who are desirous to become teachers;—to be managed under their own superintendence, by a resident Clergyman, being a graduate of one of the Universities, and such other assistants (male and female), as the numbers under instruction may require. The period hitherto appropriated to the training of schoolmasters, will thus be greatly extended; the difficulties and objections which have been experienced from the lodging of probationers in different parts of London will be done away: young persons who are found to possess the natural requisites for teaching and managing children will be received into training before they have engaged in other professions: The Science of Education and the best practical methods of instruction will be systematically taught, and a course of religious and moral culture and intellectual training pursued. . . .'

2. An Account of St. Mark's College, Chelsea, 1843

This account of St. Mark's College by the Revd Allen, H.M.I. gives a full and interesting description of the background, life and work of students in this early training College. Because of its position as the central training college of the Church, the approach taken by St. Mark's to problems of training students had a considerable effect on the aims and methods of other colleges scattered through the dioceses.

SOURCE: Report of the Committee of Council on Education for 1842-3, pp. 290-303.

General Time Table (Winter)

	Occupation	Begins Hrs. Min.		Continues Hrs. Min.	
	Rise, &c.	5	30	0	30
	House-work	6	0	0	45
	Study	6	45	1	30
	Breakfast	8	15	0	25
	Preparation for Chapel	8	40	0	20
	Morning Service	9	0	1	0
	Preparation for Study	10	0	0	10
	Study	10	10	1	30
Monday	Garden &c.	11	40	1	5
	Preparation for Dinner	12	45	0	15
	Dinner	1	0	0	40
	Preparation for Grounds	1	40	0	20
	Garden, &c.	2	0	2	0
	Study	4	0	1	45
	Preparation for Music	5	45	0	15
	Music	6	0	1	0
	Preparation for Tea	7	0	0	10
	Tea	7	10	0	20

	Occupation	Begins Hrs. Min.		Continues Hrs. Min.	
Monday	Preparation for Prayers	7	30	0	5
	Evening Prayers	7	35	0	25
	Study	8	0	1	0
	Leisure	9	0	0	30
	Leave for Bed	9	30	0	30
	Gas extinguished	10	0	—	
Tuesday	Note—The Forenoon Work as above				
	Dinner	1	0	0	40
	Preparation for Music	1	40	0	20
	Music*	2	0	1	0
		3	0	1	0
	Preparation for Drill	4	0	0	5
	Drill	4	5	0	50
	Study	5	0	2	0
	Tea, &c. as before	—		—	
Wednesday	Morning Work as before				
	Dinner	1	0	0	40
	Preparation for Drawing	1	40	0	20
	Drawing	2	4	2	0
	Leisure	4	0	1	45
	Preparation for Music	5	45	0	15
	Music	6	0	1	0
	Tea, &c. as before	—		—	
Thursday	Morning Work as before				
	Study, Music &c. as on Monday				
Friday	Morning Work as before				
	Dinner	1	0	0	40
	Preparation for Music	1	40	0	20
	Music	2	5	2	0
	Garden, &c.	—		—	
	Study	5	0	2	0
	Tea, &c. as before	—		—	
Saturday	Morning Work as before				
	Dinner	1	0	0	40
	Preparation for Drawing	1	40	0	20
	Drawing	2	0	2	0
	House-work	4	0	1	0
	Music	5	0	2	0
	Tea	7	0	0	30
	Evening Prayers	7	30	0	30
	Private Study &c. as before				

Qualifications of Pupils on admission—The age at which the youths
are admitted into the college ranges between 14 and 18 years,
15 or 16 being considered as the most desirable age. A ground-
work of good must be apparent in the character, for though
much may be done for youths afterwards, yet much cannot be
undone. The college is not a school of correction, therefore the
principle of selection cannot be dispensed with. The testimonials required (all of which must be countersigned by a
clergyman) are: '1. A certificate of baptism; 2. A declaration
from the parents or guardians of the youth, stating that he has
attended the services of the Church of England, with their consent and approbation, for the space of, at least, one twelve-
month previous to the date of the application; 3. A medical
certificate, according to a printed form; 4. A recommendation
from a clergyman, who is requested to state, as particularly as
possible, the grounds on which it is given, as well for the
satisfaction of the National Society as to prevent disappointment
and needless expense on the part of the youth and his friends.
Good moral character, amiability, truthfulness, and diligence,
are indispensable requisites. Further information is solicited as
to the youth's temper and disposition, his abilities and attainments, his tastes and habits, his age, size and physical strength,
and as to any other matters from which his general fitness for
the office of schoolmaster may be inferred. A certain degree of
bodily as well as mental vigour is deemed indispensable. A
strong healthy well-grown lad, of amiable disposition and promising talents, who shows an evident desire of knowledge, and
has made good use of the opportunities which he has already
enjoyed, though these may not have been great, is considered
to be the description of youth best fitted to fulfil the designs of
the institution.
Mode of Admission—'These certificates having been received and
approved, the youth is directed to present himself for examination at the college. He is expected to read English prose with
propriety, to spell correctly from dictation, to write a good hand,
to be well acquainted with the outlines of Scripture history, and
to show considerable readiness in working the fundamental rules
of arithmetic. Any further knowledge which he may possess, of
whatever kind, is in his favour, not only, or so much, for its own
sake, as on account of the studious turn of mind and aptness for

receiving instruction which it may appear to indicate. A talent for vocal music and drawing is particularly desirable.

'In the event of his passing this examination with credit, he is received into the college, and remains there on probation for the first three months; after which, if his conduct shall have been satisfactory and he shall have been satisfactory and he shall be found to possess the necessary qualifications, he is apprenticed to the National Society. From this period, till the age of 21, the society is responsible for his education, clothing, and maintenance, being at liberty to make use of his services as a schoolmaster at any time and in any way that may be thought proper. In general the period during which the apprentices are expected to remain under instruction at the college is three years, after which time they are to be placed in situations either as the masters of small schools, or more commonly as assistants in large ones.' At the time of my examination only one pupil had left the institution to be employed as a teacher. He is engaged as assistant to Mr. Irvine in the instruction of the first class in the lower school attached to Greenwich Hospital.

Cost of Maintenance to Pupils—Three annual payments of twenty-five pounds (the first to be paid at entrance) and one outfit of clothes are required with each youth. The above payments (which taken collectively may be regarded in the light of an apprentice fee) are in particular cases commuted for a single sum. The outfit of clothes is not required till the end of the first three months; it costs seven guineas. Each pupil is required to come decently provided with apparel, which is returned to his friends, if required.

Circumstances of the Pupils—At the time of my examination there were 46 pupils under instruction. . . . Of these 46 pupils, 4 were the sons of parents in a superior class of life, 4 were the sons of schoolmasters, 13 were the sons of artisans and tradesmen, 3 were the sons of labourers, 10 were the children of fathers that were dead, 3 were youths brought over from Syria in October, 1841, by Assaad Y Kayat for education in this country, and especially with a view to acquiring some knowledge in medicine, in the hope that they will prove useful as teachers and missionaries on their return to their native land.

The number of pupils has, subsequently to my examination, been filled up, and there are at present several candidates for

admission. The Syrian youths have left the institution; and as
the number of applications is on the increase, it is probable that
the College might have been filled twice, or nearly so, before the
expiration of the first three years, in May, 1844. Great exertions
were made in the first instance to find out suitable candidates,
but spontaneous applications are rapidly on the increase.

Training of Pupils—Pains are taken to secure the health of the
pupils, and for this end, as well as with a view to the moral
effects, they are trained to habits of continual industry and some
self-denial. They are required to rise early, to labour in the farm
and in the garden, and their fare is simple; to borrow again, Mr.
Coleridge's [the Principal's] words: 'The object being to produce
schoolmasters for the poor, the endeavour must be on the one
hand to raise the students morally and intellectually to a certain
standard, while, on the other hand, we train them in lowly
service, not merely to teach them hardihood and inure them to
the duties of a humble and laborious office, but to make them
practically acquainted with the condition of that class of the
community among whom they will have to labour. I say,
"on the one hand," and "on the other," not that there
is any real contrast either in the means taken or the ends
proposed. The labours of the house, the field, and the garden,
are intended to elevate, not depress; the studies of the schoolroom, not to exalt, but to humble. Both alike may be made to
develop the understanding and furnish materials of useful
knowledge, both alike may inspire true elevation and true
humility. The exercises of religion, and those studies by which
knowledge is added to faith, when duly performed, will be
allowed by all to have this double effect. These will be our first
and principal care; while a religious spirit will, it is hoped,
temper and chasten our other occupations, dignifying what
might else be thought menial, and making lowly what might
tend to lift up. The schoolmaster, though his path of duty lie
among the poor, must all the more be raised, not lowered, to his
office.'

Industrial Occupation—'The advantages, I had almost said the
necessity, of balancing the intellectual pursuits of the students
by manual labour scarcely need to be further insisted on. It is,
in the first place, the only way in which such an institution
could be supported, except at an enormous expense; but this is

the least consideration. It is almost the only mode in which the hours not occupied in study could be profitably and innocently passed by a promiscuous assemblage of youths, almost all of whom have so much both to learn and to unlearn. Above all, that which is learnt in this way is itself a most valuable acquirement, more especially to the schoolmaster of the poor. Not merely will it enable him to increase his own comforts without cost, but it will make him practically acquainted with the occupations of those whom he has to instruct, and thus procure him an additional title to their confidence when he comes to act among them, not merely as their teacher but as their adviser and friend.'

... 'The business of the house is partly performed by the students, and partly by female servants. The former clean all the shoes, and knives, &c., lay the cloth, &c. and wait at meals, sweep and dust the school-rooms, keep the courts clean, light and attend to all the fires except those in the kitchen department, regulate the gas lights, keep up a constant supply of water throughout the college by means of a forcing pump, and attend to the drainage, which is also effected by means of a pump. It has not been thought advisable that they should make their beds or wash the floors. It is not likely that they will ever be called upon to perform these offices when they leave the college, while the loss of time, and the injury done to their clothes more than counterbalance any pecuniary saving which could in this way be effected.

'The labours of the farm are principally confined to the care of domestic animals—cows and pigs, and poultry of various kinds. The cows are milked by the youths, and an accurate account kept of the produce of the farm and dairy, which is consumed almost entirely in the establishment. The utility of this part of the establishment is too evident to require a comment.

'The gardens, lawns, and shrubberies furnish abundant employment for those not otherwise engaged; and though a considerable portion of time and attention is necessarily allotted to ornamental horticulture, yet this will be found by no means the least useful or the least appropriate feature of the scheme. There is perhaps no form in which habits of manual industry can be encouraged more easily or more beneficially, either with a view

to the immediate or to the ulterior effect, than by the occupations of the garden. Not to mention their effect upon the health
and happiness of the youths, or the lessons which they teach of
patience, order, and neatness, they are decidedly favourable to
the growth of intelligence, and this of the best kind, more
particularly when connected with the study of botany, which
may with peculiar propriety be called the poor man's science.
When studied on physiological principles, its close connexion
with the best and holiest truths give it a yet higher claim to our
attention.

'Looking forward to the future position of our students,
almost every country schoolmaster might be, with much advantage, both to himself and to his neighbourhood, a gardener
and a florist. The encouragement lately afforded to cottage
gardening has been already attended with the most pleasing
results. The parochial schoolmaster who shall be able to assist
by example and precept in fostering a taste so favourable to the
domestic happiness, and in fact to the domestic virtues of a
rustic population, a taste by which an air of comfort is communicated to the rudest dwelling, and a certain grace thrown
over the simplest forms of humble life, will, it is trusted, in this
as in so many other ways, be made an instrument of good, and
an efficient assistant to the parochial clergyman.'

'The pupils leave their beds at half-past 5 in the morning,
and are again in bed at 10 at night, when the dormitory lights
are extinguished by one of the elder youths; two of whom,
under the inspection and control of the industrial teacher, are
entrusted with the duty of lighting, regulating and extinguish-
ing the gas-lights throughout the establishment. This gives
seven hours and a half for sleep. The remaining 16 hours and a
half are thus divided: they are allowed to remain,—

'One hour in their bed-rooms, half an hour in the morning,
and the same time in the evening. This, however, includes the
time spent in coming and going &c. Habits of personal cleanliness, neatness, and order, are carefully enforced. It is with this
view, as well as for the purpose of private devotion, that a
separate bed-room has been allotted to each youth.

'Four hours and a half are assigned to industrial occupations,
of which half an hour is consumed in coming and going, getting
out and putting by their tools, washing their hands, &c.

'The studies of the college commence at a quarter before 7, with the reading of a collect from the Prayer Book (Prevent us, O Lord, &c). The period of time allotted to study and united devotion amount to about 8 hours.

'Half an hour is allowed for each of the three meals, including the laying and removing of the cloth, &c. They breakfast at 8, dine at 1, and drink tea at 7. Before tea they sing for an hour.

'Two hours and a quarter are reserved for voluntary study and recreation, viz. the half hour before and after dinner, the half hour after tea, which is spent in family devotion, and an hour before bed-time, when the repetitions are learnt which are to be said next morning.

Diet—'The food is of the plainest description, but is the best of its kind, and carefully prepared. It is not given out in rations; if any youth were to eat habitually to excess, he would be reproved for it, as for any other fault; but with this exception (if exception it may be called), there is no stint. Intemperance in eating, where the opportunity is given, is indeed a common vice among boys, but it should be corrected as far as possible by admonition and moral treatment. A discipline so strict as to exclude all temptation appears to be inconsistent with the formation of character. The dietary varies with the seasons; but a general notion may be gathered from the following table:

'Sunday	Cold boiled beef and plum-pudding
'Monday	Soup during winter
'Tuesday	Roast legs of mutton
'Wednesday	Mutton and potatoe-pies
'Thursday	Boiled pork, with suet-dumplings; occasionally roast-beef
'Friday	Irish-stew and rice-pudding
'Saturday	Boiled beef

'One cup of small beer is allowed to each youth at dinner.

'The cost of maintenance, including meat, beer, bread, milk, butter, vegetables, and groceries, has been reduced to 5s. 6d. per week for each person, including masters and servants, and indeed during the last quarter to 5s. 2d.'

Public Worship—At 9 o'clock the pupils of the college, together with the entire school, attend a full cathedral service in the college chapel. The solemnity and devotion with which this is celebrated must impress every one that takes part in it, and doubtless exercises a great influence in the spiritual culture of the inmates of the college. I am not a judge of music, but I have heard from those competent to give an opinion that the skill with which the fine old services of Tallis and others are performed by the pupils without the assistance of an organ is very remarkable. The building, which is a very striking one, in the Byzantine style of architecture, has been so fitted as to leave the nave for worshippers not connected with the institution. The extreme length within the walls, exclusive of an ambulatory round the eastern apse, is 120 feet, the width at the transepts is 60 feet, the breadth of the nave 30 feet, the breadth of the transepts 20 feet. The school children are arranged in the galleries which extend over the north and south transepts; below these, and round the centre of the building, are the pupils in training as schoolmasters, with their teachers, and a few of the children whose voices specially fit them to take part in the choir. On either side, at the steps to the chancel, are the desks of the officiating clergy, the principal, and vice-principal. The windows at the east end, and a circular wheel window in the west side have already, by the piety and munificence of some of the friends of the college, been fitted with painted glass, in harmony with the structure.

The service here is with respect to the college as it were the keystone of the arch—the highest point yet that to which every other part is referred, and from which are derived the stability and consistence of the whole. It is obvious that a private chapel affords facilities for gaining an extensive and practical acquaintance with congregational psalmody and church music in general, that could not otherwise be supplied, owing to the distance of the parish church; but there are other considerations in comparison of which these are as nothing; when we take into account the devotional habits that may here be formed, the religious teaching that will here be given, specially adapted to the students and the children, yet delivered with ministerial authority, and with those devotional accompaniments which add so much to its fitness and weight, and the thorough practical knowledge that may be gained of the formularies, practices, and liturgical discipline—of the characteristic sentiment—the undefined but pervading spirit of the national Church.

At half-past seven the evening service (with some omissions) is read in the lecture-room, lasting about half an hour. On Sundays and holidays the morning service in the chapel commences at eleven; there is also on these days an evening service in the chapel, commencing at four, a short form of family devotion with a psalm or hymn being used in the early morning and evening. The studies of these days are exclusively of a religious kind; the industrial occupations (with the exception of the feeding of the animals, and other necessary works) are suspended. A portion of the day is given up to leisure and quiet recreation. All the Scripture lessons appointed by the Church are read in course; and when there are proper lessons, the chapters omitted in the public service in the chapel are read in the family devotion of the early morning and evening.

It may perhaps seem that in thus stating the aim and circumstances of the institution, I have quoted too largely from Mr. Coleridge's writings, and that in my endeavour to throw together the leading features of his plan, it would have been better not to leave my composition in such a piecemeal state, through an over carefulness to preserve his own forms of expression. But I feel that his attempt deserves the sympathy of all friends to sound education. This Report may possibly fall into the hands of some who will never have an opportunity of reading his own papers, and his forms of expression, however incomplete in their disjointed state, will indicate his views more perfectly than any description which it is in my power to frame.

3. The Official Syllabus for Training College Students, 1854

From the beginning of the system, the central government's inspectors were closely concerned in the preparation of students for teaching. The syllabuses were centrally prescribed and the examinations were conducted by H.M.I.'s until the years between the two World Wars. In the nineteenth century there was a certain degree of conflict between those who felt it was enough to teach students material they might themselves later need to teach and those who saw the training college courses as concerned with the personal education of students and therefore favoured the introduction of a wider curriculum.

SOURCE: Report of the Committee of Council on Education for 1854–5, pp. 17–21.

16

Subjects Proposed for Annual Examinations of Students in Training Schools under Inspection

Note.—In this programme no addition is made to the subjects in which the students of training schools have been accustomed to be examined. The only alteration lies in this,—that, whereas heretofore every student has been examined without distinction of standing, it is proposed for the future to graduate the examinations according to the different years of residence. It will be seen that this arrangement, whilst it prescribes no new subject, does not limit the subjects of instruction in any year to those in which the student is to be examined at the end of the year.

It may often be judged expedient by the authorities of training schools to teach to the students in the first year subjects not prescribed for examination by Her Majesty's Inspectors until the end of the second year; and so of the second and third years.

The examination at the end of the first year offers a parallel to the first examination of undergraduates in the Universities.

Every student will be required to have passed the examination of the first year before he is admitted to that of the second; and so of the second and third years.

FIRST YEAR

Holy Scriptures

1. The History, chronology, and geography of the Bible.
2. More particularly (December 1855) the text of St. John's Gospel.

The Catechism and Liturgy

1. The text. 2. The Scriptural authorities.

Church History

The outlines of Church history, to the Council of Chalcedon.

Reading

To read (December 1855) with a distinct utterance, with due attention to the punctuation, and with a just expression, a passage from Mr. Warren's 'Select Extracts from Blackstone's Commentaries.'

Penmanship*

To write a specimen of the penmanship used in setting copies.
1. A line of large text hand.   2. A passage in small hand.

Arithmetic

1. To prove the usual rules from first principles.

2. To compute with precision and accuracy.

3. To make (with a knowledge of the principles) simple calculations in mensuration.

Mechanics

1. To make (with a knowledge of the principles) simple calculations on the work of mechanical agents, and on the mechanical powers.

2. To know the structure and action of simple machines.

School Management

1. To teach a class in the presence of the inspector.

2. To answer, in writing, questions on the expedients to be used for the purposes of instruction in reading, spelling, writing, and the first four rules of arithmetic.

English Grammar

1. Its principles.

2. To parse (December 1855) a passage from the Chapter on 'The Doctrine of the Hereditary Right to the British Throne,' and 'The History of the Succession of the British Monarchs,' in Warren's Extracts from Blackstone.

3. To paraphrase the same passage.

---

* SIR,   Whitehall, 24 May 1854.
   I am directed by Viscount Palmerston to request that you will submit to the Committee of Council on Education, for their consideration, that one great fault in the system of instruction in the schools of the country lies in the want of proper teaching in the art of writing. The great bulk of the lower and middle orders write hands too small and indistinct, and do not form their letters, or they sometimes form them by alternate broad and fine strokes, which make the words difficult to read. The handwriting which was generally practised in the early part and middle of the last century was far better than that now in common use; and Lord Palmerston would suggest that it would be very desirable that the attention of schoolmasters should be directed to this subject, and that their pupils should be taught rather to imitate broad printing than fine copper-plate engraving. I am, &c,
                                   (Signed)   H. Waddington.
The Secretary of the
Committee of Council on Education.

Geography

1. To be able to describe the outline maps of the four quarters of the globe.

2. To be able to describe the map of each country in Europe.

3. To be able to draw the outlines of the above maps from memory.

History

The outlines of the History of England (to be known thoroughly).

Euclid

The first four books.

Algebra

As far as quadratic equations (inclusive); with problems.

Drawing

1. Drawing freehand from flat examples.

2. Linear geometry by aid of instruments.

3. Linear perspective of horizontal planes, and of rectangular solids having one side parallel with the picture plane.

4. Outline drawing from models.

Vocal Music

SECOND YEAR

The Holy Scriptures

1. The Acts of the Apostles.

2. The Epistle (December 1855) to the Romans.

Church History

The history of the Reformation in England, with the outlines of Church history in the fifteenth and the early part of the sixteenth centuries.

Reading

To read with a distinct utterance, with due attention to punctuation, and with a just expression, a passage from Milton's 'Paradise Lost,' or from Shakspeare.

Penmanship

(As in First Year)

Arithmetic

1. The use of logarithms. 2. Compound interest and annuities.

School Management

1. To teach a class in the presence of the Inspector.
2. To answer questions in writing on the following subjects:
    a. The expedients to be used in teaching the elements of geography and history, the higher rules of arithmetic and book-keeping.
    b. The different methods of organising an elementary school.
    c. The form of, the mode of keeping, and of making returns from, school registers.
3. To answer questions on the subject-matter of the Reading Lesson-books used in schools.
4. To write a theme on some practical questions of education, founded on moral considerations.

English Grammar and Composition

1. To paraphrase (December 1855) a passage from Milton's 'Paradise Lost' (Book III.), or from Shakspeare's 'Henry V.'
2. To analyze the same passage (according to Mr. Morell's work).
3. To answer questions on the style and subject-matter of the work, or part of work, named.

Geography

1. Physical. 2. Political. 3. Commercial. 4. Popular astronomy.

History

1. The Constitutional history of England.
2. The progress of the people, and of manners and customs in England.

Physical Science

1. The instruments most commonly used in mechanics, hydrostatics, pneumatics, electricity, and optics.
2. The elements of inorganic chemistry.

Higher Mathematics

1. The sixth book of Euclid, with problems in the first four books.

2. The subjects which follow quadratic equations in Lund's edition of Wood's Algebra.

3. Trigonometry.

4. Levelling, land-surveying, and the first steps in practical astronomy.

Drawing

1. Advanced freehand drawing from flat examples.

2. Advanced linear geometry by aid of instruments.

3. Linear perspective: 1, of rectangular forms, none of whose sides are parallel with the picture plane; 2, of polygons, plane and solid; 3, of cylindrically spherical forms.

4. Shaded drawing from objects.

5. Drawing of objects from memory.

Vocal Music

THIRD YEAR

The Holy Scriptures

1. The Bible generally.   2. The evidences of Christianity.

School Management

1. To teach a class in the presence of the Inspector.

2. To write an essay upon a thesis embracing the principles of education.

Vocal Music

Drawing

In addition to the above subjects, students of the third year will be examined in one of the following subjects, at their option. They will be required to specify the subject at the commencement of the third year.

1. Mental science as applied to education.

2. Experimental science (especially as applied to manufactures and agriculture).

3. Higher mathematics.

4. Languages (ancient or modern), as a means of intellectual discipline.

5. History.

4. The Warwick and Leamington Schoolmasters, Association

The efforts made by Kay-Shuttleworth to improve the schools by offering wider facilities and inducements to young people to train as teachers had its effect on teachers already in service. Local Associations of teachers organising lecture courses and summer schools became a feature of the educational scene in many areas.

SOURCE: Report of the Committee of Council on Education for 1850–1, pp. 231–2.

Objects of the Warwick & Leamington Schoolmasters' Association as stated in its annual report.

'In consequence of the high standard of qualification set up by the Committee of Council of Education, for masters of National and other schools, it is necessary that the masters should make themselves fully acquainted with the various branches of knowledge specified in the Minutes of the Committee of Council on Education. In order to do this, an accurate knowledge of arithmetic, grammar, geography, sacred and profane history, algebra, land-surveying, levelling and mensuration, is absolutely necessary. Several of the schoolmasters of this part of Warwickshire have only a partial acquaintance with some of these subjects, and desire to increase their information by meeting together at stated periods, when they may assist each other by mutual instruction, and occasionally obtain the advice and direction of those who may countenance their efforts, and fully qualify themselves in the subjects for examination at the yearly inspection'.

Its operations are thus described in the Report for 1850:

'For the information of those unacquainted with the same, the Association was established in May, 1848, for the "mutual improvement of schoolmasters, whose schools are in connection with the Church of England". The meetings of the Association have been held regularly every three weeks, alternately, at Warwick and Leamington National Schools, when papers of an educational character (compiled by the several members themselves) have been read; the various subjects advanced have been discussed, the several branches of education required by the Committee of the Council of Education have been studied, and all with the same desire, on the part of the members, as expressed in the last Report, viz. that they might acquire the best

views and means whereby they might promote the sound education of the children committed to their care, and also that they
might become better qualified themselves to fill the important
stations assigned to them, viz. that of training up the young to
do their duty "in that state of life unto which it shall please God
to call them". With respect to the promise made in the last
Report, that it was proposed that extra attention should be paid
to the 13th rule of the Association, the Secretary feels great
pleasure in being able to show that the said promise has been
fulfilled, by having it in his power to lay before the members
and friends of the Association a list of the subjects on which
papers have been read to the Association during the past year,
which at once shows that it is a good one, and that some progress has been made in the right direction.'

The following is a list of subjects on which papers have been
read:

1. On 'English Grammar and Paraphrasing' by Mr. Newn-
ham of Hill, 2. On 'The Geography of Europe' by Mr. J. E.
Baker of Snitterfield, 3. On 'Astronomy' by Mr. R. Baker of
Leamington, 4. on 'Church History' and 5. On 'Agricultural
Chemistry' by Mr. Town of Napton, 6. On 'Religious Teach-
ing' by Mr. Hunter of Claverdon, 7. On 'Physical Geography'
by Mr. Wynn of Warwick, 8. On 'Music' by Mr. Smithom of
Fretton, 9. On 'The Rites and Ceremonies of the Apostolic
Age' by Mr. J. E. Baker of Smithfield, 10. On 'Ancient Geo-
graphy' by Mr. Baker of Leamington, 11. On 'Drawing' by
Mr. Fretton of Southam, 12. On 'The Reformation in England'
by Mr. Bolton of Warwick. The Association would here tender
their grateful thanks to the Rev. Herbert Hill of the College,
Warwick, for an interesting lecture delivered before the
Association on 'English Literature', and they also beg to express
the hope that new friends may be found during the coming year
to assist in a similar way. In reference to the working of the
Association, the Secretary begs to mention one point especially
which has been, and still must be, productive of much real
good. It is that of members arranging sets of useful questions on
school subjects, and laying them before the Association in order
that each member may have an opportunity of solving them in
the interval that elapses between the meetings. In this way the
whole of the information that can be obtained on the subjects

by the various members, is brought before the whole, and leading, as it does, to much discussion, must necessarily tend greatly
to the mutual improvement of the members. In the last Report
it was stated, that the operations of the Society had been much
hindered for want of funds. In this respect there has been a
decided improvement during the past year caused in the first
place by an increase of subscriptions, and, in the second, by the
kindness of the Committee of Council of Education, in allowing
the Association to purchase books at reduced prices, thereby
causing an advance towards obtaining that most important
desideratum, a 'Schoolmasters' Library'.

5. A Letter from a Schoolmaster giving his Experience of Assistant Schoolmasters, 1868

This letter from a headmaster was sent to one of the Assistant Commissioners employed by the Schools Inquiry Commission. It throws
some interesting light on the supply of teachers for schools that
catered for children of the middle-classes.

SOURCE: Report of the School Inquiry Commission, Vol. IX,
    1868, pp. 846–8.

SIR,

I have been in the habit of employing, as under-masters,
graduates of some University—generally a Scotch University,
and trained certificated masters of a high class. The latter
generally come to me from Battersea, or the Boro Road T.C.
But a few years ago I happened to open a quite new vein; in
fact, the vein of the regular School assistant, the young (and
sometimes old or middle aged) man, who has drifted into this
kind of work from want of ability or strength of will to gain a
footing in a trade or profession. These men—and there are
thousands of them—have in many cases been educated at some
good school, and have even had a year or two at some University; but they have never been able to rise to anything like a
feeling of the importance or necessity of accurate scholarship.
Nor are their teaching powers superior; in fact, they have no
idea whatever of teaching. All they can do, and all they do do, is
hearing lessons.

There is one case, the details of which I remember very
distinctly—a young man of about two and twenty, of fair manners, 'gentlemanly' appearance, and generally presentable

ways. He has been the sole assistant-master in a grammar school in the north of England—a grammar school of fair reputation. I wrote to the Headmaster of this grammar school, and was informed that Mr. —— had been a very good master—had taught what is called 'junior Latin'—had taken a 'Virgil' class, and had prepared pupils for the Oxford local examinations. I therefore considered him quite equal to the work I had for him which lay in some of the lowest forms. In the course of the first week two or three suspicious signs showed themselves which made me rather uneasy. For example, he had written on the blackboard the word 'compositive'; and he appeared to me to look rather unappreciative and restless when I one day taught a class in his presence a page of Ellis's Latin Exercises. This was one of the subjects he had to teach. It occurred to me that it would be well to ask him to write out the night before the page which the class had for next day; and I volunteered to correct any 'minor errors' he might have. The page was one between the 12th and 20th. He did so. His version of the page contained fourteen errors of the worst description; errors which no fairly-taught boy of ten ought to commit. Among these were hominoram, viribus (for the dat. pl. of vir), surgaverat, and other fine specimens of 'junior' Latinity. Of course I immediately looked out for a successor for him. I was, however, still unfortunate enough to follow the same vein. I could find no one by the private means I usually employ, and my advertisements called up letters in which there was a fair variety of careless spelling and weak composition. I selected two or three of the best. In an interview with one of these I proposed that as a kind of examination he should write out a page of Ellis. He accepted the proposal cheerfully. I left him for an hour. On my return he had not written a word; and he was obliged to admit that he was unequal even to that very junior test. The same test was politely declined—not from a feeling of offended dignity, but confessedly from inability—by a B.A. of Trinity College, Dublin. He said he had forgotten his junior Latin!

I believe from what I have heard from other heads of schools that there is a perfect army of such men, who travel from school to school of the lower 'middle class' and 'train' the boys committed to their care in every kind of blunder and inaccuracy.

But I do not think this the greatest evil that haunts English schools and diminishes their power. There is one which is to be found in every school in the kingdom, from Eton down to the cheapest school for the poorest classes. Until this evil is recognised and the right means taken for its cure and future prevention, Government may issue a commission every year, and no good will come of them. The prime evil under which *all* schools without exception labour, is want of power. That is, they are under-officered. In the public schools, there are too many boys in each form, generally two or three times more than the master can do justice to; in the private schools, where the proportion of master to pupils is much more favourable to the interests of the latter, the private schoolmasters take care to put themselves on an equality of inefficiency, by teaching too many subjects, and by taking too many boys of too many different ages, and at too many different stages of advancement in too many different subjects. What is the reason why the education of the majority of boys in Great Britain is not a fair one? Simply that there has been no one to see that every boy does his work, and that he does it in the best style. Even if there were nothing done of what is called teaching, but if every schoolmaster could see that every boy did his best, the mental and moral effects of the attention and notice on the part of the master and of the constant efforts 'to do his best' on the part of the boy would be incalculable. At present, and I am sure that this is the case in nine schools out of ten, it is a lottery whether a boy is 'heard his lesson', and he often leaves it undone altogether on chance or leaves it to chance to get a little help to enable him, not to satisfy the fair demands of his own conscience and of his master, but to 'pull through'. The subjective element, the constant effort to do one's best, is the prime element of education, is in fact itself education, and the best and highest education in the world. The corresponding objective element—the necessity—supplied by the pressure and authority of the master, of doing one's best, ought to exist in every school in the highest degree of power and ought to supplement all that is wanting in the boy of the former element. Omnipresent encouragement and cheer, all-sufficient force to compel, these constitute the ideal school. When one thinks of the 'conspicuous absence' of these in almost every school, when one thinks of the numerous causes at work to prevent even a weak growth of these, one must either laugh horribly or be very near to the melting mood. The result is what we know. A large number of boys are more or less neglected; and they form moral and mental habits of the loosest, most irregular and inaccurate kind. In fact their training and discipline is not a training to strength, clearness and self-respect, but to weakness, shuffling and slovenliness of thought and expression. What would be thought of a locomotive establishment which boasted that two out of every ten locomotives turned out by it were good, while three were only fair and the rest useless? We are an uneducated people, but, uneducated as we are, I would rather see introduced into all schools the Philistine principle of paying for results than have things continue as they are at present. Impracticable! absurd! shout a chorus of schoolmasters. I don't know about that. One good immediate effect would be that no schoolmaster would take a boy without a definite limitation as to what he proposed to teach him. At present, the private schoolmaster is too amenable to the whim of the parent, who asks for Natural Philosophy, Botany, Natural History, two or three languages, two or three Mathematical subjects, and a large group of other subjects included under the all-embracing term English to be taught his boy; while public schoolmasters are far too much subjected to the school boy's laziness. There are several other helps towards the same great end. One is to make the salaries of schoolmasters higher, and to do all in the power of Society and the State to elevate his social standing (though indeed schoolmasters could do this for themselves, if they would endeavour to cease being mere Dominies); another is to have training colleges for middle-class teachers, and these, if begun by Government, would quickly pay as a money speculation; and a third is to erect large schools, where there are plenty of masters, where the forms are properly graduated and where there is a well organised system of promotion for each boy'.

6. Teaching Practice in the Nineteenth Century, 1877

This usually took place in schools attached to training colleges as practice or 'demonstration' schools and the regular work of pupils in such schools had to be subordinated to the arrangements for students' teaching. One such school was Holy Trinity National School at Ripon which was much used by Ripon Diocesan College and the log book gives some idea of the heavy load of school practice and students' 'criticism' lessons.

SOURCE: Log Book of Holy Trinity National School, Ripon.

1877

Monday, October 1st.   Three criticism lessons given by students of the second year. Subjects of lessons 'Volcanoes', 'The House-Fly' and a Conversational Spelling lesson on A Hat. The Revd. E. B. Badcock present during the lessons and criticism. The Revd. J. H. Goodier took classes 1 and 2 to Scripture in the morning.

Friday.   Three criticism lessons given by students of the second year, the subjects being 'Division of Decimals' to class 1, 'Chalk' to class 4 and 'Birds of Prey' to class 2. The Revd. E. B. Badcock was present during the third lesson. Students are not practising teaching today having had the time given them to prepare for the examination in Religious Knowledge.

Monday, October 8th.   Attendance good both in the morning and in the afternoon. Miss Woods absent in the morning, superintended the infant school. Four students instead of five are practising this week and that number will be the number in future serving at one time.

Friday.   Three criticism lessons given by students of the second year, two of them being to Infants, one on 'The Ostrich' the other on 'The Idea of an Island'. The Revd. J. Gilcare and the Revd. J. H. Goodier visited during the afternoon.

Tuesday, October 16th.   The Revd. Canon Tinling and the Revd. H. Sandford, Her Majesty's Inspectors, visited the school to hear lessons given by students of the second year.

Thursday.   Lessons given by Students of the second year before Her Majesty's Inspector until 11.15. Criticism lesson given by a student of the first year in the presence of the Revd. Canon Tinling and the Revd. H. Sandford and the Revd. E. B. Badcock.

7. Science in the Training Colleges, 1884

The only training colleges in England up to this time were denominational and residential. The Royal Commission on Technical

Instruction found a paucity of science teaching in these colleges and recommended that the denominationalist monopoly of training facilities should be ended by permitting school boards to set up day training colleges.

SOURCE: Second Report of the Royal Commission on Technical Instruction, Vol. 1, 1884, p. 526.

The teaching of art and science subjects, in the Training Colleges of Great Britain for elementary school teachers, is very defective. The inspection on the part of the Science and Art Department has, until lately, been greatly neglected, owing to the divided responsibility for the Colleges, of the Education Department and the Kensington authorities. The answers received by the examiners to such questions as the following— 'Write out the heads of a lecture to an elementary class on the chemical and physical properties of water, mentioning the experiments that you would show, and your object in showing them' prove conclusively that the students have no idea as to how such a simple matter ought to be brought before a class. It would greatly conduce to sound and efficient training in science, and particularly in the methods of teaching, if those students in training who have shown an aptitude for science work could be sent annually to the Normal School of Science at South Kensington, or to other approved efficient institutions. The provision for art teaching in most of the training colleges is inferior even to that at present made for science, and an entire reform in this respect is urgently needed; and similar measures should be taken for systematic instruction in art as in science. Considerable attention is, as we have said elsewhere, paid to drawing in the Normal School at Dublin, where it is taught by a competent art master.

The School Boards of our great cities are fully alive to the defective character of the instruction of pupil-teachers. In London, Liverpool and elsewhere, they have endeavoured to apply a partial remedy by introducing joint instruction under special teachers, qualified in each subject, instead of having each headmaster to instruct the pupil teachers of his own school in every subject. The Education Department has also taken a small step in the right direction, by somewhat limiting the number of hours that the pupils may be employed in teaching, so as to give them a little more leisure for learning. No considerable improvement can, however, be expected until the great school boards are authorised to establish colleges for training teachers. These colleges would be day schools and need not receive from the State enormous capitation grants like those now given to the English Denominational Training Colleges, but only small allowances like those granted to day students in those of Scotland.

8. The Education of Pupil Teachers

From 1846 it became possible for a senior boy or girl in an elementary school to be apprenticed to a head teacher under Committee of Council Regulations for a five year period. During the five years the pupil teacher taught in the school and was taught out of school hours by the head teacher. At the end of the period of apprenticeship, those who gained the best results in their examination were awarded Queen's Scholarships enabling them to study in training colleges. The pupil-teacher system was a great advance on anything which had existed hitherto but one weakness was the limitation placed on the apprentice's study both by its being confined to the period following the normal day's work and by its depending on the wisdom and resourcefulness of a head teacher who might have little energy left by the end of the day. Thus in the later years of the century pupil-teacher centres—sometimes called 'colleges'—were set up to supplement the efforts of head teachers. Extract (a.)

After 1902 it became the aim of the Board of Education to encourage future teachers to attend a secondary school and to proceed from there to a training college and the number of pupil teachers began to decline. Quite a few of pupil-teacher centres were eventually absorbed into new local authority secondary schools—as at Brighouse. Extract (b.)

(a) SOURCE: Second Report of the Royal Commission on Technical Instruction, Vol. V, 1884, pp. 209–10. Pupil Teachers' College, Liverpool School Board—evidence of the Chairman.

Pupil Teachers' College—Liverpool School Board

With a view to give their pupil teachers, by means of collective classes, the benefits of a broader kind of instruction than they could otherwise receive, the Liverpool School Board, by the advice of H.M. Inspector, established early in the year 1876 a college for its female pupil-teachers; and about two years later extended similar advantages to its male pupil-teachers. The college is managed by a council appointed by the Board. The premises for the female teachers consist of two private houses, which one of the members of the Board has placed at the Board's service free of rent; the male teachers are accommodated in rooms specially set apart at one of the Board's schools. The subjects taught are arithmetic, grammar, music, history and (for males only) Latin, mathematics, magnetism and electricity, and acoustics, light, and heat, and (for females only) the art of teaching, French, domestic economy and animal physiology. The lecturers were at first selected without regard to their being certificated teachers, but owing to recent changes in the wording of the Education Code, they are now chosen from the certificated head teachers of the Board and other schools in the city. For music, Latin and science subjects, however, the choice is not limited to such persons.

The classes meet for instruction as follows, viz:

> Females—First year pupil teachers. On Wednesday afternoons from 2 to 6.30 including 1½ hours for tea and recreation.
>
> Others—On Tuesday evenings from 5 to 8, including one hour for tea and recreation, and
>
> All meet on Saturday mornings from 9.30 to 12.15.
>
> Males—All meet on Friday evenings from 6 to 8.45, including three quarters of an hour for tea and recreation, and on Saturday mornings from 9 to 12.30.

For facility of their instruction the pupil teachers are divided into two groups, according as the schools to which they respectively belong are examined in the Spring or the Autumn, and in each group are classified according to the years of their apprenticeship. Out of private funds tea is provided at both centres for the pupil teachers, so that the inconvenience and loss of time is avoided, which would necessarily occur if the teachers had to go to their homes for this purpose before coming to the classes. Central reference libraries (including a valuable collection of scientific works presented to the Board by a local science committee) have been provided for the pupil teachers, and a small sum per head per annum is devoted by the Board to their extension. The female pupil teachers have the privilege of practising on the pianos which are provided for the use of the teacher of vocal music. Omnibus tickets are given from a private source to those pupil teachers who come from a distance, but only on condition of their regular attendance at the classes. By means of these College classes, the following advantages are secured:

1. The lessons, being each of about one hour's duration, give an opportunity of treating the subjects more broadly than is possible in the very limited time at the disposal of the ordinary teachers.
2. The emulation and interest produced by collective oral teaching.
3. The pupil teachers receive instruction from teachers specially selected for their proficiency in their respective subjects.
4. The influence of social intercourse.

The responsibility of the head teachers for the instruction of their respective pupil teachers is not removed or interfered with in any way by the college training, such training being held to be merely supplementary to the head teachers' instruction.

The results of this system, as shown by the positions taken by the Board's pupil teachers in the scholarship examination, are very encouraging. Last year the proportion of the successful female candidates from all England and Wales who gained a first class was only 29·6 per cent. In Liverpool the proportion was about the same, say 30 per cent, for the candidates who had not the advantages of class instruction, while for those from Roman Catholic Schools it was 42·8 per cent and from the Board schools 52·3 per cent. Among the successful male candidates the contrast is still more striking; the proportion of candidates securing places in the first class being, for all England and Wales, 25 per cent; for Liverpool voluntary schools, 28 per cent; for Liverpool board schools, 57 per cent.

The expense to the Board (without rent of premises) of carrying on the College is about £450 per annum, being at the rate of about £2. 8. 0. for each pupil teacher.

(b) SOURCE: Board of Education, Report of First Inspection of the Pupil Teacher Centre, Brighouse, Yorkshire, 1906.

17

Number of Assistant Teachers: 2; including one permanent and one visiting.

Local Education Authority or other Body providing the Centre and receiving grants: Brighouse Town Council.

In Receipt of Grants under the Board's Regulations for the Instruction and Training of Pupil Teachers.

Number of	Boys	Girls	Total
Pupil teachers	—	25	25
Pupils in the Preparatory Class	—	8	8

Local Education Authorities maintaining the Elementary Schools in which the Pupil Teachers are employed.

Local Education Authority	No. of Pupil Teachers
Brighouse Town Council	24
Yorks. West Riding County Council	1

Ages of	14	15	16	17	18	19 and over
Pupil Teachers	—	—	7	14	2	2
Pupils in Preparatory Class	2	6	—	—	—	—

Fees (Yearly): Nil.

Governing Body: The Education Committee of Brighouse Town Council.

PREMISES & EQUIPMENT

This Pupil Teacher Centre for Girls serves the needs of Brighouse and district and is financed and managed by the Education Committee of Brighouse. Apart from one or two small private ventures, there is no provision for the secondary education of girls in the district. The need of a Public Secondary School for girls is recognised both by the Local Authority and by the West Riding County Council.

When in 1905 application was made to the Board of Education for the recognition of this Centre, the Education Authority at Brighouse expressed its intention to establish a Girls' Secondary School and transfer the Centre to it. Upon this understanding recognition was granted to the Centre to be held temporarily at the Mechanics Institute and the Board expressed its opinion that these premises were quite unfitted for anything beyond temporary occupation. Up to the date of the Full Inspection no definite step had been taken by the Brighouse Authority towards the erection of permanent premises.

The Mechanics' Institute at Brighouse in which the classes for Pupil Teachers and Intending Pupil Teachers are held is situated in the centre of the town. It contains, besides a public reading room, laboratories, Art room and class rooms used in the evening for technical instruction.

The centre has the use of two class rooms upon the first floor, both of which have recently been redecorated. Of these one is a long room fitted with antiquated long desks and so ill-lighted that the back of the room is always useless without artificial light and in the front of the room pupils face such light as there is. The other room behind it and smaller is furnished with new single desks and has good light. In both rooms the noise of passing traffic much interferes with the teaching.

There is no cloak-room accommodation whatever; hats and coats are hung upon pegs in the two class rooms; there is no separate accommodation for the teachers, and the office accommodation is inadequate. The only playground is a small and narrow yard rather resembling a passage than a playground.

The laboratory and lecture room which are used by the pupils on Saturday morning only are good and the apparatus is adequate.

Such accommodation as these premises provide is only tolerable pending the erection of permanent buildings and on condition that all despatch is used in providing them. The present premises do not admit of extension or improvement.

CURRICULUM

The pupils in attendance fall into four distinct groups: 1. Pupil Teachers in the second year of engagement; 2. Pupil Teachers in the first year; 3. Intending Pupil Teachers of a second year; and 4. Intending Pupil Teachers of a first year.

These groups differ from each other so much in attainment that in such subjects as French, Mathematics and Science it is impossible to take the groups together without great loss of time and sacrifice of efficiency.

The present staff of two teachers is insufficient to cope with the work; often while instruction is being given to one section another has to do private work. Should one teacher be absent through illness, the work of half the pupils would come to a standstill. Both the teachers are seriously overworked, and have no free time for preparation of lessons and correction of work. It is unfair to both pupils and teachers that such conditions should continue. The appointment of at least one further assistant, preferably to take Science and Mathematics, is indispensable.

The arrangement of curriculum and time-table is as effective as the present unsatisfactory conditions permit.

GENERAL SUMMARY

Within the narrow and unsatisfactory limits, which the present premises and the insufficient staff impose, the Centre is well organised. The girls are well behaved, industrious and intelligent, and the relations between pupils and teachers are satisfactory. As no playing field has been provided for them by the Governors, teachers and pupils have joined a local Hockey Club, and thus get some opportunity for outdoor exercise.

Responsibility for the many defects of the Centre rests upon the Governors and upon them alone. Unless they are prepared both to improve facilities in the temporary premises and to proceed at once to erect permanent premises for the proposed Secondary School, the Governors would be well advised in closing this Centre and sending their girls elsewhere.

9. An Early University Department of Education

Departments of Education had their origin as day training departments attached to University Colleges from about 1890. They were designed to provide students with a way of training for the profession of elementary school teacher without having to go into residence in a denominational training college. It can be seen from the extract that students were obliged to practise in the whole range of elementary school subjects. Some of the detailed instructions here seem tiresome and unnecessary today but some of the advice offered is undoubtedly sound.

SOURCE: The University of Leeds, Education Department, undated, early present century. *Practice Work in Schools*, pp. 1–6.

Time

Any time unavoidably lost during the period of practice, except for Government Examinations, must be made up after its close. If any student is compelled by illness to be absent, communication of the reason must be made at once both to the Head Teacher and to the Member of Staff in charge of the school.

Students must be at the schools at least five minutes before the regular times of opening, except when train service renders this impossible. Whenever this is the case a written permission signed by Professor Welton must be obtained by the student and shown to the Head Teacher.

Each student, on entering school both in the morning and in the afternoon, should enter the time of arrival in the Time-book provided by the Head Teacher.

Inspection

H.M. Inspector will inspect and examine in Practical Teaching and Reading and Recitation during the practice time. He will examine the students' note books and inspect their teaching and class management. Each student should bring his Criticism book and last year's report to school on the day of the inspection in order that it may be examined.

Discipline

Each student should realize that he has full responsibility under the Head Teacher for the discipline of his class, and should, on taking charge of it, at once assume that responsibility, and show in manner, attitude and tone, that he intends to secure obedience.

One who is quite convinced that the pupils are going to obey has no real trouble in maintaining order; therefore, make up your mind beforehand that you are going to be obeyed.

Your relations with the class should be pleasant and kindly, yet firm and authoritative. Do not be lax in your dealings with the class on the first day in the hopes of strengthening the discipline later. Remember that you are strangers to the children and that the first step is to establish your authority. As you and the children get to know each other the relations may become gentler and more familiar, and the government freer. It is easier to relax than to tighten the reins of discipline.

Aim at winning the confidence, respect and willing obedience of the children. You will find that calling them by their Christian names is a great aid in getting on good terms with them; therefore, make a special effort to learn all their names on the first day. The class teacher should be asked to furnish a plan of the class-desks with the children's names entered on it, and the children should be required to occupy those positions, at any rate until you are thoroughly familiar with their names.

Try to learn the individual character of each child, that in cases of bad behaviour you may be able so to deal with the individual as to secure the co-operation of the child in his own improvement. You will find few ways of doing this more effective than taking part in outdoor games and helping to organise them. Without this, indeed, you cannot hope to be successful. When you know a child you can generally speak to him with more effect in private than in public.

Do not be continually finding fault. The eye is a better instrument of discipline than the tongue, and less likely to get out of control. Use tact and judgement in expressing disapproval or approval, blame or praise. Be economical of threats; punish as seldom as possible. Never threaten any punishment which you do not impose. On no account must you, on any provocation whatever, inflict corporal punishment in any form. Breaches of discipline so serious as to require corporal punishment should be reported to the Head Teacher, before whom you may also bring instances of continued neglect of work or obvious carelessness or indifference. But remember that every such report implies to some extent a comparative failure in your own powers as a disciplinarian.

General Syllabus of Work

The students should practise teaching in the following subjects:

		Lessons per week
1.	Literature	3
	Reading	
	Composition, with Spelling and Writing	
	Grammar	5
	Music	
2.	History	3
3.	Geography	3
4.	Nature Study	2
5.	Mathematics, including Arithmetic and Geometry	5
6.	Drawing	2
7.	Physical Training	2
8.	Needlework (Women only)	1

Writing

Formal Writing Lessons should be given in Classes 2 and 3 only. These should take the form of transcription of a continuous copy, which may be a paragraph constructed by teacher and pupils on matter already learnt. The teacher should write the copy before the class drawing attention as he does so to points needing special care. These points may require special detached practice before the writing of the paragraph begins.

In Classes 4, 5, 6 and 7 the practice in written composition and in transcribing summaries of lessons should be sufficient. Formal lessons in writing should be taken only if necessary to correct special faults. Though rapid writing should be aimed at in the upper classes, the writing should not become slipshod or careless. There should be a steady improvement both in legibility and in rapidity during the three weeks.

Attention should be paid to the position of each child's body. The position in writing should be an erect one, facing square to the desk. The position of the left arm is important. Special watchfulness will be found necessary to prevent bending over the book, which should, under no circumstances, be allowed. Slouching attitudes should be prohibited. The pen should be held freely and easily. Stiffness in holding the pen hinders free and rapid writing.

10. The College Rules of the Westminster Training College

One of the features of the system of resident training colleges was until very recently the degree of control exercised by the College over the lives of the students. This example is quite typical of its period.

SOURCE: F. C. Pritchard, *The Story of Westminster College, 1851–1951*, Epworth Press, 1951, pp. 204–5.

WESLEYAN TRAINING COLLEGE: RULES
(in force during the whole of Dr. Rigg's Principalship)

Domestic Routine—The students shall rise at six o'clock; assemble in their day-rooms at half-past six, and in the dining-room for breakfast and Family Worship, at eight. They shall dine at one o'clock, have tea at five, supper at a quarter to nine and meet for Evening Worship at nine. All shall retire to their dormitories at or before ten, and all lights shall be put out at twenty past ten.

Dormitories—1. Before leaving his room in the morning, each student shall strip his bed and open the window.

2. The students shall be responsible for the order and cleanliness of their own rooms, and the time from 7.40 a.m. to eight o'clock will be allowed them to do whatever is necessary for that purpose.

3. The dormitories shall not be used during the day, except for half an hour after dinner and tea.

4. No student is allowed to deface, or stick anything on, or drive any nail into, the walls of his bedroom.

5. The use of candles and lamps in the bedrooms is strictly prohibited. All boxes must be removed into the rooms provided to receive them.

6. There shall be no gathering of the students in the bedrooms.

Absence from College—No student shall be absent from the College without permission from the Vice-Principal, except during the time prescribed for holidays and recreation.

No student shall be called away from class exercises to see friends.

Every student shall regularly attend drill.

Officers—The following officers will be appointed, viz.—a Censor, four Curators, two Monitors from the students of each year, and a Precentor and Librarian.

The Censor shall keep a record of the attendance of the students at their general assemblies and render such general assistance as the Vice-Principal may from time to time require.

The Curators shall be responsible for the order of the day-rooms during the hours of private study.

The Precentor shall lead the singing at Family Worship, assist the Music-Master, and have the charge of the library and the distribution of the books.

Two Monitors shall be appointed weekly for each day-room, who shall ring the bell according to the daily routine, and be responsible for the management of the gas in the day-rooms and corridors.

Public Worship and Religious Exercises—The students shall attend the Wesleyan Chapel, Westminster, on the morning and evening of every Lord's day, and on Wednesday evenings, and shall, in the matter of religious observances, conform to Methodist rules and usages.

General Discipline—The students will be held subject in their general conduct to the direction and control of the Principal, and of the Vice-Principal as usually representing him. The Committee have power to expel from the Institution any student who may be found deserving of this severe penalty. It is expected that the students will, by the propriety of their general appearance and behaviour, honour the character of the Institution with which they are identified; and by orderly habits, and an earnest and devout life, seek to prepare themselves for the fulfilment, in its highest sense and spirit, of the calling, to which, as Christian teachers, they have devoted themselves.

JAMES H. RIGG, D.D.
Principal

11. School Practice about 1920

One of the distinctive features of the training college has been the amount of time and effort devoted to school practice. There is little doubt but that it bulks as large in the minds of many students today as it appears to have done in the period with which this extract is concerned.

SOURCE: Angel Lawrence, *St. Hilda's College, 1858–1958*, passage contributed by M. Dibb, pp. 86–8.

About 1920 the pattern of school practice was something like this. On returning to college after a vacation either the first year students or the second years would be sure to be going straight into a period of school practice—the dreaded 'S.P.'. It would have loomed like an uneasy shadow at the back of the mind during the holiday and there would be an eager rush, after depositing luggage, to look at the notice-board in the lecture-room to see to which school you were allocated and whom your S.P. mates would be. This matter had all been arranged by the College staff and was accepted without question. There were various less-liked schools, there were the more distant ones, there were the nearby ones, there were the known-to-be-difficult ones. Having seen your allocation you went to commiserate with your less fortunate friends or yourself receive sympathy in your ill-luck.

In any case, school practice meant a period of very hard work, long hours, early rising, much discomfort and the anxiety as to whether you would be able to satisfy the college tutors, the head teacher and the children, and whether you would secure a reasonable teaching mark. It was the recognised vogue to look with dread upon school practice and senior students painted the picture with full horrors before the juniors, yet for all that worry a student met the challenge and enjoyed the experience and after each period felt a little more able to meet the real job of teaching when she left college.

The easiest schools to be posted to were schools within the city, the very nearest being the old Blue Coat School. This meant that you need not leave college so early in the morning, and you would be home earlier in the evening and be able to get on with some of the next day's preparation. The hardest hit were those who had to set off at an early hour and walk to North Road or Elvet Stations, take a train and then have quite a distance to walk at the end of the journey to reach the school. The same journey had to be retraced in the evening. The most pleasantly placed, I think, were those at Gilesgate Moor or Sherburn Hill, for in this case there was the thrill of being conveyed by horse-drawn waggonette from the top of Gilesgate Hill. You were able leisurely to continue your breakfast while others had hurried off to walk to the station, then, at the respectable hour of 8.15 you hurried up to the top of Gilesgate carrying your case, various items of school practice luggage and your famous lunch tin, and there at the top the waggonette was waiting for you. You climbed in with a 'How-do-you-do' to the driver and a remark about the weather and then scanned the hill to see who came puffing up at the last minute. Finally, and most anxiously, everyone looked to see which member of the college staff came gracefully up at the last, for she would be staying with you all day.

Each group in a school had to be responsible for such mundane things as the kettle, the tea-pot, the tea-towel and the day's ration of tea and sugar. You each took your own cup and saucer, towel and soap. It was pleasant to trundle along the level stretch to Gilesgate Moor in the fresh morning air, going over in your mind your plans for the day's lessons. Students taught a full class for the whole day, and some of the classes were very large ones. It was quite probable that you would have a special 'crit' lesson to give, to be heard by the college tutor or perhaps by the rest of the students in that school as well. For physical training lessons you hurried into the often quite inadequate cloakroom accommodation or even hid behind the blackboard, while you struggled into your gym tunic and shoes before giving the lesson and this caused mixed expressions of amusement or amazement from your class because class teachers seldom or never presented this picture of a properly turned-out P.T. instructor.

Lunch time provided a welcome break. The children went home to their dinners, the school door was probably locked and there descended on the building a calm and a quiet. Out came those 'horrible tins'. They were about $6'' \times 6''$ square and $2''$ deep with nasty sharp-edged lids and a rather scratched and battered look, for they had carried many, many school practice lunches. The contents were four rather thick sandwiches of bread and butter spread with jam, marmalade or a smear of Bovril. Many an old student has looked on Bovril's famous beefy advertisements and thought of school practice.

During the break you might be fortunate enough to be given the criticism of your lesson by the College tutor and this saved time in the evening. If the tutor were safely cloistered with the head teacher in a separate room you were free to 'let off steam' to each other, and many pent-up fears and anxieties were got rid of and feelings relieved in this free and easy gossip time.

On returning to college in the evening there was a hot meal, and then the mad scramble to get the next day's notes written up, notes of every lesson, and get into the queues waiting to bear these marked by the various members of staff and trembling for fear some might have to be re-written. There was also the tutor to be seen to have your 'crit' lesson criticised and commented on. This evening work and the 'queues' took a great deal of patience, physical endurance and ingenuity, from staff as well as students. All had to be up early and all worked late into the night. Long after 'Lights Out' there were pale glimmers of candle-light showing over the top of the old dormitory bedrooms, as students struggled with notes or illustrations which needed finishing touches, or the many little models in cardboard or paper which they needed for the next day's lessons, or even a story to be memorised. There was a full day's work to be done in school with the necessary tensions of supervision and criticism and nothing short of an earthquake would have released you from school before closing time. You were indeed practising the craft of your calling and it was done in all thoroughness.

9 Primary and Secondary Schools, 1902—1950

1. The Maintained Secondary or Grammar School

One important provision of the Education Act of 1902 was that which permitted the new local education authorities to establish and maintain secondary schools. Morant, the Permanent Secretary of the Board of Education, ensured that these schools were moulded in the pattern of the traditional grammar schools through the Secondary School Regulations of 1904 and subsequent years. The grammar schools increased rapidly in number with the local authorities' new foundations and within a few years they were sufficiently numerous to offer a full secondary education to a considerable proportion of the abler pupils throughout the country. The following extracts from the Regulations of 1904 and 1907 and from the Board of Education Report for 1905–6 give some idea of these developments and of conditions in the schools themselves at this time.

(a) SOURCE: Regulations for Secondary Schools, 30th June, 1904, pp. 17–18.

For the purpose of these Regulations the term Secondary School means a day or boarding school which offers to each of its scholars, up to and beyond the age of 16, a general education, physical, mental and moral, given through a complete graded course of instruction, of wider scope and more advanced degree than that given in Elementary Schools. . . .

Courses of Instruction

1. The curriculum of the school must include an approved Course of general instruction extending over at least four years.
2. In classes in the school below those taking the Course the curriculum must be such as will prepare the scholars fully for entering on the Course. It must include English, History, Geography, Arithmetic, Writing, Drawing, and Physical Exercises. It should also make provision for work to develop accuracy of observation and skill of hand, and for Singing.
3. The average age of the scholars in any class commencing the Course must not be less than 12 years, and the Inspector must

be satisfied that the class as a whole is qualified to commence the Course.

4. The Course should provide for instruction in the English Language and Literature, at least one Language other than English, Geography, History, Mathematics, Science and Drawing, with due provision for Manual Work and Physical Exercises, and, in a girls' school, for Housewifery. Not less than $4\frac{1}{2}$ hours per week must be allotted to English, Geography and History; not less than $3\frac{1}{2}$ hours to the Language where only one is taken or less than 6 hours where two are taken; and not less than $7\frac{1}{2}$ hours to Science and Mathematics, of which at least three must be for Science. The instruction in Science must be both theoretical and practical. Where two languages other than English are taken, and Latin is not one of them, the Board will require to be satisfied that the omission of Latin is for the advantage of the school.

5. In a girls' school in which the total number of hours of instruction is less than 22 per week, the time given to Science and Mathematics may be reduced to one third of that total, provided that at least three hours are given to Science.

6. By special permission of the Board, Languages other than English may be omitted in a school which can satisfy the Board that its English course provides adequate linguistic and literary training, and that the staff is specially qualified to give such instruction. In this case not less than $7\frac{1}{2}$ hours per week must be allotted to English, Geography and History.

7. The curriculum for scholars who continue in the school after completing the Course may provide for specialisation in a subject or group of subjects to such extent only as may be approved by the Board in any case.

8. The curriculum for each year of the Course must be taken in the prescribed sequence; but scholars may, with the sanction of the Inspector, commence with that year of the course for which they are qualified by previous instruction. The retention of a scholar in one year of the Course for more than one session must be approved by the Inspector. . . .

(b) Source: Board of Education, Report for the Year 1905–6, pp. 52, 55, 61. Conditions in the Schools.

Another general statement that can be made about these

schools is that in almost all of them, whatever their type, the staff of assistants is underpaid and often overworked. As a result, teachers with inadequate qualifications are entrusted with the instruction of children who, when they are grown men and women, should do the brain work of the nation. Even where the teacher is properly equipped he is depressed and disheartened by the conditions under which he is obliged to work, and a feeling of restlessness among the staff is engendered which results in too frequent changes; the prevalence of short service teachers impairs the continuity of tradition. A typical case of this is referred to in the following report of the Inspectors on an Endowed School for Boys:

'The present staff, with one exception, have been at the school two years or less; the cause is simply that after a short stay at the school men have been able to go elsewhere to better paid posts. At the salaries now paid, this will inevitably be the case, unless quite inferior men are engaged.

In the smaller schools the headmaster or headmistress is frequently too much occupied to be able sufficiently to supervise the work of the assistant staff; yet in such schools, owing to the small salaries and to the poorer quality of the teaching, the need of supervision is greatest.

'Valuable as is the work of the Headmistress as a teacher' runs the Report on . . . Endowed School for Girls, 'it seems quite essential that for the present she should be set free entirely from the necessity of teaching herself.'

The Municipal Secondary School has frequently, indeed almost normally, been developed out of the older Technical Institute or out of an Organised School of Science. As a result of this past history the curriculum of a large number of Municipal Secondary Schools is too predominantly scientific for their present purpose, and far too little attention is given to English and other literary subjects.

Of one such school (. . . Council Secondary School for Boys), the Inspectors report:

'The teaching of English throughout the school needs to be thoroughly re-organised. The importance of the subject has not as yet received the recognition that it demands, and, though careful and painstaking work is done in some of the classes, it is unfortunately true that, taken as a whole, the English work is weak, and the weakness is due to a general lack of interest in the subject and to a failure to recognise and to appreciate its great educational value in a school where the future occupations of the great majority of the scholars must of necessity give a predominantly scientific bias to the curriculum. The very fact, however, that a comparatively short time can be spared for the study of English Literature renders it all the more necessary that the work that is done should be most carefully and thoroughly organised in all its branches. With a staff of teachers appointed almost exclusively for their qualifications in science and mathematics, it is only natural to find the main interest centred in the teaching of these subjects. The soil is not favourable for the development of literary study, and it is hard to avoid the conclusion that, in certain instances at least, the time devoted to the study of English is somewhat grudgingly bestowed. Indeed in one instance that came under observation a lesson in practical science was allowed to encroach upon the time assigned to a literature lesson, and the master defended this as a habitual practice on the ground that no other time was available for the completion of the laboratory notes.'

[The] question, on the solution of which the whole character of the system to be adopted will depend, is how the type of super-primary education represented by the Secondary School may be organically connected with the national system of primary education open to the children of the whole nation and maintained wholly by public funds, without lowering the standard of work to be attained.

Secondary education differs from Elementary education in two ways, and the difference between them may be expressed in two sets of terms according to the point of view from which the matter is approached. The difference is, from the one side, a difference of stage, from the other a difference of kind. The Secondary School, that is to say, may be regarded either as taking over, at a certain age and a certain stage of proficiency, the children of the Elementary School, and developing their education in a larger manner to a higher point; or as providing for children an education, which either from the very beginning or from a very early stage, is differently planned from that of the Elementary School and directed towards a different though kindred object. Both these types of Secondary School are well established, and, under existing social conditions, both are alike necessary. But the former is, and must tend more and more to be, the predominant type as regards the bulk of the nation; and it is in that the problem of continuity is at once most difficult and most acute.

Education is one. Any dislocation in its course is at the best but a necessary evil. It ought to be continuously progressive from the time when a child first passes beyond the home and goes to school, up to the time when school life ceases, when the boy or girl ceases to be under educational tutelage, has been taught how to learn, and can thenceforth go on to learn for himself or herself. In an ideal commonwealth, this process would be complete for the whole youth of the nation. This is a high ideal, and how far removed it is from existing facts, or from any state of facts which can be contemplated as soon to be possible, is at once obvious. But short of it there is no finality; and the higher the aim is fixed, the higher the attainment is likely to be.

The problem which has to be faced is how to unify education by liberalising the whole of it. A break of gauge is harmful and wasteful; but much may be done to ease it and alleviate its drawbacks. It is difficult to imagine that the social organisation can, at least for a long time to come, be so adjustable and elastic as to be able to do away with it altogether. A class-education in compartments after the fashion of Plato's *Republic* is contrary to the essence of democracy. It is true that in the civic scheme of the *Republic* provision is made for transfusion of children from the ruling to the labouring class, and *vice-versa*; and such in effect was the system of the Middle Ages in England. But a democracy is naturally jealous of a privileged class; and one of the dangers that have to be guarded against is that this jealousy may restrict the province or contract the scope of higher education.

(c) SOURCE: Regulations for Secondary Schools, 30th June, 1907, pp. V–VIII.

2. The Regulations for Secondary Schools grew up round the old provisions of the Directory of the Science and Art Department. . . . In 1904 the Board re-cast the Regulations so as to

18

bring all schools aided by Grants within the general definition of a School offering a general education up to and beyond the age of 16 through a complete graded Course of instruction, the object of which should be to develop all the faculties and to form the habit of exercising them. In view of the limited funds at the Board's disposal, and of the importance of concentrating aid where it would be most useful, grants were made in respect of a four years' Course only, covering the period from 12 or 13 up to 16 or 17 years of age. This Course was regarded as the minimum which any Secondary School should provide. But the earlier education leading up to it, and the later education continued beyond it, were regarded as forming together with it a single organic system, and the whole curriculum of the School was brought under the review and made subject to the approval of the Board. . . .

4. The additional funds placed this year at the disposal of the Board enable the formal limit of a four years' Course to be enlarged as regards the eligibility of scholars for grants, and also allow of the merging of the Special Courses, whether for the whole or part only of the four years, in a curriculum admitting of large variation and flexibility in its content according to the requirements of the area and the aim which the School sets before itself. The essential core of the education which all recognised Secondary Schools have to provide must at least include progressive organised instruction in certain specified subjects or groups of subjects, to an amount which the ordinary scholar beginning it about the age of twelve may be expected to cover in about four years. But emphasis is now laid rather on the full curriculum of the School than on this indispensable minimum. It is expected that the School will normally include junior classes leading up to it, and that in a large number, if not the majority of Schools, provision will be made for continuing instruction beyond it.

5. A uniform grant will accordingly now be paid on scholars following an approved curriculum and between 12 and 18 years of age. . . .

6. In the main portion of the School, the curriculum must, as hitherto, provide instruction, duly graded and duly continuous, in the English Language and Literature, in Geography and History, in Mathematics, Science and Drawing, and unless by

special dispensation in exceptional cases, in at least one language other than English. But the Board have now determined to dispense with the rules under which in each year of the Course a certain definite minimum of time had to be given to these subjects or groups of subjects. That rule was necessary when instituted, and has been of great service in practically impressing on Schools the necessity of a certain breadth and solidity in the education given. But it was contemplated from the first as being only a temporary expedient. The measure of its necessity was the measure of its success; and the measure of its success is now in turn the measure of the degree to which it has ceased to be necessary.

2. At School in Edwardian England

SOURCE: Edmund Blunden, *Edwardian England, 1901–1914.* (Edited by S. Nowell-Smith), Oxford University Press, 1964, pp. 564–8.

The master of the grammar school suggested to my father that I might become a pupil. Cleave's School, established 1665, to give it its full title, stood on a high site looking down at the church and high street; a building ornamented in local style with rich red half-moon tiles, and guarded with a line of chestnut trees. The village green sloped down from its gate to the cross-roads, and just at the corner of its wall was the primitive lock-up with iron-studded door. This school, though its history was one of gaps and mismanagements, had long been held in honour. Many farmers in the district had had their schooling at Cleave's, especially since Mr Samuel Williams had been headmaster. In my day about sixty boys attended, half of them boarders, and of those one or two came from France or Germany. The curriculum printed on the terminal reports might impress even a German parent, for I fancy it included (mensuration was one of the simpler items) callisthenics and astronomy. There was an usher; he had one classroom and Mr Williams the other.

So in the Spring of 1907 I was committed to the charge of the junior schoolmaster, in the long classroom with the leaded window running its entire length; and after the diligent work of my father's school I was rather surprised at the amiable leisure here. Under desks the boys kept stacks of private reading—magazines and serial adventures of Sexton Blake and Jack, Sam, and Pete; and the young master was urged to give opinions on matters far removed from even algebra. But algebra there was; and parsing and analysis; and Euclid. Why? Nobody stopped for that, and I wandered along with the rest—*omnes eodem cogimur*. One thing was sure: Mr Williams himself was a learned man and learning was a desirable state rather than a number of things memorized. But we were given much to remember.

The school day began with a general assembly in the senior classroom for prayers. Mr Williams, marching in fresh and puffing importantly, read these with little melodies at phrases like 'neither run into any kind of danger'. Then he would select a hymn, and very often it was one with angels in it. Seated at the harmonium, he would brush back his scarecrow gown and execute the tune with flying fingers; the boys were well used to his system, which was to take the first three lines of a stanza at a gallop and the fourth with solemn delay.

full *speed*	{ Around the throne of God a band Of glorious angels ever stand, Bright things they see, bright harps they hold,
dead slow	And On Their Heads Are Crowns . . . Of . . . Gold.

When the music was over the lesser boys receded into their schoolroom, the others heard an address or exhortation from Mr Williams, usually on character. Behind him as he spoke we saw the gilded names of former scholars who, presumably possessing character, had passed several public examinations; and on the notice board he had perhaps pinned a column out of a newspaper concerning some old boy who was now on the frontiers as a mounted policeman, or otherwise making his way in the world. Character, that was what mattered, it was something each boy must take out to his future mission, now was the time to develop character. Now, boys, if you cut your finger, is that worse than losing your cap? No. Your finger will heal up again; but you won't get a cap so easily. Character. Sometimes Mr Williams would resume the music with a song which might almost be called our school song, and which was poured out with energy:

> Whatsoe'er you find your duty,
>   Do it, Boys, with all your Might;
> Never be a little truthy,
>   Or a little in the right.
> Trifles even lead to heaven,
>   Trifles make the life of man;
> So in all things, great and small things,
>   Be as thorough as you can.

How he loved his boys! We had some difficulty to perceive this at the time. He liked to be thought a bit of an ogre. As we filed in still chattering from the playground, he suddenly appeared with large eyes at the window, and then we were expected to give an 'eyes left', which he acknowledged with a military salute. How curiously he smiled as this happened! Cleave's was all a little state, himself the president of it, and no other state at war with it. Sometimes he dealt out justice, which was always betokened by his setting up a violent clatter with his new cane on his desk, and sometimes by his repeating loudly 'The Lord hath spoken unto Samuel'. It was not at me that he was looking one day as he said this, but he meant me. I had absented myself the Saturday before, and thought I had escaped notice altogether; but he had found out by his uncanny power where I had been, and he thrashed me without appeal.

The homework on which he insisted was considerable. He would write up on blackboards a table, thus:

| City | On What River | Country | What Famous For |

and add a great string of place names, for which we were to get the required information that evening. At Congelow I had a private corner for my work, not far from the family's barrel of beer, which I tried in very modest samples for the good of the grammar school. Mr Williams taught us French so well that when I reached a great school I was much in advance of almost all competitors; he had the grammar and the spoken language. A time was given for writing our diaries, contained in thick books of abominable paper which nevertheless had the shield of Cleave's School on their cardboard covers, and cost only two-pence each. Each entry had to be begun with a weather report

('Beastly weather' was often enough) and Mr Williams read and marked all we wrote. In my time I suppose the cleverest boy in the school was Tom Singyard, who was a born mathematician and, generally, understood whatever was put before him. He lived some way below Congelow in a house near a disused brickworks, which had become a chain of ponds hidden in thickets and sagebeds, full of carp and tench and water lilies and moorhens. He kept me in a state of misery all the road home by pulling my hair and swinging me round and using me as a butt for his wit; but I was devoted to him. One day I appeared at school wearing some knickers of a certain breadth hurriedly made by my mother. Tom Singyard raised his eyebrows, and, to the boys round, he uttered the sufficient description 'Bells'. Thereafter, when he would torment me, he merely uttered this word in a lovely tunable voice, 'Bells', and it became my knickname, which he does not live to use. He and his promising young mind were not to survive the first world war. Everything that we could do at all he could do well, including cricket and football. I envied him this superior gift, but perhaps even more his home in that lonely old place with the kiln overgrown with ivy and ash, the pools only separated by narrow paths, the swans winging to and fro out of the forest of reeds.

One advantage I had—some say it was not an advantage— even over clever Tom Singyard. At Congelow there was a good-sized cupboard off the sitting room and into it my father bundled (for it had good shelves) a number of his books. Either I had not had access to them before or I had not been interested, but now I was. They were miscellaneous, but they included some old literature—sets of the *Tatler* and the *Spectator*, a few eighteenth-century plays like *Oroonoko* bound together, the works of Paley, of Josephus, *British Battles by Land and Sea*, an early Victorian Encyclopaedia, Bacon's essays, *New Atlantis*, and other pieces, apocryphal plays of Shakespeare, two quarto Bibles with copper engravings, and much else. One tall book, which had been deposited on my father in acknowledgement of a loan, had my attention for years: it was Thomas Stanley's *History of Philosophy*, a seventeenth century masterpiece, with alleged portraits of the Greek philosophers. These were not the best books in the house, but such as they were they aroused in me some sense of bygone tastes, studies and feelings.

Boys came from remoter parts of the parish and from other villages to Cleave's School. The two Readers from Laddingford way, the Featherstones from East Peckham were among my special friends. The Readers had, in their father's farms, a lovely little river, all twists and turns, called the Teise, and we had afternoons with rod and line there. The Teise runs into the Medway at last round a place called the Ring, an ancient cricket ground, which at that time was girdled with many splendid trees and one or two white pillars that had been trees but had been struck by lightning. This circle of greensward, invaded by coarse tussocks of swamp grass, was the school's cricket ground, and sometimes we played a match against a Maidstone school. Cricket was a great thing in the village, and I had the honour of being scorer often and sometimes last man in for the second eleven. The away matches might mean a delightful ride in a horse brake, and songs on the way home under skies of golden glow, past unknown parks and orchards, yet at last down our own familiar hill with its spring-well and stacks of fruit baskets by the farm gates. Sometimes Jack Cheeseman would inspect a little book in which scores of our private contests (Alf Cheeseman, Harry Excell, and me) were kept if creditable enough. Alas, going in last for the men's eleven was not always without responsibility. I once did so when Herbert Cheeseman (and he is still a batsman to be reckoned with) had gone all through the innings and was within sight of his century. My orders were to stay, naturally, and I was being wary, when the grandly moustached enemy bowler had an idea and sent me down a lob on the leg side. I saw an obvious gift and took a bang—just what he wanted, for the ball sailed straight into someone's safe hands in the distance, and poor Herbert Cheeseman was not out 92, no more. He was scoring well forty years after that.

Mr Williams had no special affection for cricket, which he knew was a menace to common sense and useful knowledge, but he sent the school off to afternoons at Tonbridge when the county side was playing, and he obtained very cheap tickets for the railway journey and the ground. As for play, I cannot now recall much. Kent certainly disappointed us once by being overwhelmed by lunch time, and a fine attacking innings by K. G. MacLeod of Lancashire placed him among my heroes. All who figured in county cricket were indeed heroes to me, and when my father pointed out to me (after some such match) Mr E. W. Dillon actually standing on the railway platform I gazed as on 'the herald Mercury, new lighted on a heaven-kissing hill'. My father took me to Chichester among other scenes of the summer game, and sweetly still I hear the words 'the Priory ground', which that day lay bathed in sunshine and Sussex serenity.

3. Educational Facilities in Portsmouth

This extract gives some idea of the facilities offered by a medium sized local authority under the Education Act of 1902 and illustrates the emphasis which the new authorities placed on their work in higher education—a term which included secondary education before 1944.

> SOURCE: *Social Conditions in Provincial Towns*—Portsmouth, edited by Mrs Bernard Bosanquet, Macmillan, 1912, pp. 9–11.

The elementary council schools in the borough are 26 in number, while there are in addition nine non-provided schools, only the latter having school managers. There are no schools or special classes for physically or mentally defective children. The medical inspection of schools is carried out by a school medical officer, an assistant and two nurses. No treatment is provided at present by the Education Authority, although the question of the provision of a school clinic is under consideration, and defective cases are simply notified to parents requesting them to obtain the necessary treatment. However, in 26 per cent. of cases notified, no treatment has been obtained for the children. The only special provision for school children is made at the Eye and Ear Infirmary, where the staff devote one morning a week to their treatment. The tickets entitling the children to attend are obtained through the teachers or from private sources, and not through the Education Authority. The need for some special provision for mentally defective children is felt alike by social workers, medical men, and teachers; but the Education Authority have declined to adopt the permissive Act of 1899 and these children are consequently left without training or education of any kind, becoming later on a danger to the community. The school medical officer reports that 61 mentally dull or defective cases passed through his hands during the year, and he considers that the presence of such children with normal ones is not desirable. Numbers of children, however, are too seriously afflicted to attend school, and therefore are not included in any register. We believe that one of the most pressing needs of the town is some suitable provision for these feeble minded children, and it is satisfactory to know that the subject is to be discussed at an early meeting of the Council.

The recommendations contained in the Majority Report of the Poor Law Commission with regard to the extension of the school age appeal with peculiar force to social workers in the town on account of the large number of boys who enter the Services at the ages of fifteen and a half to sixteen, and who are obliged, as a rule, to spend two of the most important years of their lives in casual work, as newsboys or errand boys. The opportunities for entering skilled employment in the town are comparatively few, if we except the opportunities of apprenticeship in the Dockyard and the excellent preparatory training given in the secondary school for engine-room artificers to a limited number, and the establishment of Juvenile Advisory Committees will be a great boon to lads leaving school. No organised efforts have been made hitherto, either by the Education Authority or by voluntary workers to induce boys and girls to enter skilled employment on leaving school.

The Provision of Meals Act was adopted by the Council in January 1910, and the local branch of the National Union of Women Workers was asked to organise a band of helpers to assist in dispensing the food, and as an ample number of volunteers came forward, no paid supervisors have been necessary. The canteen committee, a sub-committee of the Education Committee, are in charge of the feeding arrangements, and they gave the contract to a local caterer who supplies the meals at the present time at a cost ranging from $2\frac{1}{2}$d to $3\frac{1}{2}$d per child, according to the numbers fed. The food is prepared at the central kitchen, and sent on from thence to the ten feeding centres. The helpers are organised under an honorary secretary who, in addition to regular helpers, has a special reserve to fill temporary vacancies. The arrangements have been so successful that the Council have co-opted the honorary secretary and two other lady supervisors to the Canteen Committee. The average number attending elementary schools is 29,000 while the average number fed daily in January is 725 only. Parents of necessitous children make the application for meals at the Town Hall, to the Education Authority. Inquiry is made by the school attendance officer, and if it then appears necessary, the names are added to the feeding list. Up to the present time the Council have not recovered any part of the cost of the meals from the parents. There is little doubt that the logical outcome of the medical inspection in schools and the adoption of the Provision of Meals Act, will be the formation of Children's Care Committees, and the voluntary helpers should form a good nucleus, if the work of the committees is supervised by a trained organiser.

Great strides have been made by the Higher Education Committee during the last few years. The building of excellent secondary schools for boys and later on for girls was followed by a venture of great importance—the opening of the Municipal College in 1908—which was built and furnished at a cost exceeding £100,000. Within the building provision is made for the Technical College, the Day Training College, and Pupil Teachers' Centre, the Municipal School of Art, and the Central Free Library. The College is organised on the lines of a University College, having its various courses of study under the immediate direction of the Heads of Departments. The Technical College provides instruction in chemistry and natural science, mathematics, mechanical, electrical, and civil engineering, in arts and commercial work, in domestic science and other subjects. The educational needs of the whole community are catered for without any distinction of class, and those in less affluent circumstances may compete for the many studentships and scholarships in connection with the College. The Pupil Teachers' Centre provides instruction for all pupil-teachers serving under the Portsmouth Education Authority, while the Day Training College receives 90 students only each year, the majority of whom are working for the certificate of the Board of Education. There are four hostels for the students in connection with the Training College. The provision of this Central Municipal College is an immense boon to the town and neighbourhood.

4. Basing Church School in the 1920s

SOURCE: *Basing Church of England School, 1866–1966*, The School Managers, 1966, pp. 23–25.

I was at Basing School from when I was six years old until I was twelve, during 1920–30. I'll not pretend that they were the happiest days of my life, because I never did like school. Despite this, I left Basing School with an extremely good basic education, and the ability to settle down to learn. There was no way out, one had to . . .

Mr Moss was the Headmaster at the time. I remember him always wearing a bow tie. A thin man with thinning red hair and a moustache, with a temper to match his hair. He was very quick to anger and wielded his cane with abandon when roused. In memory I may be maligning him, but I remember I was frightened of him, or rather, frightened that I might raise his wrath. Although I spent only one year in his class (he taught the seniors) he was a good teacher. He had a great love of music, as far as I am concerned this was his saving grace! During his headship, the school used to perform wonderful operettas each year in the Village Hall. These were great fun. We also used to go to church each Friday, where, over the years we learned the various lovely settings for the Sung Eucharist.

Miss Blackmore was the Infants teacher. My memory of this period is very hazy, but I vividly remember being taught to knit on needles that seemed as large as crowbars.

Mr Foote joined the staff during this time. I always think of him as the Handwriting king. He was superb, and he made us feel that good writing was an asset. I enjoyed the lessons with Mr Foote, despite the book one occasionally got round the ear!

Mrs Hewitt taught some of the juniors. She was a very alert, vital person. Reminded me of a starling, even to the slightly bowed legs. She had grey hair, and when angry, which seemed often, her hairpins used to fly all over the place. We enjoyed this immensely, and we used to like to make her angry so that we could be amused by this. Mrs Hewitt was never slow to rap one, jolly hard with a ruler. She was a good teacher, who expected the best of which one was capable. She knew your capabilities, and heaven help you if you offered her less than your best.

Miss Tyler taught, amongst other things, needlework. A hopeless task for her, as far as I was concerned. Despite her sweat and my tears, I still sew with a hot needle and a burning thread, nothing ever stays together!

The staff were all disciplinarians. We were left in no doubt as to what was right or wrong—what we could or could not do. We were given certain standards, and I'm quite sure that this imposed discipline helped us to become self-disciplined and enabled us to accept responsibilities at a comparatively early age. School buses were unheard of then, and some pupils walked great distances to school. Walking to school was a good thing. We had exercise and fun on the way, and by the time we reached the school we were physically awake and mentally alert and quite ready to settle to work. The bell summoned us to school, and if you weren't in the playground by the time the bell sounded, you took to your heels and ran. Lateness was frowned upon, and quite often the seriousness of unpunctuality was driven home with the help of the cane!

One thing I remember with absolute horror was the lavatories—bucket affairs. Certainly not conducive to regular habits, as one used them only in dire straits. Evidently the school authorities didn't subscribe to the idea that cleanliness was next to godliness, as in the girls' cloakroom were two hand basins with cold taps. There were no towels, and the basins were usually a delicate shade of black, through non-use, dust and ink powder, but enormous 'Basingstoke' spiders lived with obvious pleasure in these basins.

School dinners were started during the time that I was at the school. These were cooked in a big black gas stove in the boys' cloakroom by dear old Miss Harmsworth. None of today's balanced diets and variety. I seldom stayed to dinner, but I can remember nothing other than thick soup, bread pudding or rice pudding, eaten out of enamel bowls or plates. The noise as spoon scraped enamel! As I said at the beginning, I did not enjoy life at Basing school but it was certainly an experience, but such was the education and the training that I received there, that learning was very easy when I went on to High School and University.

5. A Day at a Public School in 1934

This extract gives a brief picture of school life standing in considerable contrast to that experienced by the majority of children between the wars who were accustomed to seeing no school other than the local elementary.

SOURCE: W. F. Ewbank, *Salopian Diaries*, Wilding & Son, 1961, pp. 51–2.

October 23, Tuesday: Fine. I have meant for some time to give a detailed description of an ordinary day. First and second bells did not wake me, but I did wake just before third bell to the patter of feet going off to the swills. Up at 7.30, a quick dash to the cold bath; in and out; dry; dress. If the clock says no later than 7.35 a.m. as I begin to dress, I am reasonably safe. As I brush my hair the school bell starts. Downstairs to the study, get books, on with shoes, and tow full speed to arrive at the School Buildings just in time. Street took us in first lesson for Juvenal, with his own touches of humour to enliven it. Back again to the house with Cartmell, at a more leisurely pace, for breakfast, which consisted of porridge and scrambled eggs on toast. The scrambled eggs were cold. Breakfast ended by 8.55 a.m. and I spent part of the time before chapel revising my Tacitus for the head man. Pegg and I set off at 9.25 a.m. for chapel, and Hoskyns took the service. In the first period of second less (9.45–10.35), Mossy put me on to 'strue the Euripedes, which I did badly. In the second period (10.40–11.30) we discussed our essays on "Broadcasting" without receiving them back. During the ten minutes' break (11.30–11.40) Cartmell and I strolled up to the board and found nothing on it, as usual. In the third period (11.40–12.30) Hardy did most of the Tacitus himself, and filled up the remaining time by reading the wordy translation by Murphy—'old man Murphy', as he always calls him. I had meant, after 12, to read an article on *The Lyric* by M. R. Ridley in *Essays and Studies, 1933*, but Shegog dragged me off to prepare our speeches for the debate on Friday. This we did in the bedroom. Lunch consisted of our dear old mutton, relieved with mint sauce, and followed with Dead Man's Leg. This is a roll of solid suet, half-heated and spotted with currants, and Kitch himself gave it its name (so the story goes) one day at lunch. We had an 'erection' immediately after lunch on ground 7, for first leagues and others, in which I had to play; which was followed by six-a-side. I missed a number of goals through bad ball-control, and felt miserable about it. During the lock-ups, before third lesson the house was unusually empty, as most men had gone to the run-in of the Bomere Pool Run, in which Petrie came fourth. I went over with Foster Pegg to third lesson. In the first period, which was a Dawson period, there was less milling than there sometimes is and I managed to get most of my Euripedes done for tomorrow. In the second period, Street discoursed on the MSS of Juvenal, and told us how an undergraduate, working on Juvenal for mods., obtained permission to read the MS which is in the Bodleian. He stumbled on thirty lines which appeared in none of the standard texts. When he told the librarians and dons, they would none of them at first believe him, until he compelled them to see for themselves. A notice came round in the second period, giving the schedule of lectures for Cert A Written [a Cadet Corps test]. The first was tonight. I was due to go to a tuition set with Tucker, and tried to catch him after third lesson to say that I could not come; Cartmell was due to help Hoskyns with his scout troop. In the end I cut the tuition set and went to the lecture; Cartmell went to his scouts; and I answered Cartmell's name at the roll-call. Tea was rather rushed for the lecture, and I sped over on a bike in the dark without a light. It lasted an hour (7.0–8.0 p.m.), and was rather a waste of time—the West, talking on the 'platoon in attack', all the stuff we had learnt after a year in the Corps. Barwick, MacConnell and Munro were with me; Colebrook and Smith were in another part of the room. MacConnell had the papers to give out, to men whose names he didn't know. The Bull took digs at 9.40 p.m., and so to bed.

6. The Evacuation of 1939

The wholesale evacuation of children from the large towns to rural areas in early September, 1939, had both educational and social consequences that have proved to be far-reaching. These two extracts illustrate a few of the more common problems of schooling and of social adjustment encountered in the early weeks.

(a) SOURCE: *The Times*, 18 September, 1939, p. 3

Reception Area Schooling

Beginning Made in Lancashire

Two-Shift Working

Manchester, September 17th

Lancashire education authorities are getting to grips with the task of providing instruction for evacuated children, and the problem is found to differ in each area. It may have been illegal for a Manchester head teacher to begin lessons for his school only three days after the evacuation—illegal because he was ahead of instructions—but who will quarrel with him?—he was one of the lucky ones.

Liverpool children sent to rural districts in Lancashire should begin school tomorrow: their fellows sent to Cheshire have already resumed, but in Denbighshire some have and some have not. Each category has its vagaries. Obviously a school of 1,600 pupils evacuated and scattered between neighbouring villages where the local schools accommodate only 50 each is in a difficulty. Here the solution may be to absorb the children into the village classes.

Cost of Bus Transport

Where possible children of the same age have been billeted in the same village, and their schooling is not too hard to organise. Where an attempt at double shifts is made by taking children to school in buses plying between villages, the question of cost is arising. Cost, too, governs the renting of buildings where village schools are inadequate. Education authorities receive only 50 per cent. grants for approved extra expense, and Liverpool, with its large schools moved to rural areas, is perturbed by this.

A rough scheme for dividing responsibility is being worked in some places. If a school is working on a double shift, using the full accommodation of the local school for half the normal teaching hours, it supplies all its own staff and materials, the main problem being one of transport and of securing supplies of books, stationery, apparatus &c. But where a village school has 'digested' the newcomers some repayment by the evacuating authority has to be devised, generally on a *per capita* basis. The hundred and one items of school equipment complicate the reckoning.

The advantageous dispersal of the available teachers is less troublesome to resolve, and the usual method is to settle such problems round a table. Elementary school teachers are as a whole pretty resourceful, and where a master finds himself in charge of a miniature and very mixed school he is generally sufficiently well equipped to cover most other subjects until re-settlement comes. The secondary school teacher is much more of a specialist, but in the secondary schools the difficulty rarely arises because they are moved as units, complete with teachers.

Effect on Examinations

Largely because of the lack of accommodation, many secondary schools are joining with local schools in working shifts. Contrary opinions are held as to the effect this will have on the standard attained by pupils in their leaving examinations a year or so hence. Many feel that the change will work to the advantage rather than to the disadvantage of the children: it will possibly encourage a new angle of attack on the syllabus. Actual teaching will be halved, and the pupil will work more on tutorial lines, doing more home work. The English tradition of science teaching is based on much practical work by the pupil, but some educationists prefer the continental method of instruction by demonstration, a method perhaps not so lasting in its effects, but certainly wider in its scope. The new system seems assured of a good trial because in the winter the afternoon shift will be shortened if pupils are to go home before dark.

School meals are a difficult problem. The Board of Education stated in an earlier circular that one of the best services to householders in the reception areas would be to feed the children at school, but it now states that there will be no free meals because the 8s. 6d. or 10s. 6d. [per child per week] paid to the host is for board as well as lodging. Community school feeding is proceeding mainly in the urban districts. In the rural districts it takes the form of a school canteen, but in general the problem of feeding has been shelved until the necessary teaching adjustments have been made.

(b) SOURCE: *The Times*, 18 September, 1939, p. 3.

Lancashire Children in Wales
Effect on Village Life

Cardiff, September 16th

Though most people who have been evacuated from the Midlands and Lancashire to places in Wales are now settling down to their new surroundings, some have for some reason or other returned to their homes. The change to new surroundings has already proved beneficial; the open air life and wholesome and plain food have benefited the children, while the discoveries made in the local flora and fauna have been sources of unending wonderment.

In the nature of things some complaints were to be expected, most of the children evacuated to North Wales were from the poorer parts of Liverpool and other Lancashire towns. Some were said to be dirty, verminous and scantily clad, and had to be bathed and given a change of clothing immediately on their arrival. Acquired home habits, however, were not so easily shed. Some children stared blankly at the clean beds prepared for them, and insisted on sleeping on the floor in their clothes as they said they did at home. Vegetables were refused by some at dinner because they had never tasted them. Fruit trees were looked on as legitimate prey, and in one village an apple tree is alleged to have been stripped bare in the first few days of their arrival. Complaints of uncleanliness were not confined to children. A party of women are said to have been refused at three villages, and were eventually put up at a village institute until other arrangements could be made.

The addition of so many thousands to the scanty population of the small villages of North Wales is bound to create some difficult problems where social and other facilities are limited. Already some fears are expressed as to the effects on Welsh village life and institutions. Can the native speech and culture withstand the impact of alien influences and habits? Will children whose mother tongue and daily converse is Welsh lose it in daily contact with playmates speaking another language?

7. City Schooling in Wartime

Many schools which remained in or returned to the cities encountered difficulties of aerial bombardment in full measure in 1940 and 1941. These extracts give some idea of the circumstances which were encountered.

(a) SOURCE: C. P. Hill, *A History of Bristol Grammar School*, Pitman, 1951, pp. 207–8.

. . . It was not until after the capitulation of France during the summer of 1940 that the war began seriously to interrupt school life. Then broken nights made it advisable to begin the day at ten o'clock instead of nine, and to curtail the number of boys playing games at Golden Hill. First-aid classes were held: the

19

School contributed a platoon to the Local Defence Volunteers. Eighty of the O.T.C.'s rifles were sent, for some oblique reason, to the Warwickshire Police, and the School's German howitzer was turned to scrap metal. Eleven members of the staff joined the armed forces before the end of the summer term of 1940. The *Chronicle* of December, 1939, recorded the first O.B. casualty, and the next issue contained the first list of O.B's in the forces. A fair number of boys left the school and Bristol through private evacuation, but this loss was offset by new entrants whose parents had come to the city as official migrants.

It was a hectic but scarcely a perilous year, this first one of the war. The second brought sterner trials. On the night of Sunday, 24th November 1940, Bristol had its first big raid, and many incendiary bombs fell on Tyndalls Park. Mr Moore [then headmaster] has described what followed.

We put out many incendiaries, but one lodged in the rafters of the Prep. proved intractable; when the fire engines came the water mains had failed; and the building burned steadily to a shell. That night, as on other nights, the School site was ringed by fires, in the University and in the adjacent roads. The wind was in the west, and all night burning tinder from a house in Elton Road fell on our house. We evacuated it and stood by; but wonderfully it did not catch fire. A small stick of bombs fell on the blazing Prep. but they were of small calibre and did little harm. In the early hours Sargeant and I put our heads together and decided that we would carry on school next morning if possible. It did prove possible; we had salvaged a fair amount of equipment from the Prep. and somehow we fitted in its forms in the big School.

There were six large fires in the neighbourhood that night; and the glare from blazing buildings reflected in the windows of the Great Hall added the illusion that that too was aflame. This was the worst raid; three more—on 2nd December, 1940, when part of the Preparatory Hall roof, hitherto little harmed, was burned off, and on 3rd January and 11th April, 1941—brought relatively minor damage to the School premises. The main school stood unhurt: but the latest of the Tyndall's Park buildings, Fenwick Richards' Preparatory School, was, its hall apart, a blackened shell.

The Preparatory Department was housed in drawing-room

and dining-room of the Headmaster's House, and in accommodation provided by Western College. Its numbers fell; the School's total declined by almost 100 during the year 1940–41, and nearly all those who left were younger boys whose parents thought it best to remove them from so heavily bombed a city. This fall added to the financial worries of the governing body which, at a time of steeply rising costs, had to face additional expenditure on the rent of extra premises and on air raid precautions; and which had lost much of the income from its trust funds, through the heavy damage caused by enemy action to the Redcliffe Street property of Dr Owen's Charity. Parents inquired whether the School was to be evacuated from Bristol; the Governors took a unanimous decision against this course. Events justified them. As 1941 wore on air-raids grew less frequent and less intense; there were other British targets, the summer nights were shorter and after the German attack on Russia in July the major fury of war moved to the east. The worst of the war was in fact over, for the School as for the nation as a whole. But 1940–1 had been a profoundly difficult year.

(b) SOURCE: Log Book of Northam Girls' Elementary School, Southampton.

1939

September 1st.   Evacuation took place. 160 people altogether.

1940

April 1st.   School re-opened. Each child attending for two hours each day.

April 2nd.   I visited school group in reception area to make arrangements for transfer of senior children to the Henry Harbin School (Poole).

September 24th.   On account of severe air raid, school started at 2.45. Another raid followed. After which at 4 p.m. children were sent home. Raid did severe damage to houses nearby.

September 26th.   Heavy gunfire 3.20–3.40. Severe air raid when Northam Gas Works received great damage.

November 19th.   Owing to severe air raid in neighbourhood many people had to be accommodated and fed on school premises, therefore no school could be held. Staff assisted with feeding.

November 25th.   Owing to damage in air raid on 23rd., water and drainage was affected—craters in playground and outside school.

December 2nd.   Further very severe raids on Nov 30th. and Dec 1st. have destroyed most of the centre of the town and many other parts. School was damaged and many people have been evacuated.

December 3rd and 6th.   Staff visiting homes—helping with evacuation and finding of homeless.

December 9th.   Staff continuing to help with meals and visited all children attempting to find out where they were. Many houses were demolished or empty but after repeated visits information was obtained as to where the children had gone except in a few cases. 34 children only were found to be home—these were informed that school would be open on Monday.

1941

March 12th.   Air raid damage during the night resulted in severe damage in the locality. Unexploded bomb reported in Kent Street. No school as roads were closed.

March 13th.   School re-opened as no bomb was found. Few children attended.

July 8th.   Severe raid during the night. Extensive damage done. Infants' School destroyed. Shelters unsafe. Top storey not usable—still burning. Huge crater in playground. School closed to children remainder of week. Homes visited by staff.

8. Post-War Aspirations

Wartime conditions produced the Education Act of 1944; possibly the main achievement of that measure was to confer a right to 'secondary' education on all children attaining the age of eleven regardless of means or ability. The generally accepted form of provision was to be tripartite, the established grammar and technical schools continuing to provide for the more able minority while modern schools were to offer a 'non-academic' secondary education to the majority. The Ministry's view of the tripartite system and of the secondary modern school was set out in ' *The New Secondary Education* '.

SOURCE: *The New Secondary Education*, Ministry of Education
Pamphlet No. 9, 1947,
loc. cit. p. 7.

For the first time in the history of this country, genuine secondary
education is to be provided for all children over 11. The Education Act of 1944 lays down that at this age children are to pass
in future from the primary stage to 'full-time education suitable
to the requirements of senior pupils'. Secondary education is to
be the right of all, and no longer the privilege of a few.

There has been some confusion about the meaning of the
phrase 'secondary education for all'. Until 1944 a 'Secondary
School' meant a particular sort of school to which only a small
proportion of the population could aspire, one which had better
qualified and better paid staff, smaller classes, and more attrac-
tive premises and amenities than most of the other schools in its
neighbourhood. It was attended by some of the ablest pupils
selected by a highly competitive examination, and by a certain
number of other pupils of varying abilities whose parents could
afford to pay fees. This sort of secondary school will remain,
doing its own special job, and it will be at the service of all
children for whom its educational provision is considered to be
the most suitable. But it is now only one type of secondary
school, to which pupils with particular leanings and aptitudes
will go.

In future there will be various types of secondary schools and
various courses within secondary schools, which will offer
children an education specially suited to their particular needs.
All these schools will have the advantages and the amenities
hitherto exclusively associated with the limited number of
schools called secondary schools up to 1944. They will have
equally good buildings. They will enjoy the same holidays and
play the same games. There will eventually be boarding facilities for all types of secondary schools. In all these schools the
studies will be related to the abilities and aptitudes of the pupils.
The maximum size of classes will be the same for all.

As a mere matter of finance it will, broadly speaking, cost as
much to build, equip and staff one type of secondary school as
another, and the jibe that the new types of secondary school
have been advocated because they are cheap should be heard
no more.

loc. cit. p. 23.   [The Tripartite Theory]

Experience has shown that the majority of children learn most easily by dealing with concrete things and following a course rooted in their own day-to-day experience. At the age of 11 few of them will have disclosed particular interest and aptitudes well enough marked for them to require any other course. The majority will do best in a school which provides a good all-round education in an atmosphere which enables them to develop freely along their own lines. Such a school will give them the chance to sample a variety of 'subjects' and skills and to pursue those which attract them most. It is for this majority that the secondary *modern* school will cater.

Some children, on the other hand, will have decided at quite an early stage to make their careers in branches of industry or agriculture requiring a special kind of aptitude in science or mathematics. Others may need a course, longer, more exacting, and more specialised than that provided in the modern school, with a particular emphasis on commercial subjects, music or art. All these boys and girls will find their best outlet in the secondary *technical* school.

Finally, there will be a proportion whose ability and aptitude require the kind of course with the emphasis on books and ideas that is provided at a secondary *grammar* school. They are attracted by the abstract approach to learning and should normally be prepared to stay at school long enough to benefit from the 'sixth form' work which is the most characteristic feature of the grammar school.

Both 'books' and 'activities' are essential in all three types of secondary course; no school can afford to base its work exclusively on one or the other. The person who has no kind of skill with his hands is as imperfectly prepared for life as one who cannot read. The proportions in which these two ways of learning are to be combined should be determined by the capacities and needs of the individual pupil, and the basic principle is that whatever his native ability a child must be guided towards the kind of work in school over which he can acquire some sense of mastery. This means, for instance, that it is of little use to present subject-matter to him which he is unable to appreciate or to press him to labour in an atmosphere of frustration. It will be evident that it is as unfair to the child to expect him to develop through a study of Latin or advanced mathematics, if he shows no sign of attaining any standard in them, as it is to restrict him to a practical or scientific approach if his more characteristic outlet is through the humanities. No organisation, indeed, will adequately meet the situation that involves the sacrifice of the best interests of one type of child to those of others. This is a sacrifice our country cannot afford.

loc. cit. pp. 29–30.   [The Modern School]

Perhaps the main difference between a modern school and other types of secondary schools is its very broad outlook and objective. It has to provide a series of courses for children of widely differing ability, aptitude and social background. It has to cater for the needs of intelligent boys and girls, for those with a marked practical bent, as well as for the special problem of backward children. To quote the Spens Report: 'By no means all who succeed in commerce or industry are of the type which benefits at all obviously from an academic and scientific education, and it is very probable that many such men would have gained more from the curriculum of a modern school especially if, as might well have been the case, they were more attracted by such a curriculum and more industrious in pursuing it'. On the other hand, The Ministry's pamphlet on Special Educational Treatment makes it clear that a number of educationally sub-normal children will be attending modern schools.

With such a wide variety of ability the modern school must be free to work out its own syllabuses and methods. Teachers must be ready to ask themselves 'Why?', 'When?', 'Where?', 'How?', and 'What?', and be free to act on the answers. And since neither teachers nor teaching conditions nor children are mass-produced to a uniform pattern, the answers to these questions will vary not only from school to school, but, even more widely, within a school.

The aim of the modern school is to provide a good all-round secondary education, not focussed primarily on the traditional subjects of the school curriculum, but developing out of the interests of the children. Through its appeal to their interests it will stimulate their ability to learn and will teach them to pursue quality in thought, expression and craftsmanship. It will interpret the modern world to them and give them a prepara-

tion for life in the widest sense, including a full use of leisure. It
will aim at getting the most out of every pupil that he is capable
of, at making him adaptable, and at teaching him to do a job
properly and thoroughly and not to be satisfied with bad work-
manship, and to be exact in what he says and does. Freedom
and flexibility are of its essence and are indeed its great opportunity.

The best existing modern schools offer already convincing
examples of the lines on which this general objective can be
attained. They are providing a broad and balanced general
curriculum, and they are giving it reality by means of many
kinds of practical activity. They are achieving on the one hand,
a standard of effort and performance that is raising the common estimate of the capacities of the children attending them,
and, on the other, they are showing themselves as much concerned, and not less successful, in dealing with the needs of the
more backward pupils.

The modern school will be given parity of conditions with
other types of secondary school; parity of esteem it must achieve
by its own efforts. Local education authorities can help to hasten
this development in several ways. They can show in their public
policy that they have faith in the modern school; they can treat
it with the same trust and confidence as they treat the grammar
school and administer both with a loose rein that allows plenty
of scope to the heads and their staffs. They can staff the schools
liberally, so as to allow of the sub-division of forms and some
free time for the staff for preparation and marking of work.
They can give modern school heads the same measure of responsibility in the appointment and retention of their assistant
staff as is commonly enjoyed by grammar school heads. They
can give stability to the modern school staff, so that its members
can feel that they are genuinely members of a team and not
merely so many individual teaching units liable to be moved
from school to school. They can encourage generous expenditure on books and equipment. They can advertise the school's
secondary status by such apparently trivial acts as the provision
of school uniforms, caps and blazers. And they can establish
residential modern schools.

10 The Universities

In 1800 the only universities in England were Oxford and Cambridge; at that time they were hardly fulfilling the functions which are associated with universities today. The nineteenth century witnessed the reform and modernisation of the two older universities as well as the foundation of universities in the rapidly expanding centres of industry and commerce.

University College	Date of Foundation
London, University College	1828
London, Kings College	1831
Durham	1833
Manchester, Owens College	1851
Newcastle, College of Physical Science	1871
Leeds, Yorkshire College of Science	1874
Bristol, College of Science	1876
Sheffield, Firth College	1880
Birmingham, Mason College of Science	1880
Nottingham, University College	1881
Liverpool, University College	1882

All of these institutions were the product of local endeavour and philanthropy for the first grant in aid from the government was not made before 1889.

There was a considerable increase in the amount of state aid during the first half of the present century but there were few new foundations; University colleges were opened at Leicester in 1921 and at Hull in 1928 and both of these had to rely heavily on local financial support during their early years.

The group of twenty of so universities which have either been founded or developed out of existing technical colleges during the last few years have all received very substantial capital and recurrent aid from the state from their inception. Nowadays there are, perhaps, at least four groups of universities, the new ones built on green fields, the ex-technical colleges, 'Oxbridge' and 'Redbrick'. The first two groups are still establishing themselves.

In this chapter, the first group of extracts illustrate the transformation of Oxford and Cambridge since 1800 (Nos. 1–5), while the second group mainly illustrate some aspects of the emergence and growth of the older universities situated in the large cities (Nos. 6–10).

1. Oxford University about 1850

The Reports of the two Royal Commissions appointed to inquire into Oxford and Cambridge in the middle of the nineteenth century provide a fascinating account of the way in which those two institutions were adapting themselves to the more modern concepts of universities. The seven extracts given here from the Report on Oxford show that the University had already travelled far from the conditions of the late eighteenth century and point the direction that further reform was to take.

Source: Report of the Royal Commission on the State, Discipline, Studies and Revenues of the University and Colleges of Oxford, 1852.

(1) Discipline (loc. cit. pp 23–7)

... It is satisfactory to find, when we compare the discipline, the order, and the morals of the University with what they are reported to have been even within the memory of living men, that a decided reform has taken place. . . .

The habit of extravagant expenditure is more widely extended than either of the evils just mentioned [vice and gambling]. But flagrant instances of misconduct in this respect, such as come before the courts, and raise the indignation of the public, are less frequent than formerly; and a large number of undergraduates are disposed to practise as strict an economy as their position admits. This is attested by the fact that nearly one half of the students deal for grocery with a tradesman who refuses credit in all cases. But between the small class which is guilty of disgraceful extravagance, and the larger body which is prudent, there is still a considerable number of young men who spend far more than they have any right to spend. . . .

'The debts', Professor Browne observes, 'into which undergraduates are led, by the growing taste for furniture and decorations, totally unsuitable, are ruinous'. This language is strong, but the evil to which it points is very serious. We cannot forbear from alluding also to the excessive habit of smoking, which is now prevalent. Tobacconists' bills have, and that not in solitary instances, amounted to £40 a year. A third cause of expense is the practice of dining at inns, taverns, and clubs, in or about Oxford, a practice which may be checked, as has been proved, under the administration of active Proctors. . . .

Driving, hunting and riding are also causes of great expense.

The University regulation, which imposes a heavy fine on those who are found driving, unless they have obtained permission from an officer of their College and one of the Proctors, is more or less enforced, and restrains the practice to some extent. Undergraduates are forbidden by Statute to keep horses without the sanction of the head of their College; a rule which, however, is only partially enforced, and may be easily evaded by the use of hired horses. Of these amusements the most expensive is hunting. It seldom costs less than four guineas a day. Some of those who indulge in it are accustomed to it at home, and can afford it; and on this ground, as well as on the supposition that it often takes the place of worse pursuits, it is in several Colleges overlooked or permitted. It is, however, a matter which ought to be under strict control. A moderate indulgence in it has, in some cases, been found compatible with serious study and academical distinction. But the present licence ought to be repressed; and hunting ought at least never to be permitted by the College authorities without the express sanction of parents. In such cases the temptation held out by those who can afford the amusement to those who cannot, should always be taken into consideration. . . .

Finally, it is important to observe that no permanent good results can be expected from these or other means, unless a change is effected in the habits and the temper of the students themselves. Those who are studious at present are, for the most part, moral and frugal. But a large proportion of students are now unemployed, and require additional incentives to study. Without this there is no effectual security against vice. The University, therefore, applied what we trust will be found a great and real remedy, when, in a recent Statute, it determined that more frequent proofs of diligence should be required from the young men. Extravagance, like other vicious habits, springs from idleness. 'To correct these evils', writes Professor Wall, 'we must make study and not amusement the law of the University'. 'The most effective mode of preventing idleness', says Sir Charles Lyell, 'and thereby promoting good conduct, is to interest the great body of the undergraduates in the studies of the Universities'.

(2) Distinctions of Rank and Wealth (loc. cit. pp. 28–9)
Several of those who have given us evidence lay stress on the bad

effect caused by the distinctions of rank and wealth which the University still retains among the students. Young noblemen wear a distinctive academic dress, take precedence of their academical superiors, are permitted to take degrees at an earlier period than other students, and in general treated in a way that seems to indicate too great a deference to rank in a place of education. The sons of Baronets and Knights are also permitted to graduate earlier. This is a relic of the past state of things when the different orders of society were much more widely separated than they are at present. Among the Fellows and Tutors of Colleges, whatever may be their birth, their fortune or their social position out of the University, a perfect equality subsists. This is very beneficial, and among the junior members of the University it might at least be expected that there should be nothing in the institutions of the place to encourage an opposite feeling.

If distinctions of birth, even where they are in some measure warranted by the law of the land, are objectionable in a place of education, those made on the ground of mere wealth are still more objectionable; and the distinction between Gentleman-Commoners, as they are called, and Commoners, rests on no other ground. . . .

A Gentleman-Commoner is well known to be marked out for every kind of imposition. He is usually courted by the worst among his equals: he receives less instruction, and is subjected to a less careful discipline; and thus both the College and the individual suffer from the continuance of the system.

'This class may be regarded, taken collectively,' says Professor Daubeny, 'as the worst educated portion of the under-graduates, and at the same time the one least inclined for study. If the qualification were even that of rank or station, something might be said in its defence, but it is notoriously only that of wealth; and if it be alleged in its behalf that its existence tends to set up a wholesome line of separation between those who can afford to indulge in expensive luxuries and those who cannot, and thus to diminish the chance of rivalry between the two, with respect to their habits of living, it may be replied, that in the largest and most aristocratical Colleges it fails in effecting this, now that so many wealthy parents are wise enough to enrol their sons in them merely as Commoners, whilst it might be expected that if the class of Gentleman-Commoners were abolished there would be then no inducement for men of fortune to resort elsewhere, excepting it were to secure the advantage of superior tuition, or more careful discipline, and hence that the remaining societies would either consist wholly of youths of moderate means, or that, if they contained an intermixture of young men of wealth, the latter would consist of such as were studious in their habits, and disinclined to extravagance.'

(3) Examinations (loc. cit. pp. 60–2)

Two great improvements were effected by the change in the Statutes [1800]. First, distinctions were awarded to the ablest candidates. Twelve of these were to be classed in order of merit; and in case more than twelve were found worthy of distinction, a second list was to be drawn up on the same principle. The lists were to be made public. Thus the University acknowledged that Degrees were not of themselves adequate honours for students of merit. The second improvement, which indeed was rendered necessary by the first, and was scarcely less important, was that examiners should be paid functionaries, selected by responsible officers, and appointed for a considerable period. . . .

By a Statute passed in 1825, in consequence (as the preamble states) of the increase of students in the University, the distinction between the two Schools of Classics and Mathematics was still further recognised by the appointment of separate Examiners for each. The classification of the honorary distinctions was rendered still more definite by giving the name of 'Third Class' to the lower division of the Second.

But the increase in the number of candidates produced an effect which had not been foreseen. It became necessary that the examination should be conducted more and more on paper, and therefore a knowledge of Philosophy, together with skill in composition, increased gradually in importance, and perhaps skill in Construing proportionably declined.

In 1830 these changes were carried further in the same direction. A Fourth Class was established; and the examinations of candidates for an ordinary Degree were separated from those of Candidates for Honours. The 'Literae Humaniores' now included Ancient History, with Political Philosophy, as well as Rhetoric, Poetry and Moral Philosophy; and the important permission to illustrate ancient by modern authors was then first introduced. . . .

The examinations have become the chief instruments not only for testing the proficiency of the students, but also for stimulating, and directing the studies of the place.

The general effect of this change has been exceedingly beneficial. Industry has been greatly increased. The instruction in the Colleges has become indirectly subject to the control of the University. The requirements of the examinations for an ordinary Degree, slight though they be, have yet a great effect on that period of the Academical course which immediately precedes them. The idlest and most careless student is checked in his career of idleness by the approach of his examinations. The severity of the final examination may be judged of by comparing the number of those rejected at Oxford with the number of those rejected at other Universities. It appears from a return made to the House of Commons, that, on an average of the same four years (1845–1848), the number of those who presented themselves for examination, and of those who passed the examination, were, respectively—at Dublin, 259 and 242; at Cambridge, 370 and 342; at Oxford, 387 and 287.

The stimulus of the examination for Honours is found to be very strong. The average number of candidates for Honours in Classics is not less than 90 out of nearly 500 candidates for a Degree. Of these 90, about 10 obtain a First Class. This Honour, then, is no mean distinction. That it has been honestly and deservedly awarded is proved by the confidence which the examiners, for the most part, enjoy, and by the success in afterlife of those who have won it. . . .

We have said that the number of candidates rejected in examinations for an ordinary Degree is considerable. But, notwithstanding this, the amount of attainment commonly exhibited in these examinations is small. An ordinary candidate has prepared usually four plays of Euripedes, four or five books of Herodotus with the History, six books of Livy also with the History, half of Horace, four books of Euclid, or (in lieu of Euclid) Aldrick's Compendium of Logic to the end of the Reduction of Syllogisms. He is also expected to translate a passage from English into Latin, and to construe any passage of the four Gospels, to repeat and illustrate from Scripture the XXXIX

Articles; and to answer questions on the historical facts of the Old and New Testament. The examiners are satisfied with a very slight exhibition of knowledge as regards many of these subjects. 'If decent Latin writing should be insisted upon, the number of failures would be more than quadrupled.' The Latin and Greek authors are commonly got up by the aid of translations. The knowledge of Logic insisted on is very meagre.

(4) Proposal to Establish an Examination before Matriculation (loc. cit. p. 68)

It appears to us that it would be very beneficial to establish a uniform examination for all young men before they are admitted as Members of the University.

The recent Statute has made an approach towards this great improvement, though it has shrunk from carrying it out. The Responsions, or First University Examination, which was formerly to be passed between the sixth and ninth terms of standing (inclusively), must now be passed between the third and seventh.

The advantage of an examination before Matriculation may be at once inferred from the fact that the best Colleges have already adopted it for themselves. These Colleges require some facility in Latin writing, and a fair acquaintance with the grammatical principles of Greek and Latin. To this is now generally added Arithmetic and a portion of the elements of Euclid. Several Colleges also require some knowledge of the Elements of Religion.

This ordeal, however, varies greatly in the different Colleges in which it is applied, and perhaps in the same College at different times. It is well known that a youth who is rejected at one of the better Colleges can gain admission elsewhere, the scale of requirement descending in proportion to the character of the College. From Gentlemen-Commoners and Noblemen, and from members of Halls, such an examination is usually not required at all.

The introduction of this test has proved a great benefit to the Colleges in which it has been systematically applied; but the extreme facility with which young men are admitted in many Societies, prevents the University at large from reaping the benefits which now accrue to particular Colleges.

One or two gentlemen, in their evidence, oppose any such examination, on the ground that students come to the University as learners, and therefore 'ignorance rather than knowledge must be presumed on the part of those who come to be taught'. No doubt students come as learners, but not as learners of everything; and it is precisely to secure learners capable of receiving the instruction proper to their age that an examination at Matriculation is required.

The Professional Value of an Oxford Education
(loc. cit. p. 71)

Now the Statute of 1850 was an effort in the right direction; but its present regulations, which still retain the compulsory study of the Literae Humaniores to the end of the course, will scarcely remedy the evil. At present not only have the studies preparatory to the professions of Law and Medicine ceased to be followed in the University, but even Theology has suffered.

It is important to note the extent to which all separate branches of learning, both professional and preparatory to professions, have been suffered to decay; nor do we believe that any measures which the University has as yet adopted are sufficient to remedy the evil.

Oxford still educates a large proportion of the clergy; but learned theologians are very rare in the University, and, in consequence, they are still rarer elsewhere. No efficient means at present exist in the University for training candidates for Holy Orders in those studies which belong peculiarly to their profession. A University training cannot indeed be expected to make men accomplished Divines before they become Clergymen; but the University must be to blame if theological studies languish. Few of the Clergy apply themselves in earnest to the study of Hebrew. Ecclesiastical History, some detached portions excepted, is unknown to the great majority. The history of Doctrines has scarcely been treated in this country. It may be safely stated that the Epistles of St Paul have not been studied critically by the great majority of those in Orders. It is true that the English Church has produced great Divines, and may boast at this moment of a body of Clergymen perhaps more intelligent and accomplished than it ever before possessed. But they might well acquire more learning. We hope that the Theological

School of Oxford may yet be frequented by earnest students, as of old; so that many among her sons may gain a profound acquaintance with the history and criticism of the Sacred Books, and with the external and internal history of the Church.

Oxford has ceased altogether to be a School of Medicine. Those few persons who take Medical Degrees there with a view to the social consideration which these Degrees give, or the preferments in the University for which they are necessary, study their profession elsewhere. This may result from causes for which the University is in no way to blame. But the University is blameable for the little encouragement which, even considering all it has done by its recent improvements, it has as yet given to those Physical Sciences which Medical Students ought to learn before they begin their strictly Professional course.

The connexion of Oxford with the Profession of the Law is also unsatisfactory. The number of barristers not educated at either University is increasing; and of those who have graduated, the majority are of Cambridge. Many other courses may have contributed to this result. It may indeed be said that Oxford was never actually connected with any branch of the legal profession, except that which is practised in Ecclesiastical Courts, and that no one can wish to revive the study of the Canon Law. This is true, but the study of the Civil Law, which occupies so large a place in the statutes both of the University and of the Colleges, ought not to have been allowed to fall into complete desuetude. Under an improved system young men might be efficiently assisted in Oxford in the attainment of much knowledge directly serviceable in training a young lawyer for his profession.

In our printed papers we proposed for consideration the question, whether 'the studies of the University might be so regulated, as to render them at some period of the course subservient to the future pursuits of the Students'. We have received a great number of answers concurring in the affirmative. It is not recommended that the University should be made a place of Professional Education, at least not for Law and Medicine. But it is suggested that if its Students cannot be made Lawyers and Physicians in Oxford itself, they may there be taught much that would prepare them for the strictly Professional Studies to be pursued in the great towns, where these professions are practised.

20

(6) Professors (loc. cit. pp. 93–7)

The operation of the system of University Instruction, or rather its failure, also requires a short description. . . .

The present Professors of Sanscrit and of Modern History have also on the few occasions on which they have delivered public Lectures been attended by numerous audiences. We cannot refrain from expressing our regret that these distinguished persons have not been encouraged by that success to renew the attempt. A considerable number of hearers has, for some time past, been secured to the Reader in Experimental Philosophy by a regulation of the Dean of Christchurch, who till lately compelled all his Undergraduates to attend one course of these lectures; and many of these, as we are informed by Professor Walker, continue voluntarily the study thus commenced. And no doubt an able and eloquent Professor can command a numerous attendance if his Lectures relate to subjects of general interest, bearing directly on the Public Examinations. Yet the general fact is unquestionable, that the Professors are not now the Teachers of the University; and that of all the functions of the academic body, that which was once, and which in the Statutes is still presumed to be, the most important, might cease to exist altogether, with hardly any perceptible shock to the general system of the place.

This cessation of Professional Teaching is designated by the Hebdomadal Board, in the document to which we have more that once referred, as a 'temporary interruption'; but it is an interruption which, so far as we can ascertain, has been the rule and not the exception, for at least a century and a half.

This state of things has been brought about by various causes acting and re-acting upon each other.

In the first place there is little demand for Professional teaching. The influence of the Colleges has continually tended to limit the Studies of the University to subjects which can be taught by their own Fellows, and within their own walls. The Public Examinations, as we have shown, have also assisted in bringing the Studies of the University within a narrow range. It is not to be expected that young men, who suppose their success in life to depend on success in the Examinations, will bestow or (as they think), waste time in attending lectures which are in no way likely to promote their main object. Students have had no motive whatever supplied by the University to induce them to study Physiology, Chemistry, and the other Natural Sciences; they have had no sufficient motive for studying even History or Theology. Under such circumstances, the teaching of the ablest Professors would be unable to serve a permanent audience.

Again, the endowments of the Professorships, with three or four exceptions, are not such as to command the services of the ablest men, especially in a country like England, where the avenues of practical life are so open and so numerous. The revenues of Colleges (as we shall have to show more fully here-after) cannot retain young men at Oxford, now that celibacy is not, as of old, a necessary condition of Holy Orders. The ablest Fellows of Colleges, who might aim at becoming Professors, are glad to accept livings, the masterships of schools, or any office which holds out the prospect of a settlement in life, and are thus, for the most part, lost to literature and Science. . . . Unless something is done to secure the services of the ablest men as professors, it is not likely that Professional teaching will thrive much more than heretofore.

It has sometimes been argued that the invention of Printing has superseded the use of Public Lectures, and that Books now convey the knowledge formerly communicated by Professors. It may be remarked, however, that, if in former days Professional Lectures were made necessary by the want of books, at the present day an able Teacher is rendered no less indispensable by their abundance. Such a Teacher furnishes the Student with a chart to guide him through the labyrinth of knowledge that surrounds him. . . .

So far we have been speaking of Professors only as Teachers. But the Professor will serve higher purposes still, by 'devoting himself' (as Mr. Pattison himself observes), 'to the cultivation of the more abstruse parts of his Science . . . it would be well to consider whether, especially at the commencement, we shall not make the process of creating and inviting powerful men all the more difficult if we impose, by unyielding rules, the same bur-den of constant instruction as a necessity upon all. It would doubtless produce more teaching, in the common acceptation of these words, but it would lead also to second-hand learning, hand-to-mouth lectures, and the instalment of a race of men in our Chairs without enthusiasm, eloquence, profundity, or venerable acquirements. Such remarks may perhaps invite one observation, that at any rate there should be some guarantee for the activity of Professors and that in providing this security large allowance must be made (as has been said) for 'the power of human indolence', to deter men from great exertions. But to this again there is a reply, the truth and sufficiency of which will appear the more, I believe, the more it is considered. The position holds true if wrong appointments are made. If right appointments are made, those will be selected to represent a branch of study in the University who are cultivating it with energy and delight. It has been, it ever will be, the tendency of men eminent in any intellectual pursuit, to be enthusiastic, to carry their exertions to the extreme limit of their constitutional strength, because they find in it, and must find in it, the purest, the deepest, and the most enduring pleasure, in comparison with which, so long as vigorous health remains, idleness is privation and amusement a meagre pastime.

(7) Actual State of the Colleges (loc. cit. p. 143)

Nowhere has the number of Fellows been increased as the revenues of the several societies have increased. In some Colleges, it has been diminished. A surplus, sometimes a very large surplus, in money, is divided between the Head and the Fellows, in addition to the allowance for food which is their statutable right; and this dividend forms the principal portion of their emoluments. . . .

Fellows of Colleges are no longer bound to live as members of a community subject to a rigid rule of life. They are never brought together, except at Elections, and on other rare occasions. Residence, which Founders looked upon as essential for all the purposes of a College, is required of none but Probationer Fellows in the First year, and that not universally. Those who live in Oxford, with few exceptions, do so because they find profitable employment there as Tutors or College officers. Two-thirds of the Fellows pass their life at a distance from the University, and employ themselves as parochial ministers, as schoolmasters or tutors, as students of law or medicine, as literary or scientific men, or have no occupation at all.

2. Science at Cambridge, 1884

In the last thirty years of the nineteenth century the study of science came to be an important activity within the University.

SOURCE: Second Report of the Royal Commission on Technical Instruction. Vol. I, 1884, pp. 420 et seq.

XIII—Cambridge

The Commissioners were informed that, previous to the year 1871, no practical teaching of science was carried on in the University, with the exception of Chemistry. In that year the late Professor Maxwell was appointed Professor of Physics, and designed the Cavendish Physical laboratory presented to the University by the Chancellor, The Duke of Devonshire; and Professor Michael Foster was elected as lecturer on Physiology in Trinity College. From the above year, up to the present time, science teaching in almost every branch has been instituted, of at once the most advanced and the most practical character.

Maxwell's influence on the examination system of the University, by introducing physical problems in addition to the more purely mathematical subjects formerly in vogue, has been of the highest importance; and that of Professor Foster equally so in another direction, viz, that of encouraging and developing the teaching of the biological sciences, as forming an important part of the scientific training for the profession of medicine. Other eminent Cambridge men, Lord Rayleigh, Professor Stokes, Humphreys, Liveing, Dewar, Vines, Mr. Coutts-Trotter, and the late Professor Balfour among the number, have done much to assist in this matter; and there is no doubt that the authorities of the University generally are at the present time fully alive to the importance of these practical scientific studies, and are determined to push forward and coordinate the still somewhat unsystematic efforts which are being made by the different colleges in this direction. The energy and activity which is thus being displayed at Cambridge is very remarkable.

Of the various scientific institutions and laboratories now existing at Cambridge, the most important are: (1) the Cavendish Physical Laboratory under Professor Lord Rayleigh; (2) the Physiological and Morphological Laboratories under Professor Foster and Mr. Sedgewick; (3) The Chemical Department

HOW THEY WERE TAUGHT

under Professors Liveing and Dewar; (4) the Geological Museum under Professor Hughes; (5) the Mineralogical Collection (Professor Lewis); (6) the Mechanical Workshops of Professor James Stuart; (7) the Fitzwilliam Museum; besides (8) the purely professional department of medicine under Professor Humphreys and others.

(1) *The Cavendish Laboratory*—This laboratory, which is one of the most complete of its kind, was designed by Professor Clark Maxwell, and since his death the direction has devolved on Lord Rayleigh. There are special rooms for optical research, for exact measurements of different kinds, and for special physical research in all its branches. The Professor is assisted by two demonstrators, Messrs Glazebrook and Shaw, who undertake the elementary instruction of about 45 students, carrying on a specific course of practical work. The demand for this tuition is steadily increasing, the attendance having trebled in the last three years. The fee for working in the laboratory is two guineas per term. There is no endowment in connection with the Department but a fund amount of £2,000 has been raised at the instigation of Lord Rayleigh, for the purchase of apparatus. The senior students attend lectures on advanced electricity, given by Lord Rayleigh, who is himself engaged in original physical research, and great stimulus is thus given to the higher work of the students, who assist him.

(6) *The Mechanical Workshops of Professor Stuart*—An interesting feature of the present scientific activity at Cambridge is the experiment inaugurated by Professor Stuart about five years ago, by the establishment of a department for carrying on practical work in machine construction. Professor Stuart's intention of establishing this department is to enable the sons of manufacturers and others who are sent to the University, to obtain instruction of a kind likely to be of immediate practical value in their subsequent calling. On inspecting the workshops, which are still unfinished and in gradual course of erection, the Commissioners were impressed with the bona fide character of the work. The department contains a fitting shop, smithy, a small erecting shop, and a draughtman's office, together with a cuprea and casting shed. About forty two students were working at the time of our visit. All the men go through a regularly prescribed

course of work, special attention being paid to the instruction in mechanical and machine drawing, which is made the foundation of all the teaching in the shops. The system of tuition is arranged on the basis of an actual mercantile establishment. The rate of wages of each student is fixed, the cost of material and the time employed being accurately noted and entered in a ledger, so that the cost of every article produced can be ascertained. An examination of the register of attendance showed that twenty students had in eight weeks attended 725 times and worked 2,121 hours, giving an average of $4\frac{1}{2}$ attendances of three hours duration per student per week. For the purpose of instructing the students, five or six skilled mechanics are employed, who are paid the average wages of their class. Of these, two are former students of the University who, having gone through the course, remain as paid workmen. The work in progress during the Commissioners' visit was of a most diverse kind; some of the most advanced students were constructing dynamo-machines, steam engines, telegraphic and electrical apparatus, etc.

In conversation with the University Professors on the subject of scientific instruction, the Commissioners were told that the great drawback at present in Cambridge is the want of coordination of the different scientific studies. This, however, thanks chiefly to the efforts of Mr. Coutts-Trotter, of Trinity College, is gradually being remedied, so that a student coming up to Cambridge, and desirous of adopting a scientific career, will in future have equal facilities with one who goes in for purely classical or mathematical studies. The tendency has hitherto been to make a man feel that a liberal education must necessarily conduct him to the Church or to the Bar. The college tutors, whose business it is to advise the freshmen, and inform him of how he is to get his teaching, have, as a rule, been ignorant of science, and even of the facilities which Cambridge possesses for carrying on a scientific education; moreover, the science Professors have more or less been free lances, each doing the best he cared for his own subject. It is intended that the system of intercollegiate lectures shall bring the subject chosen by the senior Professor into coordination.

Respecting the method of teaching science, Professor Foster expressed his opinion that the first duty of a good Professor was to create men who should carry his own work further, and that the highest work of the Head of a Department is the education of a few good men who are to be equal to himself. His plan was therefore, to train up his demonstrators so that they could take the advanced men. He believes that so far as the students are concerned, the Professor should take the elementary lecture classes, leaving the advanced lectures to the men he had trained.

3. Oxford and Cambridge between the Wars, 1922

The Royal Commission in the two ancient universities which reported in 1922 found that the reforms initiated in the nineteenth century had gone a very long way and that these universities were giving valuable service.

> SOURCE: Report of the Royal Commission on Oxford and Cambridge (Cmd. 1588), 1922.

(1) *Self-Reform and Development Since the last Royal Commission* (pp. 25–6)

Oxford and Cambridge are totally different places from the establishments reported on in 1850–2. Yet so persistent is the impression left on the public mind by their historic past, of which the trappings and outward form are still largely preserved, that it is believed in many quarters that 'dons' and undergraduates at the two senior Universities are still following much the same courses of studies and living the same kind of lives as when the first Commissioners penetrated into their midst.

The actual facts are very different. 'Dons', whether Professorial or Collegiate, are in close and constant intercourse with undergraduates. The personal instruction of students by College teachers has been carried to the furthest reasonable limit in the great majority of subjects. Most of the Oxford and Cambridge undergraduates are serious and hardworking students, if not entirely divested on all occasions of the exuberance natural to congregated youth. A large and increasing proportion of these students are poor men, maintained at the University out of College endowments, public grants, loans or personal assistance, yet the poorer men are so much a part of the social life of colleges that their great or less means, their more or less humble origin are things indifferent and un-noticed.

(2) *Changes in Studies* (pp. 33–4)

(ii) Cambridge

The growth of science at Cambridge since the era of the Royal Commissions has been perhaps the greatest fact in the history of the University since its foundation. In the middle years of the nineteenth century the Natural Sciences Tripos had been founded in a congenial soil where studies connected with inductive reasoning had been at home since the time of Bacon, and more particularly since the time of Newton. But the development was at first slow, largely for want of financial resources and material equipment. In 1861, when Professor Liveing was appointed to the Chair of Chemistry, he had assigned to him for a laboratory two small rooms devoid of all apparatus, which he was expected to supply as best he might; there are 1,200 students in the Chemical Laboratories today. In 1863 the erection of a block of buildings known as the 'New Museums' was begun. In this block, accommodation was provided for the departments of Astronomy, Botany, Chemistry, Natural Philosophy and Zoology, for the Zoological Collections of the University and for the Philosophical Library.

In 1871 William Cavendish, Seventh Duke of Devonshire, gave to the University the Cavendish Laboratory, and the University in commemoration of this magnificent gift established the Cavendish Professorship of Experimental Physics. Up to this time the study of Physics had not been represented separately in the University, but under Clark Maxwell, Lord Rayleigh, Sir Joseph Thomson and Sir Ernest Rutherford the Cavendish Laboratory has been a prominent centre of physical research and thought during the past fifty years.

It has been found that large numbers of students in the schools form the only security for the supply of first-rate science teachers and researchers. Only by casting the net wide can the haul be satisfactory. It has become the custom of the Cambridge Colleges to encourage and facilitate the passage of men from the study of one subject to another, and many of the most distinguished scientists were originally classical students or mathematicians. It was also found that science was so big a study and so dependent on team work and on large material equipment that it could not be satisfactorily conducted on the old college system. In Science not only lecturing, but to a large extent supervision also is now done on the University, not the College, basis; and the College laboratories, useful at one stage of development, have all been abolished in favour of University laboratories. . . .

The effect of this immense development in the range and to some extent in the character of University studies, and the number of men of scientific minds who have now for a generation been taking part in College life on equal terms with men of the older studies, rising to the headship of Colleges, and sitting on University Boards and Syndicates, have affected the attitude of mind of the teachers of the Humanities. In Classics, History, Modern Languages, Philosophy and Economics, the value set upon research, new thought, and modern treatment is partly owing to their scientific environment. They have gained much by this juxtaposition and competition. On the other hand, they stand in charge of being overshadowed by the importance and popularity of science, and of falling behind in the matter of endowments which the State and private individuals are too apt to lavish solely on what is considered to be 'useful' in some obvious sense.

(3) *Oxford Tutorial System* (*Cambridge Supervisors*) (pp. 37–9)
The individual teaching of students, as distinct from public lecturing, is normally conducted by a College Tutor or Supervisor of studies, who instructs students of his own College, or of other Colleges by intercollegiate arrangement. Personal instruction is and should remain the basis of Collegiate as distinct from University teaching, implying as it does a more constant and more intimate contact of teacher and taught than in the case of the lecturer and his audience. It becomes, however, more difficult to keep even this form of teaching on strictly Collegiate lines, as the number of subjects, and the branches of each subject increase. For instance, where there is only one History Tutor in a College, he may find so much of his time taken up in mastering all the different historical subjects which his various pupils study, that he has neither time nor energy left for research or even for fully efficient teaching. And in many subjects it is not possible to have a Tutor in every College.

At Cambridge, in Science and Modern Languages and to a certain extent in Law, an inter-Collegiate arrangement of individual instruction has begun. But it is probable that College organisation of individual instruction will continue in the Humanities generally, by the help of mutual aid between the Colleges in special cases. . . .

With all its characteristic difficulties, drawbacks and exceptions, which are on the increase, the system of College instruction is largely accountable for the educational achievement of the two senior Universities. The teaching of the undergraduate, man to man, by his Tutor or Supervisor, who is very often resident in College alongside of his pupil, gives to the education at Oxford and Cambridge something scarcely to be got elsewhere in such full measure. The rudiments of the system existed in the worst days of 'old corruption', increased with the growing efficiency of the Colleges in the early nineteenth century, and were brought to perfection in Balliol by the example and influence of Jowett. The system became general in Oxford and subsequently in Cambridge. The fact that private coaching, which was said in 1852 to cost £50,000 a year to Cambridge undergraduates and was still very common thirty years ago, has now very greatly diminished in both Universities, is a measure of the great increase of teaching by the recognised College authorities. But there is still a certain difference of views between Oxford and Cambridge as to the amount of individual teaching which should be given to each undergraduate, and the amount of time which academical teachers should be expected to give to this function, at the expense of time for forwarding the growth of new thought and knowledge. So far as there is a difference of point of view—and it must not be exaggerated—Cambridge ideas are naturally coloured to a large extent by the experience of Science, Oxford ideas by the experience of 'Greats'. Without attempting to adjudicate in so nice a controversy we may point out the indisputable fact that great sacrifices are made by College teachers at both Universities to the personal education of the undergraduate, and that for this reason there is pressing need of the further endowments and encouragement of research.

It is interesting to note that whereas the earlier Royal Commissions were concerned with providing against the indifference and want of conscientiousness of some of the Fellows, the charge now made in some quarters is that the Fellows overwork themselves at teaching and administration. However this may be, they have their reward in supplying the country with a system of higher instruction which perhaps gives more attention to the individual student than is given anywhere else. If complaint is made that education at Oxford and Cambridge costs more per man than elsewhere, one reason is that the undergraduate gets more teaching in return for his money, over and above the peculiar residential advantages.

4. Tutorials

It is sometimes said that the most distinctive feature of teaching at the ancient universities is the emphasis placed upon weekly tutorials. The value of this method of teaching depends on the personal relationship between the tutor and his tutee; consequently there must be almost as many assessments of the value of tutorials as there are tutorials. These extracts give two views.

SOURCE: Oscar Browning, *Memories of Sixty Years at Eton, Cambridge and Elsewhere*, Lane, 1910, pp. 32–3.

I do not know that we profited very much by Shilleto's lectures, but his private tuition was the best in the University. Does any coach work as hard nowadays? It is difficult to say. He took, I believe, twenty-four pupils, and gave each of them a full hour's tuition by himself three times a week. He read a book with you, and you did for him three pieces of composition a week. He lived in what was then called 'The Red House' in Trumpington Street, now, I think, called 'Kingsley House', but it should have a tablet to mark it as the abode of Richard Shilleto. He received his pupils in a large room on the first floor. They passed through an ante-room, where there was a dish, full of English pieces to be turned into Latin and Greek prose and verse, all in Shilleto's very clear handwriting. You chose a piece and took it away with you, bringing back your own version of it when you returned and receiving a fair copy composed by Shilleto himself. A collection of these has been printed, and remain a monument of Cambridge scholarship. He preferred to find fault if possible, and you were rarely allowed to think that you had done anything worthy of commendation; but a bad mistake was a dishonour which you felt as a wound. You did very little reading with Shilleto and not much translation, but you imbibed the real spirit of scholarship, and he also gave you an enthusiasm for English literature. I derived from him my best knowledge of Burke. This distinguished scholar, working twelve hours a day in hard individual teaching, held no University office, and was not recognized by any public body until he became a Fellow of Peterhouse. It was always imagined that if he only had leisure he would write a great book, probably a palmary edition of Thucydides. Private munificence set him free to do this, but it proved a failure. All honour to his memory! Those who read with him were proud to be his pupils. Alas! I never knew him as a colleague. When I returned to Cambridge, in 1876, the first public function which I attended was the funeral of my old friend.

SOURCE: Dacre Balsdon, *Oxford Life*, Eyre and Spottiswoode, 2nd ed. 1962, p. 169.

A Professor's lecture is sometimes like the *pas seul* of a prima ballerina; he lectures; he retires. And then, after an interval, he lectures again. But the College tutor's public lecture is an interruption in a week otherwise devoted to teaching pupils in his rooms listening to their essays and talking about them. These are 'private hours'—'tutes', as undergraduates call them, or tutorials. Sometimes a pupil comes alone, sometimes in a pair, sometimes with two or three others. Once tutors taught in this way for ten hours a week; now, in an inflated University, they teach for fifteen or sixteen, sometimes even for twenty. Is it surprising if they teach less well?

Young tutors find the hour too long, old tutors find it too short. Undergraduates find it very long indeed and if there is no clock in the room they find it even longer. When you reach a tutor's age, it is less easy to listen than to talk; and observant undergraduates quickly realize that their tutors criticize in detail the final sentences of their essays but give little evidence of having absorbed the rest. There is the splendid story of the great Ingram Bywater.

'Ah', he said in greeting, to his pupil, 'what is the subject of your essay? Expediency? Splendid. Then will you read what you have written?'

At the end, he roused himself. He said, 'For next week, will you write me an essay on—er—Expediency? That is all.'

Had he slept through the whole of the essay? Or was he uttering the most devastating criticism? The pupil never knew.

5. Some Aspects of Life at Cambridge since the Second World War

SOURCE: R. J. White, *Cambridge Life*, Eyre and Spottiswoode, 1960.

Going Up (pp. 29–31)

Three times in every year, some seven thousand young men and women converge upon the town of the twenty colleges in order to 'keep' fifty-nine nights of residence there by way of part-fulfilment of the statutory requirements for the acquisition of the degree of Bachelor of Arts. They don't talk of converging. They talk of 'going up'. Men and women always talk of 'going up to high and holy places' like London or the older universities. Similarly, they 'keep' there, which is their way of saying 'reside'. They 'keep' their fifty-nine nights, very much as budding barristers 'eat their dinners' at the Inns of Court. When they have kept their nights, which compose the term, they 'go down'. To 'keep' literally means to sleep, or otherwise to spend the hours between midnight and six a.m., within statutory distance of Great St Mary's, the University Church, the ancient centre of Cambridge. In order to supplicate the Vice-Chancellor for the degree of Bachelor of Arts, it is necessary to produce unimpeachable evidence that nine terms of fifty-nine nights have been 'kept', and normally in succession. Then, having passed the necessary 'Tripos' examinations, or, failing these, having been allowed to proceed to an 'ordinary', as distinct from an honours degree, and having afforded your college sufficient evidence to assure the Vice-Chancellor that you are sound in both mind and morals, you will acquire the privilege of wearing a hood trimmed with something passably like the fur of a white rabbit and of writing the letters 'B.A.' after your name. It is as simple, or as complicated, as that. Whether, during your nine terms of fifty-nine nights of residence, you have attended any lectures is your own affair, though your elders and betters will have seen to it that you have read some books, and written some essays, and engaged in some weekly conversation of a more or less intellectual character with a person known as a 'supervisor'. Of course, you will have done a great many more things having little or no ostensible connection with academic studies: debating, singing, acting, sport and talking until three in the morning about everything under the sun. But, by and large, the fulfilment of strictly academic requirements for the award of your bachelor's degree amounts to little more than keeping your terms, passing your examinations, and maintaining a mediocre reputation for virtue and sober living.

And is this why seven thousand come? Is the University first and foremost a degree factory? More than six thousand of them would tell you so if you asked them. Another thousand will murmur something about 'liberal education', or 'learning to think', or 'a sense of values'. They have been reading some elderly person's book on *Culture and the University*, or mugging up Newman's *Idea of a University* for an examination. Regard them not. The six thousand know they are right. To them the University is the place to which young men and women, in a highly competitive world, come to get a good degree, and thereby to get a good job. The fact that they are honest enough to say so is the best tribute they could pay to the University as a patron of clear-thinking and plain-speaking. Nor need this imply that they are any more barbarous than their thousand thousand predecessors of more leisurely generations. The fact is that they have had the devil's own job 'getting in', and they are not to be blamed for making the most of it, in very practical terms indeed, once they have succeeded. Besides, although they are too decent to talk about it, they know perfectly well that they get a good deal more by their stay at the University than could ever be expressed in terms of spurious rabbit's fur or diplomas. Perhaps it is just as well that no one but the more solemn dons ever try to say exactly what it is that they get, or ought to get.

Cambridge Morning (pp. 79–82)

The bedmakers come into College at dawn. At least that is the theory. Mostly they arrive about seven o'clock, winter and summer alike. Only the porter on duty at the Lodge sees them come. They call at the porter's lodge for their keys which hang on several rows of hooks just inside the door. They all carry

covered baskets, and ungrateful undergraduates say these re-
ceptacles are always much heavier when they leave again at
about ten o'clock. It is the footfalls of the bedmakers as they
unlock gyp-rooms and cupboards that announce to the undergraduate, and the resident don, that the day is beginning. There
is no reason whatever to pay any attention to these sounds, for
the 'bedder' has as yet to make her pot of tea and smoke her
cigarette before she starts her magnified imitation of the death-
watch beetle on the door-panels and tunes up her cheerful voice
to the chant of 'Eight o'clock, sir. . . . Half past eight, sir. . . .
Sir, it's quarter to nine. . . . Goodness sake, sir, if you don't get
up in half a minute, you'll get no breakfast. . . .' It used to be
possible for the undergraduate to ignore these agonised cries
until somewhere near ten o'clock, and still get his bed made and
his breakfast things washed up. It is so no longer. The modern
bedder is resolute about quitting the premises at what she considers a proper trade-union hour. And there are no breakfast
things to wash up. You must race into hall before nine or go
breakfastless, which some still prefer to do.

Bedmakers are survivals of the age of the gentry. Many, indeed most, of them are still tolerant of the idle morning habits of
the young. It is important not to provoke them beyond a certain limit, however, for they are hard to recruit, and the porter
(whose problem it is) finds a legitimate source of grievance in a
rapid turn-over in bedmakers. The main qualification for
engagement as a bedmaker, apart from honesty, cleanliness and
industry, used to be ugliness. It was laid down that such serving
females must be 'horrific'. This, no doubt, descends from the
time when the University consisted of a population of 'clerks',—
clerks in Holy Orders or on the way to them. The trouble appears to have been that these horrific matrons brought with
them their daughters as 'bedder's helps', and the daughters
helped the clerks. So there set in the days of the hags, which
lasted until only yesterday, the days when bedders were a cross
between the witches in *Macbeth* and Sairy Gamp. These formid-
able and hideous creatures were one of the traditional sources of
Cambridge humour, of grisly legend, of endless anecdote. Henry
Gunning has left us his portrait of the renowned Sal Elvedge,
bedmaker to such celebrated wining and dining dons of the
later eighteenth century as Thomas Adkin and Busick Harwood.

'This woman', Gunning records, 'was much attached to her masters; and although she never scrupled supplying herself with coals, candles, etc. from their stores, yet she watched most perseveringly over their interests, in not allowing them to be imposed on in any other quarter.' . . .

It was the dawn of the Welfare State and the onset of full employment that killed off the old bedders. Alternative and better-paid employment, together with the accompanying transformation of the middle-aged and elderly women of the working-classes in the matter of personal appearance and self-esteem, has made bed-makers scarce and 'superior'. Where they still survive, they can earn some three pounds a week for two or three hours of room tidying and washing-up a day. They regard this as 'pocket-money', or perhaps 'pin-money'. Nine times out of ten the present-day bedmaker 'doesn't need the money', as her grandmother needed it, nor would she 'lower herself' to make away with her gentleman's soap and sugar and tea. She is more like a visiting housekeeper. She dresses smartly, and she is often good to look upon. The notion that she must qualify for her job by ugliness departed when the 'gentlemen' departed— the gentlemen who thought anything in a skirt fair game for gentlemanly diversion. The modern undergraduate, as often as not, would find it hard to distinguish his bedmaker socially from his sisters, his cousins and his aunts. The bedmaker of today, like the undergraduate of today, is a type-phenomenon of a silent social revolution. Likely enough she will vanish completely from the Cambridge scene within a few years, along with other survivals of the days before self-service and electric gadgets.

Likewise the 'gyp', the man-servant, her masculine counterpart. He still serves in some colleges in his old capacity of body-servant to a group of undergraduates living on his 'staircase', but he spends most of his time nowadays stoking hot-water boilers, scrubbing out communal bathrooms and lavatories, sweeping stairs and passages, removing furniture, and waiting in hall. The 'staircase-man', with his multitude of small tasks, is fast replacing the old-time valet. Some of these men, haunting college staircases while generations of undergraduates come and go, have been among the best-loved landmarks of undergraduate life: Charlie, and Jack, and Horace, and Sydney, not

21

to mention little Smithson, the ex-jockey; and Jeeves (it really was his name) who could never retire, after sixty years of gypping, and had to be allowed to come and sit in the gyp-room or the boiler-house during his last days because he was miserable unto death anywhere else. These men, along with their great exemplar, the porter, and their still more solemn exemplar, the butler, have often served the college from boyhood. They belong to it, they know about it, they love it (though they curse it often and long) more completely and continuously than anyone else in the place, not even excepting the oldest don. They constitute the communal memory. They are the fixed points in an ever-changing society, as undergraduates come and go like the flies of a summer, and as dons live their little day between fellowship election and departure for their suburban donnery. They live on small wages, they work at their own pace, and generally speaking they are among the few people of a Cambridge college who have time to stand and stare. They have plenty to stare at, and they store it all up, and they excel even tutors in never forgetting a name or a face. It is impossible to decide whether it is a good thing, or a bad thing, that they rarely if ever write their memoirs. A don would be the first person to acknowledge that they are, after dons, the most important people in a college.

6. Owens College, Victoria University, 1884

Owens College was the first of the new university colleges to be founded in the large provincial cities of England and was in some ways the archetype for those which were to be established elsewhere. It became the senior college of the federal Victoria University which was also to include the university colleges at Leeds and Liverpool.

> SOURCE: Second Report of the Royal Commission on Technical Instruction, Vol. I, 1884, p. 435 et seq.

The Owens College, Victoria University—The Owens College was established as a private trust in 1851, by a bequest of £100,000 from John Owens, merchant, of Manchester, to found a college in which 'the subjects usually taught at the English Universities' shall be professed. This private trust was reconstituted, and the College incorporated by Act of Parliament in 1871, and large additions to the funds of the College have accrued by donation and bequest.

The Victoria University, with its seat in the city of Manchester, and with Owens College as its single college at present, was founded by Royal Charter in 1880 and 1882. The Victoria University stands to Owens College, and the other colleges which, at a future time, may be incorporated, in the same position as the Universities of Oxford and Cambridge stand to the Colleges in those Universities. It is therefore not a mere examining board like the University of London, but a teaching University, as only those students can be admitted to degrees in science, arts, or medicine, who have studied under strict regulations at one or other of the Colleges of the University. The government of the University consists of the Duke of Devonshire as Chancellor, a Vice-Chancellor, the University Court, and the University Council, whilst the academical arrangements for examinations, are placed under the direction of the Board of Studies of the University, consisting of the examiners and of the professors and lecturers of the University, the former of whom are in part external to the teaching staff, the latter being professors and lecturers in the Owens College. Although only in existence for a few years, the Victoria University has already granted a considerable number of degrees in arts and science, both in honours and the pass subjects, and the number of candidates for these degrees, as for the more recently instituted degrees in medicine and surgery, is now very considerable, and there can be no doubt that the foundation of a teaching University in the midst of the densely populated industrial districts of Lancashire and Yorkshire, will in time do much to stimulate and extend the higher education of the country.

The Owens College is governed by a President, the Duke of Devonshire, a court of governors, an executive council, and an academical senate. This latter body consists of twenty-six professors, including the principal, Dr. Greenwood, who occupies the chair of Greek. The scientific subjects are very fully represented. Then there are two professors of chemistry, inorganic and organic, besides four assistant lecturers and demonstrators; two professors of physics, and one assistant lecturer and demonstrator; a professor of applied, and one of pure, mathematics, with two assistant lecturers; a professor of each of the subjects of botany, biology, geology, and physiology, with assistant lecturers and demonstrators in each of these departments; and, in addition, a complete staff of professors and demonstrators for all the subjects of medicine and surgery. The laboratories and lecture rooms for chemistry are, perhaps, the most complete in the country, and the same may be said for several of the other scientific departments. Large biological and geological museums, with very complete accommodation for teaching these subjects, are now in course of erection.

The total funds of the college amount to upwards of £400,000, the whole of this sum having been either bequeathed to the College or raised by public subscription. No pecuniary aid of any kind has as yet been given, either to the College or to the University, by the Government or the municipality.

The courses of study are of an extended character, leading up to the University degrees, and to the College Honour Certificates in the technical branches of engineering, and technological chemistry. The number of students of arts and science in the day classes amounts to about four hundred, that in the medical department to nearly three hundred. In addition to the day instruction, which, of course, forms the chief work of the college, systematic courses of evening lectures and laboratory practice exist, for the benefit of the large number of persons who, being occupied in trade or otherwise during the day, are desirous of continuing their education. The number of evening students amounts to about seven hundred, the subjects taught are the same as in the day classes, all the Professors and assistant lecturers taking part in the tuition, and in many subjects several courses are given; thus, in chemistry, there are three distinct courses of lectures, and three courses of laboratory practice, and in Latin five separate classes, so that persons desirous of carrying on their education up to a University standard have the opportunity of doing so at the low fee of ten shillings and six pence for the course of twenty lectures. These college evening classes serve, in the science subjects at least, as an excellent supplement to the ordinary science teaching under the Department of Science and Art, and to the elementary science instruction given in the board schools, placing a high standard of instruction within the reach of all resident in the district.

7. Mason College becomes the University of Birmingham, 1900

The financial difficulties which the university colleges faced in the nineteenth century were immense. They were dependent on philanthropic endeavour and fee income, supplemented after 1889 by very small government grants. In the case of Birmingham the personal interest and energy of Joseph Chamberlain served to raise the necessary funds to enable Mason College to be launched successfully on its career as an independent university. The interest and enthusiasm of local men of influence was essential to all of the university colleges and those that lacked such men had great difficulty in surviving at all.

SOURCE: Julian Amery, *The Life of Joseph Chamberlain*, Vol. IV, MacMillan, 1951, pp. 210–11, 217–21.

Chamberlain's interest in education was neither accidental nor merely personal. The spread of education had been an essential accompaniment, part cause and part effect, of the ascent in the nation of the Nonconformist middle class to which he belonged. Political controversy on the subject was confined to primary and secondary education; but, in Chamberlain's mind, university education was no less important. We must remember that Oxford and Cambridge had still been closed to Nonconformists when he had left school. Nor should we forget how he had once exclaimed to Morley, as they walked through Balliol quad, 'Ah, how I wish that I could have had a training in this place'.

Personal experience and sectarian interest thus combined with civic pride to implant in him the idea that Birmingham should have a university. It was some time before the idea became a clear conception and longer still before he accomplished it; but his interest in it dated from the days of his municipal career.

While Chamberlain was still Mayor, Josiah Mason founded in Birmingham the college that bore his name. Birmingham's band of civic reformers set great hopes on this foundation. But Mason's design was only to spread scientific and technical instruction; and he provided neither space nor funds for the humanities. About the same time, however, Owens College, in the North, had developed into Victoria University, a federal body affiliating Leeds and Liverpool as well as Manchester.

What had been done in Manchester could be done in Birmingham; and a few local thinkers, with Chamberlain's friend Dr.
Crosskey at their head, began to canvass the idea of a federal
university for the Midlands. A decisive impetus was given to
this idea by J. R. Seeley, who came over from Cambridge in
1887 and delivered an address on the true purpose and form of
a provincial university.

Seeley said, in effect, that, were such new seats of learning
widely created in the country, the movement 'would be one of
the grandest in the history of English culture'. Let the provinces
not seek to imitate the splendid colleges of Oxford and Cambridge. Those 'great boarding houses' had grown out of historic
circumstances. But time and expense made it impossible to
follow their example. Let them rather follow the Scottish and
German models. Colleges were not essential to the organisation
of study and knowledge, of teaching and research. 'A university
consists of class-rooms and professors'. If that simple idea were
once grasped, every great town like Birmingham might have,
and should have, its complete corps of professors; its general
staff of culture.

Seeley's address, reprinted as a pamphlet, set its impress on
Chamberlain's civic policy, just as the *Expansion of England* had
already done in his broader conception of the Empire. He now
determined that Birmingham should have a university, and, in
the following year, proclaimed his ultimate purpose. When
opening new board schools in 1888 he asked his audience not to
rest content with progress in elementary education. They
should cherish the vision of a Jacob's ladder of democracy,
'enabling the poorest amongst us, if he has but the ability, if
God has given him these gifts, to rise to the greatest height of
culture. . . . I desire that we may crown the edifice by establishing here in Birmingham a true Midland University. I hope that
every Birmingham man will keep it before him as one of the
great objects of his life. . . .

But the strangest part of this story has yet to be told. Only
with money could his ideal become reality. How much would
he need and how would he raise it? At the outset he asked
Professor Bertram Windle what was the least sum which would
justify Birmingham in applying for a Charter. Windle said
£100,000. This, as Chamberlain saw, would only be enough to

give Mason College some inadequate additions and a false
name, and he replied that he would have 'no pauper university,
no starved university'. Accordingly, at the meeting called to
launch the campaign for the University, he appealed for a quarter of a million pounds. Many thought him over-sanguine, but,
within twelve months half that sum had been obtained by his
public appeals to local patriotism and by his private canvass of
local wealth. But that was too slow for him; and he, therefore,
threw all his personal prestige into the scales in order to reach
his target.

Mr. Charles Holcroft, a local admirer, was persuaded to give
£20,000. Next, an 'anonymous donor' was induced to contribute, by degrees, another £50,000. This latter benefactor was
Lord Strathcona, the Canadian High Commissioner and
Chamberlain's friend.

Strathcona to Chamberlain

October 30, 1899.—'I should just say to you that, notwithstanding the interest I take in higher education, I should hardly have
been led to move in the matter in the case of a town or city less
attached to the cause of union and the unity of the Empire than
Birmingham has happily been under your guidance.'

In a final bid to raise the full £250,000 before the century
expired, Chamberlain approached Andrew Carnegie, the
Scottish-American magnate and philanthropist. Carnegie at
once agreed to subscribe £50,000 for the endowment of the
sciences. This gift had unexpected consequences. At the donor's
request, a deputation from Birmingham crossed the Atlantic to
study the provincial universities of the United States. When
they reported what they had seen,—the scale of endowment, the
extent of building and the provision of equipment—Chamberlain's ideas were revolutionised. His whole conception seemed
suddenly too small.

Up to this time, Chamberlain had only contemplated,—
what Seeley had advised,—the formation of a more complete
corps of professors. He now decided that building would have
to be undertaken on the grand scale. When the Royal Charter
was received at the end of May 1900, he startled his audience
by telling them that, though the fund had now risen to £330,000,
a further quarter of a million would have to be raised. It was the

least sum he could ask for in the new circumstances, and 'we must get it'. In this speech he used a vivid simile:

'We are like those who ascend mountains. Again and again we think we see the summit before us and, when we top the eminence, we find there is still something further beyond.'

Two more generous gifts were offered in response. Sir James Chance gave £50,000, and at Chamberlain's suggestion, Lord Calthorpe and his son presented twenty-five acres of land, an excellent site on the Bournbrook side of the Edgbaston estate.

Chamberlain was already sure that every inch of that space would have to be 'covered with buildings'; and Calthorpe afterwards increased the area by twenty more acres. But still it was not enough. At the first Congregation of the University, when more than £400,000 was already assured, their Chancellor announced that more was wanted. 'Half a million of money. What is it in view of the object?'

Six months later he took Birmingham's breath away, when he told the second yearly meeting of the Court of Governors that they must aspire to a university 'second to none'. It would cost, he said, not less than a million sterling.

This last vision was more than even he was destined to accomplish. But he pressed towards it by methods conventional and otherwise. One incident is typical of his shamelessness in begging for a good cause. When he read in the newspapers that an individual, whom he had never met nor heard of, had been left a fortune that worthy man found himself honoured with an invitation to Highbury. The sequel to his visit can be readily imagined.

But, in the end, voluntary generosity had to be supplemented. Following a suggestion of Chamberlain's to the Lord Mayor, the City Council decided to make an annual grant from the rates. The County Councils of Staffordshire and Worcestershire followed suit; and by these means a further income of £7,000 was provided.

This was Chamberlain's final effort in the cause. His interest in the University would continue as long as he was in public life and after. But, presently, the battle for Tariff Reform would absorb all his energies and leave him neither the time nor the strength for other things. In little more, however, than four

years, he had already created for his City a university, the first
of its type in England. In the same period he had also secured
for it direct endowments amounting to £45,000, as well as an
annual income equivalent, at that time, to the interest on
another £200,000 of capital. Out of his own diminished means
he had given £2000; and it was more than he could afford.

The achievement was not without its humorous side. Facetious
journalists in London wrote that, if Chamberlain wanted a
glorified technical school for Birmingham, by all means let him
have it, but why call it a university. Others, more concerned for
the repute of learning, feared that academic standards would be
degraded by Brummagem degrees. The inclusion of a School of
Brewing caused scandal in some quarters; but the brewers had
been among the best donors to the University; and Chamberlain
jestingly remarked that 'a School for Cocoa' could also be
founded, subject to endowment. But, as the work advanced, the
critics were disarmed; and the press, irrespective of party, wrote
with growing admiration.

Among statesmen Haldane was Chamberlain's most fervent
supporter in the cause of higher education. He, for one, never
thought that Chamberlain was unqualified for his self-appointed
task nor that he approached it with insufficient reverence. Out
of a number of letters, which passed between them in these
years, one sentence gives the tone:

Haldane to Chamberlain

March 13, 1903.—'On this matter of highest education I feel
that I am wholly at one with you—and that you are the only
man in this country who has the combination of keenness and of
power that can make it live.' Both men were deeply discontented
with the meagre amount of Government aid given to the new
universities.

The university buildings are the greatest of Chamberlain's
visible memorials in his city. The Tower was raised in his
especial honour. At his own wish, the design was taken in essen-
tials from the famous Torre del Mangia which soars above the
Piazza del Campo in Siena. The Birmingham model has sometimes been derided as a 'landmark of the Midlands'. But they
might have been worse. Without him, they might have had none
at all. Great is architecture among the arts; but, as Ruskin

suggests, not the least question about a building is what does it contain or enshrine. Birmingham will never rival the beauty of the older Universities, but, already, its spirit at least approaches theirs. Years later, Haldane once recalled a talk about All Souls and other Oxford Colleges.

'I shall never forget Chamberlain's earnestness, when he turned to me and said almost in a whisper, "Haldane, it may take us in Birmingham generations to create a spirit equal to that, but, if it does, one thing I can promise you—we will never lower the standard".'

8. Leeds University, 1929–34

Before local education authorities were prepared to offer grants which would cover the cost of residence to all who qualified for entry to a university, it was customary to attend the university within daily travelling distance and to live at home. About three quarters of the students at Leeds were 'local' in this sense between the Wars; grants to cover the cost of residence have now reduced this proportion to less than a quarter.

SOURCE: Rayner Heppenstall, Leeds 1929–34, *The Twentieth Century*, February, 1956, pp. 169–73 and 175.

My father had left school at the age of twelve, since when, he boasted, he had never read a book. He used to tell me that I should go mad with reading. All the same, he wanted me to get on in the world, and for this purpose (though he sometimes expressed anxiety lest education should teach me to be ashamed of my parents) he considered it necessary that I should be educated up to a point. This point was reached when I had taken Matriculation. Before the results were out, my father made me apply for a job in the Town Clerk's office. I saw to it that I did not get this job and then set about manoeuvring my parents into saying that I could stay on at school two years longer and subsequently go to a University with any scholarship I picked up. The notion was that I should become a schoolmaster. I had no wish to be a schoolmaster, but my parents had to have some idea what they were scraping and saving for. My father's wages, as a Co-op. drapery manager, would be somewhere between four and five pounds a week, and I had a sister growing up. From the age of fourteen onwards, I had received from the Huddersfield Education Committee a maintenance grant of ten shillings a week.

Two years later, the few Huddersfield men already at Leeds were joined by six freshers, five from New North Road (the school was officially known as Huddersfield College) and one from Royd's Hall. The home of one of them lay some miles outside Huddersfield, and formerly he had travelled daily to and from school by train. He lived in, at Devonshire Hall, the men's hostel. The others commuted. Two of them took Gas Engineering. The one from Royd's Hall did a more orthodox form of Science. Two read French. I did Modern Languages, which in fact meant French and English.

On the first day of the academic year, the Great Hall at Leeds was set out like a bazaar, the various stalls being tables presided over by the heads of departments. I had meant to do English alone, I cannot think why, since my father's most considerable outlay on education had been in sending me twice to France, while my chief interest was not so much in any form of literature as in music. Perhaps I had dimly perceived that, of all the subjects taught in universities English has most inherent *chic* (the only other subjects which seem to have any at all are History and Philosophy). And so I had made for a table under the double presidency of the new Professor of Eng. Lit., F. P. Wilson (he had just succeeded Lascelles Abercrombie), and the presently-to-move-on Professor of Eng. Lang., E. V. Gordon. They had looked up my Higher School Certificate results and shaken their heads. I had not done really well in English. Why did I not take a degree in French, in which I had done much better? Or perhaps I could do English as part of a combined Hons. course. And so I presented myself at Professor Barbier's stall.

The five who commuted (and three older students, one of whom again did French) normally caught the ten-past-eight express from Huddersfield. Four of us were lucky to live near the Lockwood station, and by travelling from there by the six-minutes-to-eight local we became eligible for the workman's rate, which made the difference between one-and-twopence and two shillings return.

Once out of Huddersfield station, we spread a coat across our knees and played cards. We usually played a game called Mucky

Liz, but if by chance there were only four or three of us that morning we played auction or cut-throat, as we also frequently did at mid-day in the refectory, where there was a sort of Huddersfield table, or in one of the dingy little rooms above the J.C.R. In the train, we also sang part-songs or, more frequently, spontaneously harmonised a variety of popular ballads. One of the gas engineers and the orthodox scientist both sang tenor in the choir at Crosland Moor Wesleyans, and I had singing lessons. In any case, Huddersfield is a town whose boast has always been that everybody there could either sing or play cricket. . . .

Unlike so many 'red-brick' universities, Leeds really was built of red brick, which had turned a nasty purple in that atmosphere. It was about 100 yards long and almost as high. To the left of the main entrance, in white Portland stone, stood a large and splendid Eric Gill relief, which showed Christ driving the money-changers from the Temple, the money-changers in top hats and frock coats, Christ (as Gill later explained to me) in a priest's alb, with modern boots showing underneath. This, originally commissioned by Sir Michael Sadler, had so shocked the present Vice-Chancellor that he had instructed the gardener to plant creepers in front of it.

There was usually a lecture at nine o'clock, and there were commonly four lectures thereafter. One cut a certain number of lectures, but not many. I cannot absolutely be certain, but I fancy that some kind of register must even have been called and that, if one cut a lecture, one got somebody else to answer one's name. Except when there was a recital in the Great Hall, the only alternatives to bridge-playing at mid-day seemed to be sleeping in armchairs in the J.C.R. and walking on Woodhouse Moor, a wilderness of concrete paths. The journey home in the evening was less gregarious than the journey up in the morning. There was a slow train at a quarter to five, and there was an express at twenty-five minutes past five. Sometimes one stayed up for an evening concert, a dance or a theatrical performance or to take a girl out or attend such a meeting of the Literary and Historical Society as the one addressed in my first year by Walter de la Mare. Then one got home very late indeed, though sometimes fish-and-chip shops would still be open.

No Huddersfield commuter took up a sport at Leeds, though one of the older students was a cadet. His parents were fairly rich, and he was, I think, the only one among us whose religion was C. of E. Another Wesleyan and I (I had in fact been an atheist since first reading Nietzsche at school, but I still went to chapel on Sunday evenings) played soccer for our school old boys for a season. During the holidays, I walked a great deal generally over Wessenden or to Darton, near Barnsley, where an uncle of mine was a collier who read Kipling, Rupert Brooke and Jane Austen and had started writing a history of the village.

One of the lecturers in English was Wilfred Rowland Childe, who had at one time a great reputation as a poet. He was a Catholic convert, and his poems were full of stained glass. He was a dear, kind man, but nobody listened to his lectures. He lectured on Wednesday mornings to a large audience composed of both Hons. and Ordinary students. He read his lectures very quietly, with no gesticulation or other playing to the gallery. The gallery repaid him by getting along quietly with its other work. Childe's mouth, when he lectured, was like that of a rabbit nibbling. He wore his hair long. His ties were broad and hairy. He lectured sitting down. If you listened intently, you could just make out what he was saying. It was evidently about Style and perhaps it was very good.

Another lecturer was called Baxter. He presently went elsewhere, but not before he had disconcertingly shouted at us a great deal of Chaucer in what he believed to have been the contemporary pronunciation. The figure of Alan S. C. Ross meant little to me, since he dealt only with such matters as Old Norse and Old High German, which I was not expected to do. Now as a professor at Birmingham, he has recently made a curious appearance in the rôle of *éminence grise* to Miss Nancy Mitford. The replacements for Baxter and Gordon were J. I. M. Stewart and Bruce Dickins.

Married to one of Sir Herbert Grierson's daughters, Professor Dickins was a nice plump man who lectured enthusiastically, but all his giggling and spitting could not overcome the repugnance I had early conceived for Anglo-Saxon, a repugnance which, at the end of my first year, narrowly escaped causing my expulsion from the English school. J. I. M. Stewart is, of course, none other than the fabulous 'Michael Innes'. We have been friends for many years, and he will, I trust, forgive me if I

22

gratify amateurs of literary gossip by describing him, on his first appearance in Leeds, as a small, pale young lecturer, with a wispy moustache and a rocking gait, as though, all his life till then, he had been hurrying along polished corridors.

Professor Wilson read poetry beautifully. He was splendid on the Metaphysicals, but seemed, to my taste, far too fond of Wordsworth. I did not care for Wordsworth. The first of the set books I failed to read was *The Prelude*. Wilson is now Merton Professor of Eng. Lit. at Oxford, as Dickins is now Elrington and Bosworth Professor of Anglo-Saxon at Cambridge. Stewart, too, is at Oxford. The point I wish to make is that Oxford and Cambridge, which already have the *chic* and the architecture, also lay claim to the concentration of talent. What in fact they have is a concentration of men now basking in established reputations they made elswhere. It cannot be assumed that they are better teachers now than they were twenty years ago. . . .

During our last degree year, those of us who were committed to following up graduation with a year on the Diploma in Education already took two lectures a week in pedagogy. On the whole, I managed to shut out from my mind the painful eventualities to come, but these two lectures a week were a disagreeable foretaste of another inferior world of the Nibelungs. It also now began to be borne in upon me that I had done too little work and that it was rather late to begin. My total syllabus was huge, and I had barely touched it, being occupied with too many other things. Unless I now worked very hard, I should be lucky if I got a degree at all. So I adopted an attitude of inward defiance and did even less work.

Clearly, this is evidence of a weak character. The other commuters were managing to deal with this living half in, half out of Leeds. Still, it was not exactly an aid to concentration. My subject, too, was horribly dividing. I could not take the same kind of interest, at the same time, in the French and the English. The two did not mix. Two foreign languages would have mixed better. The best thing would have been if I could have left Leeds that year, if I had not *had* to take a degree.

In the end, I was *given* a Third. I had evidently got through all right in French, but, at the Eng. Lang. oral, I saw a *gamma minus* on one of my papers, and Lascelles Abercrombie, as external examiner in Eng. Lit., had had my prize-essay on

Hopkins thrust under his nose as if to prove to him that I was not a half-wit.

9. The Degree of Ph.D.

If the tutorial is particularly connected in the public mind with the two ancient universities, the Ph.D degree is often considered to be particularly associated with the older city universities. This extract gives some account of the origin of this association.

SOURCE: H. B. Charlton; *Portrait of a University, 1851–1951*, Manchester University Press, 1951, p. 93.

His [T. F. Tout's] scheme for building up a graduate school (or in more familiar English phrase, a research department) led to his active interest in the setting up, towards the end of the European war of 1914–18, of a new English University degree, the doctorate of philosophy, Ph.D. The general intention of the whole plan was clear. From 1900 to 1914 there had been from England and from America a steady stream of post-graduate students to the universities of Germany. It was indeed an established academic habit; when I graduated at Leeds in 1911, and was awarded a fellowship, my Oxford-Balliol professor insisted, and I have never regretted it, that I should go to Germany and not to Oxford. So when the war was coming to an end the English universities, and especially the scientists in them, saw a means of developing their own post-graduate activities and of attracting to them the Americans who had previously gone to Germany. They were not trying to capitalise a world situation. Indeed, when the subject was first raised in Manchester in January, 1917, it was in a document by the American Association of University professors which urged that Great Britain should take such a step. Acting on this prompting, Manchester devised its plans to meet the situation. Nothing less than a doctorate would be sufficient bait. Hence the institution of the Ph.D., the doctorate in philosophy, where philosophy has the old German and Scottish connotation which comprises all and every component of knowledge. For Tout, the historian, this was a great opportunity; for medieval history necessitates a technique of research in which the methods of the scientist can be most easily accommodated to the purposes of the historian. It was a subject in which principles and techniques of research could be taught in a fashion closely similar to the practice in scientific subjects. So Tout, in the interests of scholarship as the historian saw scholarship, became the prime mover on the Arts side for the setting up of the new degree. Whatever may have been the less valuable results of the institution of the doctorate in philosophy, there is no doubt that it has provided a very useful instrument in the carrying forward of Tout's major objective, the development of historical scholarship. . . .

10. The First of the 'New' Universities, Keele

Keele was the first of the new university foundations following the Second World War and owed its inspiration to A. D. Lindsay. It was also the first university institution to be promised adequate aid from public funds by the U.G.C. from its inception.

> Source: W. B. Gallie, *A New University, A. D. Lindsay and the Keele Experiment*, Chatto and Windus, 1960, pp. 96–100.

Staff and Students

Early in 1950 thirteen professors, two readers and a few independent lecturers—the leading members of the future teaching staff—were appointed, and from February onwards there were monthly meetings at Keele between Lindsay and his administrative staff and the thirteen new professors. At these meetings there was always a great deal of talk which appeared to result in very little. But I now see that Lindsay wanted these meetings not in order to get anything done, not to get any particular arrangements 'talked into existence' (as I then used to think), but just to get to know us and to get us to know each other. At first there was something of a honeymoon atmosphere, although not without typical honeymoon frictions. It soon became clear that some of the new professors had only the haziest notion, if any, of what Lindsay was hoping to do at Keele, and were in spirit completely and irretrievably wedded to the ways in which they had been taught to teach their respective subjects. Lindsay's attempts to brush aside their difficulties were not very successful: at the time I thought that he was too brusque and would wound the sensitivity of one or other of my new colleagues. I soon learned, however, that some of these would be wounded by even the most tactful suggestions about their subjects, whilst from others the most pointed and necessary criticism would always slide like water from a duck's back. We spent a good deal of time at these early meetings, and at Senate meetings during the first year or so, discussing how the subject of Education could be fitted into our complex and crowded time-table. Most of my new colleagues had the usual university attitude to Education— that it was not really a subject, that it was an anomaly in the university and that it was part of the price one had to pay for State Grants, etc., and the young professor of Education, who had quite intelligent ambitions for his subject, was given a rather gruelling time. By contrast we all accepted the needs of the sciences with the respect that is as invariably and unthinkingly given to such subjects today as it was given of old to the claims of classics and philosophy.

By July of that year some of the first of the army huts, which had been regarded as one of the main assets of the Keele estate, were ready for habitation, and one by one the new professors and their families began to arrive. The first arrivals must have felt like new settlers in the bush or prairies, or rather like re-settlers of some frontier township that had been lying deserted for a generation or so. The newly equipped huts were, for the most part, located at widely separated points of the 'campus' so that the physical remoteness must have added to the sense of social isolation. During all this summer, Lindsay lay ill in the Clock House, as the dower house of the estate was called, seeing only one or two of the new professors who had the enterprise and the courtesy to go and talk with him regularly. And during all this time rain fell in Staffordshire almost continuously, churning up the red-brown mud of the new building site, with the result that Keele mud soon became something of a legend and that all work on the buildings came to a standstill. And during all this time the unhappy first Registrar did his best to keep the often anxious new arrivals cheerful, and usually succeeded only in making them more anxious than ever. Providence, working in the guise of lack of accommodation, kept me from arriving until the very end of September. When we did arrive, the rain was still falling and we were advised to spend the first night in an hotel in Newcastle. There next morning Bruce Williams, the professor of Economics, called on us with characteristic Australian kindness, and more or less dragged us out to buy gumboots—the first equipment one had to acquire before doing anything on the Keele campus.

Thereafter we took a taxi out to Keele and found our bungalow (ex R.E. stores) in the confused but willing and cheerful hands of bricklayers, carpenters, plumbers and cleaners, all getting in each other's way in their efforts to make the place ready for us. What we really needed, however, was a gang of R.E.s to make some kind of bridge or causeway across the pools of red mud that lay between our front door and the road. Allegedly to cheer me up, but really to test my calibre, the head porter offered to show me the students' accommodation. Since our furniture had not yet arrived, I went with him down a narrow muddy path, on either side of which sloped a row of asbestos-covered huts, rainsoaked, wind-blown, the colour of rotting canvas, many of them with window frames and eaves loose and flapping in the incessant wet wind. The last hut in the row on the right looked in slightly better shape than the others. It had been entirely re-covered and the windows were whole and firm: perhaps there was even a new door. Nevertheless, it looked bleak in the extreme as the rain poured down its grey felt-like sides. 'This is the model of what all the huts are to be', the porter informed me lugubriously, without a trace of a smile. Five years of the army had taught me to disguise my feelings and to make the right kind of noise without having a single thought in my head; so I think I passed the character test quite successfully. But inwardly and in truth I quaked and wondered. The students were due to arrive in a week or so and I suspected that if any of their parents were to come with them and to see the accommodation which they were to occupy the number of our first intake might well be reduced from the hundred and fifty we had been promised.

In fact, the opening day had to be postponed for two weeks; but, by that time, Keele Hall itself and a sufficient number of huts for some ninety men and fifty or so girl students had been got into fairly habitable condition. I remember, however, that at the first meeting of the teaching staff the main hall had to be lighted and heated by storm lanterns, and that for several weeks well-established members of staff were lending out their bathrooms to less fortunately equipped colleagues and students. On the day the students arrived, ladders and work-benches were hurriedly removed from around and inside the main building; and we saw that the grosser scars of the war years—Keele Hall had stood up to occupation by, successively, the Free French, the Poles, the Cypriots and the Americans—had been plastered over and that some of the finest rooms in the mansion had been redecorated in almost excessively resplendent style. And on that day the rain actually stopped and no anxious parents made scenes about their children's accommodation.

Next morning Lindsay addressed the assembled students—a strangely hushed and timid collection of aspirants, containing probably a higher percentage of gifted individuals but also a higher percentage of low-level students than one would usually find in an ordinary year's intake into an ordinary English university. Lindsay spoke in what had been the ballroom of the old Hall, a beautifully-designed L-shaped room, not very large but allowing plenty of room for the hundred and fifty students and for a number of the administrative and teaching staff as well. I arrived rather late, and my friend the porter apologised profusely for not keeping me a seat in the front row. I sat down, wondering anxiously how Lindsay's inaugural comments would go down, and fearing lest there should be some (to me) highly embarrassing form of inaugural prayer. Lindsay, however, had highly developed sensitivity to what was wanted on different kinds of social occasion. He came in chatting quite informally to the Registrar, and we all shuffled to our feet and stood up. He told us to sit down, but continued standing himself while he spoke, and just as he was beginning his address one of the staff's wives—as it happened the beauty of the place—slipped in late, rather rushed and embarrassed after seeing her young children off to school.

Index